BiG
GReeN
COOKBOOK

BiG GREEN COOKBOOK

hundreds of
planet-pleasing recipes & tips
for a
luscious, low-carbon lifestyle

Jackie Newgent, RD

WILEY

John Wiley & Sons, Inc.

Published by John Wiley & Sons, Inc., Hoboken, New Jersey

Published simultaneously in Canada.

For general information on our other products and services or for technical support, please contact our Customer Care Department within the United States at (800) 762–2974, outside the United States at (317) 572–3993 or fax (317) 572–4002.

Wiley also publishes its books in a variety of electronic formats. Some content that appears in print may not be available in electronic books. For more information about Wiley products, visit our web site at www.wiley.com.

Library of Congress Cataloging-in-Publication Data:

Newgent, Jackie.
 Big green cookbook : hundreds of planet-pleasing recipes & tips for a luscious, low-carbon lifestyle / Jackie Newgent.
     p.   cm.
Includes index.
ISBN 978-0-470-40449-2 (pbk.)
   1. Cookery. 2. Cookery—Energy conservation—United States. 3. Sustainable living—United States. I. Title.
TX651.N495   2009
641.5973—dc22   2008047025

Printed in the United States of America

10 9 8 7 6 5 4 3 2 1

Book design and typography by Ralph Fowler / rlfdesign

For my nephews, Aiden and Rhyus.
May you always have good health
and a healthy environment
in which to enjoy it.

contents

I didn't realize how lucky I was when I was a child with no worries in the world. My childhood is the reason I am who I am now. It's the reason I am so passionate today about this place—our planet Earth, our home.

Though my thoughts are on the big picture now, all I cared about when I was growing up was my own little world . . . in my typical house on a typical street in a typical town. But it was so much more than that—as I realize now.

We had grass and trees and flowers and, oh yeah, those stinging bees. My dad made sure I appreciated it all. We had so much fragrant mint growing in our yard I just thought that's how the outdoors smelled. I loved to rub the mint all over my hands and take nice long whiffs. Mmm, delightful! My mother would have me pick the best of this wonderful herb when she made her classic stuffed grape leaves. And the grape leaves— we grew those, too. I learned how to snap off the leaves when they were in season and just right—and before the beetles got to them! My dad even gave my brother, sister, and me our own trees. We nurtured them ourselves and planted whatever flowers we wanted at their bases. Oh, and our happy, vibrant tomato plants . . . I still have vivid flavor memories of them.

Then there were "the woods"—a seemingly endless forest behind our house. (Unfortunately, it's mostly developed land now.) Along with my brother and sister and neighborhood kids, I could spend hours and hours getting lost in them. There was a creek to which we made a "prickly" path and a "muddy" path. There was a giant crabapple tree where we climbed and challenged each other to find the "good" ones. We loved to eat big juicy slices of watermelon in a clearing in the woods and then plant all of our seeds. They never did grow into anything— but we had fun doing it.

To add to our wooded experience, my family would go on a fall hiking adventure every year just before school started. We each had our own hiking staff and were so proud to show off the badges we attached to them for each year we completed all of the trails— which was *every year*. Some of the prettiest sites I've ever seen were on those hikes . . . in northeastern Ohio!

After all of these invaluable outdoor experiences, appreciating nature became part of who I am, part of my soul.

Not to be left out are the indoor experiences with my mother. My mom was a caterer and she taught me about the importance of quality ingredients and the art of cooking the way nature intended. She made sure I understood where food *really* came from.

I was my mother's cooking protégé and food shopping sidekick. Even though we took advantage of what we did have, we were only able to grow a tiny portion of all the food we needed. That meant we had to do lots of shopping—and there was a method to our food-buying madness. High quality and freshness were the keys. And if we didn't know where it came from, it didn't come home with us. We were a couple of hard-to-please gals. I call it picky with a purpose!

We would only get produce from a specialty market. And even then, whenever the produce manager got a glimpse of my mother, he would go into the back room and then magically appear seconds later with the freshest, best of the best he had set aside for her. We would go to a meat locker and inspect the sides of beef before agreeing to buy selected cuts from one of them. We would only get chicken from a certain farm that my mother trusted—and only on Tuesdays, when it was freshest. Though it embarrassed me at times, we tasted everything we could wherever we were to make sure it met our particular taste and freshness approval.

We frequented a Middle Eastern–style bakery and watched the pita being baked before picking the puffy loaves off the conveyer belt and bagging them to go. And, my all-time favorite experience was going to the potato chip plant on Saturdays and plucking the freshly fried chips off the press and filling up a three-pound box. Yes, that was me in the backseat of a Dodge Dart with a box of potato chips sitting on my lap that was bigger than I was. It was so very good!

I'm privileged to have learned so much about what "real" food is—even the potato chips (sort of)! And I'm fortunate to realize how eating can and should be a pleasurable and important part of life.

So as my dad helped lead me to a place where nature became part of my soul, my mother helped guide me to a place where

food and cooking became part of my heart. Food and nature always went hand-in-hand as I knew it. But despite those incredible heart-and-soul experiences and lessons, I took it for granted . . . for years!

As time passed and I got out in the real world, I veered away from the teachings of nature while I was in school and then struggling to make ends meet as a single girl in the city. Eventually I came back to what was so dear to me when I was growing up. With my nutrition education and degree in tow, I went to culinary school to steer myself away from the "fat free" craze to a place of flavor and wholesomeness. I began following a natural eating and cooking style. When my dad was diagnosed with diabetes, I decided to pass on this healthful, natural approach to him—and everyone else—with my first cookbook, *The All-Natural Diabetes Cookbook*.

But then I kept digging, knowing that I was just scratching the surface of a better way to eat and live. Along with millions of others, I saw *An Inconvenient Truth,* featuring Nobel Laureate and former vice president Al Gore. It brought an immediacy to my interest in spreading my whole food philosophy to others for more than just good health. That documentary and further reading on work done by hundreds of scientists and activists around the world placed me on the path to *Big Green Cookbook*.

I started to implement "green" living in large and small ways, slowly, so they were actions I could maintain. I furnished my apartment in an eco-friendly way. I gave up my bottled water drinking habit. I joined the local community supported agriculture (CSA) program. I further changed the way I cooked.

As a so-called foodie, I spend a serious amount of time dabbling in the kitchen. But it made me uncomfortable to be unfriendly to the planet while I was whipping up goodies in my kitchen—even when I was making mostly plant-based foods. So over time, I began incorporating more and more eco-friendly philosophies and methods into my cooking habits. When I developed winning dishes, not only did they taste good, I felt good about them. They were prepared with green love, after all! I also switched my apartment's source of energy to 100 percent wind power—which meant I'd have a little less "green guilt" when cooking. It was then, finally, I had an "aha" moment. The best way I can describe it: I felt eco-completed. It sounds corny, but it's true.

Today, I no longer take all that I grew up with for granted. I've come full circle with those lessons of nature from when I was a child. It's all of those lessons that are at the root of my sincere passion for our planet today.

I'm now environmentally conscientious in both my food life and my overall lifestyle—though, I'm not fanatical about it. And for the past few years, luscious, low-carbon cooking has been a delightfully gratifying lifestyle choice of mine. Now, it's time to share.

Whether you're just a beginner at green cooking, or have years of experience with it, I encourage you to take a taste tour with *Big Green Cookbook*. I hope that low-carbon cooking becomes a passion of yours, too—or at least a pleasurable part of your lifestyle. These recipes are enjoyable for everyone, even the not-so-green folks. And I'm so thrilled to share this new way of cooking with you.

—Jackie Newgent, RD

acknowledgments

I have many people to be grateful to for their endless energy, time, and support of this book—and for helping me pursue my passion for the environment.

I'm thankful to:

My father, for the love of nature that he made sure I nurtured throughout my life.

My mother, for passing on her cooking genes and teaching me where food really comes from.

My eager-to-assist sister, Rebecca, my brother, Jim, and my sister-in-law, Sandi, for their help testing some of the recipes.

My bright and adorable nephews, Aiden and Rhyus, for motivating me to do all I can to make a better future for them—and all the other children on our precious planet.

Amy Morse, Leah McLaughlin, and Rachel Begun, MS, RD, for their gifts of friendship and adding their two cents when I needed it most.

Jesse and Jessica Freeman, for their enthusiastic food-loving palates—and making sure none of my recipe testing leftovers ever went to waste.

My very patient friends in New York and beyond, for being so understanding when I made this project my priority.

My chef assistants, Lindsay deJongh, RD, and Laura Allman, RD, without whom I couldn't have completed this cookbook.

Michael Bourret and Stacey Glick, my literary agents at Dystel & Goderich Literary Management, for always believing in me.

Beth Shepard, my spokesperson agent—and career sounding board.

My editor, Linda Ingroia, for providing me with the enormous opportunity to make a positive impact on the environment—and to the lives of all I reach. Thanks also to the motivated behind-the-scenes talent at Wiley, including Michael Olivo, the production manager; Shannon Egan, the production editor; Suzanne Sunwoo, the cover designer; and Ralph Fowler, the interior designer.

Finally, all of the environmental activists, for your trailblazing ways, never-ending commitment, and inspiring words and deeds; I wouldn't be writing this book if it wasn't for you who paved the green path before me.

Thank you so much to everyone!

Environmental Benefits Statement

This book is printed with soy-based inks on presses with VOC (volatile organic compound) levels that are lower than the standard for the printing industry. The paper, Rolland Enviro 100, is manufactured by Cascades Fine Papers Group and is made from 100 percent post-consumer, de-inked fiber, without chlorine. According to the manufacturer, the use of every ton of Rolland Enviro 100 Book paper, switched from virgin paper, helps the environment in the following ways:

Mature trees saved	Waterborne waste not created	Waterflow saved	Atmospheric emissions eliminated	Solid wastes reduced	Natural gas saved by using bio-gas
17	6.9 lbs.	10,196 gals.	2,098 lbs.	1,081 lbs.	2,478 cubic feet

BiG
GReeN
COOKBOOK

Planet Earth is cooking—literally! Most environmental scientists agree that climate change is a fact. Luckily, most people *want* to do something about their impact on our environment. The result: "going green" is a movement that is spreading across the globe.

Climate change, also known as global warming, occurs when greenhouse gases—primarily carbon dioxide (CO_2) from cars, power plants, and more—trap heat inside our atmosphere. More and more people understand the major impact it will likely have on our entire planet—major heat waves, more violent storms, severe flooding. These are a few of the serious threats climate change poses to our health, safety, economy, and future.

So what can *you* do? A lot—or a little! It's up to you how carbon conscientious you choose to be. And whether it is a little or a lot, one place that you can make an impact is right in your very own kitchen. The foods we choose, how we store them, and how we prepare them does indeed impact the environment. In fact, a University of Michigan study found that about one-third of the total energy used in the entire U.S. food system is for home preparation and refrigeration! Until now, this has been a mostly forgotten area of impact on climate change. That's all about to change. *Big Green Cookbook: Hundreds of Planet-Pleasing Recipes & Tips for a Luscious, Low-Carbon Lifestyle* is the first-ever comprehensive climate-conscious cookbook for everyday people.

In this cookbook, I merge a green philosophy into simply prepared delicious food. By following this book's tips and recipes you'll be able to reduce the amount of CO_2 that your own cooking and eating habits contribute to the environment. You'll be able to reduce your "carbon footprint." And this cookbook's recipes are so luscious you won't have to give up great tasting cuisine in order to do so.

I provide the what, why, and how to cook and eat in a planet-pleasing way—without having to make difficult changes. It's about being realistic.

In the recipes you'll find real food that real people eat . . . not exclusively vegetarian fare, raw foods, or unusually earthy ingredients. There are recipes for everyone—whatever your stage of greenness (and whatever your nutritional goals). And I don't rely on unusu-

iNTRODUC

ally artsy culinary skills. Thinking through the way food is prepared allowed me to streamline the recipes to make them green. This no-nonsense approach to cooking and eating is not a fad and not a drastic diet, but a doable approach for an eco-friendlier lifestyle. Think of it like a hybrid . . . the Prius of cookbooks. It's a savvy (and savory) step in the right direction.

But beware of green burnout. Do what you can, when you can, rather than try everything in this book all at once. Small changes do add up to big changes in the long run. And if you slowly adapt to new green ways of buying, cooking, serving, and storing food, you'll be more likely to stick to a green lifestyle—and make a difference. Just following one new recipe from time to time, or using some of the tips that are on every page, will guide you to a smarter, eco-friendlier, even more cost-conscious way of life.

Now, get ready to sink your teeth into the practical, positive, and positively delicious recipes in *Big Green Cookbook*. It'll keep your taste buds happy and, more importantly, keep our planet healthy.

TiON

recipe highlights

The recipes within *Big Green Cookbook* are full flavored and have a nutrient-rich focus. There are many features within the recipes that make them green. Here are the highlights.

- Fresh, whole, all-natural foods

- Plant-based ingredients (there's at least one fruit or veggie in every recipe)

- Seasonal produce (based on North American seasons)

- Use of environmentally conscious products

- Selective and eco-friendly use of animal-based products (when they're used):

  – Sustainable fish and shellfish

  – Petite portions of meats and incorporation of produce to boost heartiness and healthfulness of meat-focused dishes

  – Organic meat, poultry, milk, and yogurt

- No cooking required or a limit of 20 minutes of "on" cooking time

Additionally, all of the recipes have one or more of these unique low-carbon features:

- Low-carbon cooking techniques, such as use of small appliances or "lid cooking"

- Vegan-friendly adaptations if you don't want to use animal products

- Use of an underutilized highly edible food part, such as use of orange peel as a cup

Along with the recipes, you'll find plenty of practical tips and intriguing facts to add to their green appeal—and to help you slow climate change with your spoon, fork, and knife! They fall into the following categories:

- **Little Green Cooking Tip:** simple suggestions for eco-friendly cooking

- **Use It, Don't Lose It:** ideas for preventing food-related waste

- **Go Local:** tips for choosing locally produced foods

- **A Planet-Friendly Bite:** interesting environmental facts related to a recipe

big green cooking rules

Throughout *Big Green Cookbook* you'll find that there are eight recurring principles. By following these eight eco-rules, you can turn any food you prepare into "big green" recipes.

1. Prepare plant-based meals.
2. Be an energy-wise cook.
3. Eat by season.
4. Enjoy fresh foods naturally and simply prepared.
5. Go organic and eco-conscious when you can.
6. Buy locally when logical.
7. Practice the 4Rs: Reduce, Reuse, Repurpose, and Recycle.
8. Be realistic.

And, though it's not a "rule," have fun while cooking!

food miles: do they matter?

Food miles is a term for the amount of resources and energy required to transport food from farm to plate. Using it is one way to help understand a food's impact on greenhouse gas emissions. One estimate by Bon Appétit Management Company is that our food system, as a whole, may be responsible for as much as one-third of our greenhouse gas emissions! Eating more locally—shrinking your food miles—is one step in the right direction. But there's something that may matter more.

A compelling study in *Environmental Science & Technology* suggests that food transport accounts for 11 percent of food-associated greenhouse gas emissions, but production contributes 83 percent. Basically, food production makes up a much bigger part of the carbon emissions picture than food transportation.

The study suggests, for instance, that replacing meat and dairy with chicken, fish, or eggs one day a week can reduce emissions equivalent to driving 760 miles a year. Switching to veggies one day a week is like cutting 1,160 miles a year out of your driving. If the study is correct, it still doesn't mean that you need to give up meat or dairy, cold turkey. It does mean that reducing your consumption can be beneficial for our planet.

(It's important to know that there are eco-friendlier animal-based options becoming more available, too.)

But cutting down your food miles still does matter. The average distance food travels from farm to table in the U.S. has been estimated at 1,500 miles. Being a "locavore," or someone who eats locally produced foods (often from within a one hundred–mile radius), can help cut down on the environmental impact of food miles. And even if it only helps to shrink your carbon footprint by 5 percent, that's a good thing, as every bit helps!

But it's more than that. Eating more locally can help boost local economies. Plus, locally produced foods are likely to be fresher. And fresher foods can be more nutritional. Personally, I simply feel like I'm doing the right thing when I know I'm supporting an area farmer—and I actually can talk with them face-to-face about their food.

So eating locally (while thinking globally) can make a difference. But eating your veggies, period, is perhaps more important. In any case, the *Big Green Cookbook* way is to do what you realistically can, big or small, to help reduce your climate footprint. And the plant-based recipes in this cookbook will help you do just that.

where food is born

As of September 30, 2008, the USDA's Country of Origin Labeling (COOL) went into full effect. At most retailers, the following foods are now required to have COOL markings, such as "Product of the USA" or "Grown in Mexico": Muscle cuts of chicken, beef, pork, lamb, and goat; ground chicken, beef, pork, lamb, and goat; fish and shellfish (wild and farm raised); fresh and frozen fruits and vegetables; peanuts, pecans, and macadamia nuts; and ginseng.

finding your sustainable "sweet spot"

I had an infatuation with the environment as a child—thanks to my nature-loving dad and food-loving mom. But today, that fondness has turned into a great respect and everlasting green love. This sounds kind of like marriage, huh? But like any marriage, there is a balance. If a couple spent every single minute doing every single thing together, every single day for the rest of their lives, they'd probably go mad. That's the same philosophy I take with being green. It can be maddening to try to do everything as green as humanly possible. It can become nearly inhumane if it causes the rest of your life to go out of whack.

Finding balance is always important. So if that balance for you is being deep dark green . . . great. And if you've never done a single green thing until now . . . congratulations on taking your first eco-step. My hope is that everyone does all they can to be a friend to the planet, while still having balance in the rest of their lives. In other words, if you work fifty miles from your home, no one would expect you to walk to work. But carpooling, taking public transportation, or negotiating to work some days at home might be the way to find green balance in your commute. The same applies to cooking. Maybe you can plant a garden and grow some of your own food or maybe you try to buy only what you need at the market and make full use of everything you purchase.

Personally, my sustainable "sweet spot" in the kitchen is probably 90 percent. That means I try to make sure that at least nine out of every ten ingredients I use or nine out of every ten recipes I prepare are eco-friendly. I try to be energy efficient—or energy-wise—whenever possible. I feel good about this on a personal and planet-pleasing level. Now, it's time for you to find your sustainable "sweet spot" of cooking.

making a difference: green cooking

Take a look at how finding your sustainable "sweet spot" in the kitchen can make a big difference—just by the cooking times alone—by following three *Big Green Cookbook* recipes per week:

THE HARD-WORKING HAPPY COUPLE

Friday

Instead of spaghetti with a jarred pasta sauce = 15 minutes "on" cooking time

Prepare Citrus Cream of Capellini (page 151) = 8 minutes "on" cooking time

Save 7 total minutes

Saturday

Instead of homemade roasted eggplant dip = 50 minutes "on" cooking time

Prepare Baba Ghanoush à la Skillet (page 192) = 10 minutes "on" cooking time

Save 40 total minutes

Sunday

Instead of traditional skillet hash brown potatoes = 30 minutes "on" cooking time

Prepare Fiery Fingerlings (page 88) = 11 minutes "on" cooking time

Save 19 total minutes

3-Day Total

Save 66 minutes—or over 1 hour—of combined cooking energy in 1 week!

THE BUSY FAMILY OF FOUR

Monday

Instead of traditional chili con carne = 60 minutes "on" cooking time

Prepare Chili con Turkey under Pressure (page 228) = 18 minutes "on" cooking time

Save 42 total minutes

Wednesday

Instead of a side of steamed brown rice = 55 minutes "on" cooking time

Prepare Side of Supergrains (page 278) = 7 minutes "on" cooking time

Save 48 total minutes

Friday

Instead of typical chocolate chip cookies = 20 minutes "on" cooking time

Prepare Happy Planet Cookies (page 358) = 10 minutes "on" cooking time

Save 10 total minutes

3-Day Total

Save 100 minutes—or over 1½ hours— of combined cooking energy in 1 week!

Then, if the couple or family did that for one year, look what happens:

THE HARD-WORKING HAPPY COUPLE

66 minutes × 52 weeks = total yearly savings of 3,432 minutes of cooking energy.

That means significantly less CO_2 entering the atmosphere—plus less money spent on the utility bills, which means more spending money!

THE BUSY FAMILY OF FOUR

100 minutes × 52 weeks = total yearly savings of 5,200 minutes of cooking energy.

That means significantly less CO_2 in the atmosphere—plus less money spent on the utility bills, which means more money for paying off other bills!

In addition to saving all of that cooking energy, there will be other positive impacts on the environment because of the eco-friendly ingredients you use. Then toss in a few *Big Green Cookbook* tips here and there and you've got a sustainable "sweet spot" of cuisine that makes a big whopping difference!

How much energy are you consuming or saving? If you know the wattage of an appliance or electronic device, you can calculate the annual CO_2 emissions using this formula: (watts × hours used daily × 365 days)/1,000 × 1.34 pounds. Or use your state's carbon coefficient, found on the EIA Web site: www.eia.doe.gov.

the green kitchen checklist

I've compiled a handful of practical strategies for how you can make a realistic, yet significant, impact in cutting global warming pollution from your very own kitchen. Implement one tip at a time using this checklist. Hopefully you already have a head start. If not, get ready. Get set. Go green your kitchen!

☐ **Be energy wise.** Each year, households use about one-fifth of the total energy consumed in the United States. And those utility bills definitely add up. The average U.S. family spends about $2,000 a year on their energy bills; approximately 60 percent is from electricity use. As a nation, we spend about one-quarter of our electricity on lighting. Much of this energy is wasted using inefficient incandescent lightbulbs. Only 10 percent of the energy used by one of these bulbs produces light; the rest is given off as heat. So light right! If you replace 25 percent of your lightbulbs with fluorescents (start in your kitchen!), you can save about 50 percent on your lighting bill. Though compact fluorescent lightbulbs (CFLs) may cost more, they provide the same amount of light and save money in the long run. They use only one-quarter the energy of incandescent bulbs—which helps reduce the greenhouse gas emissions that lead to climate change. Plus, they can last about ten times longer! Each CFL you install can save you $30 to $60 over the bulb's life. It's important to look for recycling or proper disposal options in your area— even though you won't need to actually

do it for another eight to ten years from now!

☐ **Shop for the "stars."** You can save money while saving the environment by switching to appliances that have earned the U.S. Department of Energy's Energy Star. They generally use up to 50 percent less energy and water than traditional models. If you have a fridge made before 1990, consider buying a new Energy Star–qualified one. It might save enough energy to light the typical household for about four months! You'll be preventing pollution in the process. Plus, the money you save on utility bills (how does an extra eighty bucks in your pocket sound?) can make up for the cost of a more expensive, yet more efficient, model. So thank your lucky Energy Stars! (See Pledge to Become a "Star" on page 9 for more information.)

☐ **Reduce your refrigerator energy use.** Appliances account for about 20 percent of a typical household's energy use. The refrigerator is the biggest energy glutton in most household kitchens. Whether you have an energy smart refrigerator-freezer or a not-so-smart one, here are smart ways to use it. The obvious first step is to minimize the time the fridge or freezer doors are open. Keep it nicely stocked (though not overstocked) with food for optimal energy efficiency, as it takes more energy to cool air than it does to keep food cool! Consider getting an energy audit. Or audit yourself by checking the following: make sure that the position of the fridge is away from the oven, dishwasher, or direct sunlight; the air is freely circulating around its condenser coils and that the coils are clean; and the door seals are airtight. If you didn't pass the audit or you have an older or second refrigerator, recycle it. Visit RecycleMyOldFridge.com.

☐ **Know the Goldilocks settings.** Check your refrigerator and freezer temps. For optimal food safety and storage, ideal refrigerator temperature is 34° to 40°F. I keep my fridge set at 39°F—there's no need to go much lower than that. Freezers are best kept at 0°F. Negative temps aren't necessary—just be sure the freezer doesn't go above 5°F. This will prevent using excess energy and, at the same time, prevent food spoilage and keep food safe at "just right" temperatures.

☐ **Dish wash wisely.** If you're lucky enough to own a dishwasher, check to see if it was manufactured before 1994. If so, your best bet is to replace it with an Energy Star–qualified one—which will ultimately help promote cleaner air and slow climate change. It might save you $30 a year (or more!) on your utility bills, too! Try these other eco-friendly ideas whether you have an energy smart dishwasher or not: scrape dishes before dishwashing (but don't go crazy rinsing dishes beforehand); use the energy-saving cycle if it's an option; let dishes air-dry instead of heat-dry; and run it only when full since the energy used by a dishwasher is mainly for heating water. Use eco-friendly, phosphate-free, bleach-free dishwashing liquids or tablets, too.

☐ **Got wind?** Regardless of what kitchen appliances you use, make using them greener. Switch your power supply to green power, which is any renewable energy source or combination of sources, such as solar and wind power, hydropower, geothermal, and various forms of biomass. You don't need to have your own windmill or solar panels. (But if you do, that's fantastic!) In most states, you can have your energy sourced from cleaner fuels. Contact your energy supplier or go to the U.S. Department of Energy's "Green Power Network" at www.eere.energy.gov/greenpower to find out how. Otherwise, look into purchasing renewable energy certificates. For me, having my energy sourced from 100 percent wind power is a win-win. I'm being

pledge to become a "star"

On April 22, 2008 (Earth Day), the U.S. Environmental Protection Agency (EPA) launched a national campaign to help Americans join in the fight against climate change. The campaign, "Change the World, Start with Energy Star" was designed to help people make important energy-efficient changes that ultimately add up to significant reductions in greenhouse gas emissions. Take the Energy Star pledge at www.energystar.gov/changetheworld. If every American household took part in this pledge, it could save more than $18 billion in annual energy costs and prevent greenhouse gases equivalent to the emissions of more than 18 million cars!

more environmentally responsible and, at the same time, it supports development of more renewable energy sources. But even if you're using a renewable energy source, it's still important to be conscientious about energy use. No matter what the source, it's not free and it's not a license to cheat! Look at it like this: If you join a weight-loss program, but then pig out on whatever you want, that's obviously not the answer to dieting. So switching to wind or other green power doesn't mean that you can "pig out" and use as much energy as you want—even if it is clean energy. After all, nothing in life is truly free. Making meaningful eco-lifestyle changes are still important—and will remain important.

☐ **Get unplugged.** Throughout the recipes in *Big Green Cookbook*, I encourage small appliance use, such as the toaster oven and panini grill. Their small size means they'll use less energy than larger appliances, like the oven. But when those little appliances and other electric kitchen equipment, like toasters or blenders, are not in use, it's best to unplug them. Why? Even when not in use, just being plugged in drains a small amount of energy—called "phantom" or "vampire" energy! Another option is to use a smart power strip that will sense when an appliance is off, automatically cutting power to it—saving energy and money. The strip is so "smart," it even knows when to turn things on.

☐ **Think at the sink.** Water is one of our planet's precious resources. Conserving it is important for the continued good health of our planet—and the health of our vital drinking water supply. The friendly folks of Atlanta can tell you first-hand about this. In 2008, they had to follow specific water conservation rules due to drought conditions. So consider some of these smart practices at the kitchen sink. Place produce in a bowl of water and then scrub clean, rather than continually running water while you wash vegetables and fruits. Need extra help when removing dirt, waxes, and residues from produce? Consider using just a little bit of one of the many natural fruit-and-veggie washes on the market, which may ultimately help you use less water. Instead of a lengthy rinsing of hot pasta with cold water to cool it down for use in pasta salad, place a few ice cubes in the pot with the pasta and toss. And when using canned beans in a recipe, don't rinse them; buy organic and simply drain them.

☐ **Practice the 4Rs.** Okay, so they're usually called the 3Rs. But I always need to be a little different. So here are 4Rs worth practicing for an eco-friendly kitchen—and beyond:

- **Reduce:** Buy and use only what you need. Aim to have less waste by using all parts of foods when possible.

- **Reuse:** Wash and reuse whatever food and beverage containers that you can—as long as it's safe to do so.

- **Repurpose:** Consider other ways to use something other than how it was originally used. (For instance, a used soup can may be repurposed as a chopstick holder or pencil container.)

- **Recycle:** Recycle everything allowable . . . but don't try to recycle what's not recyclable. (Ask your local municipality for recycling guidelines in your area.)

☐ **Give composting a chance.** Aim to make your trash can the smallest bin in your house, not the biggest. Put everything allowable into your recycling and compost bins. Composting basically speeds up natural composition—and, in the process, you'll lighten your environmental footprint. It's nature's way of recycling. It makes fertilizer for your herbs, plants, and trees. You can compost outdoors with a compost pile or a bin. Or, if you prefer or don't have an outdoor space, do it indoors. If you do it inside, you'll most likely be using worms. That's called "vermicomposting"—the worms eat your kitchen scraps.

There may be other options for composting if either of these ideas sounds a bit too earthy, such as making use of composting collection centers or drop-off locations in your local area (like I do!). You'll then collect your scraps in a compost container to save them until you're ready to take them to a community composting center. Common food items safe for composting: fruits and vegetables, leaves, bread, cereal, and pasta, eggshells, nutshells, and coffee grounds.

☐ **Plant an indoor herb garden.** It's possible to find most fresh herbs year-round. But consider growing them indoors—especially if you live in an area where it's difficult to find certain herbs fresh. This will be particularly helpful for recipes in *Big Green Cookbook*. Herbs can do quite well on a sunny windowsill. And, like all plants, they're good for the environment—even when indoors. Start with three or four herbs, like mint, rosemary, thyme, and oregano. It's easiest to start from small herb plants from a local nursery or garden center. Choose a window that gets at least several hours of sun each day. Repot the herbs in larger pots or a long divided planter with drainage holes. Use potting soil recommended by the nursery or garden center. Then water your herbs sparingly. Enjoy seeing them grow—and using them in your green cuisine.

☐ **Let small appliances rule.** Green things come in little packages. When considering how to cook, the general rule is the bigger it is, the bigger the carbon footprint it will ultimately leave. In *Big Green Cookbook*, you'll find that the little appliances are used most often. Two must-haves for your low-carbon cooking needs: toaster and microwave oven.

a bright idea

If one person in every American home replaces just one incandescent lightbulb with an Energy Star qualified CFL, in a year it can save enough energy to light more than 3 million homes. That can prevent the release of greenhouse gas emissions equivalent to those from about 800,000 cars.

green pans

Is it time to toss out those nonstick skillets?

Research suggests that some chemicals in certain cookware may make its way into the food that's cooked in it. So it is prudent to get rid of anything with Teflon. There are just too many warning flags about it.

What's the problem? Perfluorooctanoic acid (PFOA), the chemical used in the manufacturing of Teflon. It's what has made most of the cookware on the marketplace, until recently, nonstick. And it's likely a carcinogen, according to the U.S. Environmental Protection Agency (EPA). Although there remains scientific uncertainty regarding potential risks, PFOA is being phased out by manufacturers.

My personal advice: Choose to cook with what you feel good about. And don't throw safe pots and pans out even if there are greener alternatives available now. It can be eco-wiser in many cases to use what you have (at least the non-Teflon-coated pots and pans) until it becomes a problem or it's lived a full life. For me, I'm not using any of my old nonstick cookware anymore—at least for cooking.

I suggest stick-resistant skillets in many of the recipes. That just means cooking in a pan that resists sticking, like a well-seasoned iron skillet, but that doesn't have a traditional nonstick coating. Stick-resistant pans are not completely nonstick, so there might be a slight bit of stickiness.

My top three stick-resistant skillet suggestions:

- Well-seasoned cast iron; it's the original stick-resistant surface and meant to be used for a lifetime!
- Enameled cast iron; it's stick-resistant if enough oil or other fat is used; it distributes heat evenly and retains heat well.
- Anodized aluminum; it's stick-resistant if kept clean and is nonreactive to the foods being cooked; it distributes heat well.

My other pot, pan, and baking dish picks:

- Stainless; they're multipurpose and dishwasher safe. I used All-Clad Stainless saucepans for most of my recipe testing when I didn't need a stick-resistant option.
- Copper-lined stainless; they hold heat well because of the copper and ultimately require less energy use; they're dishwasher safe.
- Copper with aluminum core and stainless-steel cooking surface; though pricey, they retain heat very well and ultimately require less energy use.
- Stoneware; you can prep, microwave, bake, freeze, store, and serve in it. Plus it's dishwasher safe. I used a 10-inch round (2-quart) Le Creuset Traditional Stoneware dish for several recipes—including microwave recipes.

Green skillets to consider:

- Eco-friendly nonstick hard-anodized, such as Cuisinart Green Gourmet; its ceramic-based coating doesn't contain PFOA.
- Eco-friendly nonstick hard-anodized or stainless-steel induction, such as GreenPan; its Thermolon ceramic-based coating doesn't contain PFOA.

☐ **Toaster oven.** It works just like a regular oven, but more efficiently—using only about half of the energy of a conventional oven! If you need to buy a toaster oven, pick one that has two shelves. That's because you'll probably be relying on it more as you bake eco-friendlier—and you'll want enough space to prepare a meal or fix full desserts, not just toast.

Note: I used a 1,600-watt two-shelf toaster oven for testing recipes in *Big Green Cookbook*. (See In This Cookbook on page 38 for more information.)

☐ **Microwave oven.** Due mainly to faster cooking times, the microwave oven can reduce energy use by about two-thirds (maybe more!) compared with the conventional oven. The energy heats only the food, not the entire oven. What's more, microwave ovens are now smart; they automatically shut off when a food is properly cooked. And that can shrink an environmental footprint even further. You'll probably be relying on a microwave oven more as you cook greener—and you'll want enough power to make meals, not just reheat. Higher wattage means more power is used minute per minute, but it cooks faster! If you decide, you can always use less than the full wattage by cooking at 50 percent power, too.

Note: I used a 1,200-watt microwave oven for testing recipes in *Big Green Cookbook*. (See In This Cookbook, on page 38 for more information.)

☐ **Equip for green cuisine.** Below is my essential list of cooking equipment and other tools for a well-stocked eco-friendly kitchen. They'll come in handy in the *Big Green Cookbook* recipes. It's time to get equipped!

- High-quality pans with tight-fitting lids, including a large (12-inch) stick-resistant skillet (see Green Pans, on page 12)

- Stoneware, including a microwave-safe 2-quart dish and 9½-inch oval baker

- Serving bowls that can be used as mixing bowls

- Good knives—and good knife skills (Take a knife skills cooking class!)

- Panini-style grill

- Grill pan

- Indoor electric grill

- Pressure cooker

- Bamboo and/or Paperstone cutting boards

- Salad spinners (large and small)

- Produce scrub brush

- Bamboo or silicone-coated cooking utensils, including a silicone-coated whisk

- Butane kitchen torch

- Box grater

- Microplane zester/grater

- Kitchen mallet

- *Molcajete* or large mortar and pestle

- Manual smooth-edge can opener

- Bamboo or reusable skewers, such as cast iron

- Whistling tea kettle

- Mesh strainer

- Ice cream "ball" or hand-churned ice cream maker

- Misto or similar spray-type bottle (fill with oil for "homemade" cooking spray)

- Kitchen scale

- Cooking timer

- Ruler

- Potato masher

- Pastry blender

- Citrus reamer

- Cherry pitter

Add slow cooker to this list. It actually requires very little energy—even though you generally leave it on for hours! But since the "rule" for the recipes selected for this cookbook is that they need to stay within 20 minutes of "on" cooking time, I didn't include slow cooker recipes. Nonetheless, you'll find I sort of snuck a couple ideas in anyway under Little Green Cooking Tip on pages 57 and 324. Hope you enjoy them . . . slowly.

☐ **Stock up on planet-pleasing staples.**
Listed here are ingredients you'll want for an eco-friendly kitchen. They'll come in handy in the *Big Green Cookbook* recipes. So stock up!

- Stone-ground whole-wheat flour

- Turbinado or Demerara sugar

- Mild floral honey (preferably locally sourced)

- Sea salt (preferably locally sourced)

- Quinoa

- Bulgur wheat

- Whole-wheat couscous

- Various whole-grain pastas and soba noodles

- Old-fashioned oats

- Various oils—canola, peanut, extra-virgin olive, sesame, flaxseed

- Various vinegars—apple cider, aged balsamic, aged red wine, white wine

- Various canned organic beans—black, kidney, cannellini, garbanzo

- Low-sodium vegetable broth

- Organic eggs

- Fruit spread (preferably locally sourced)

- Various seasonal onions

- Garlic

- Shallots

- Lemons

- Limes

And remember: go organic when you can.

twenty-seven clever tips for low-carbon cooking

While low-carbon cuisine strategies are already incorporated into the book's recipes, below are some of my favorites. Incorporate these savory and sweet suggestions for any of your own recipes, too.

1. **Try "earth-style" on for size.** Use every edible produce part—skin, seeds, and all—whenever possible to create less waste and add eco-flair. Scrub skins and outer peels well first. And aim to go organic when you go earth-style.

2. **All eco-wrapped up.** Since many wraps, like white flour tortillas or rice papers are overly processed, wrap foods in lettuce leaves instead. Or, if you choose a grain wrap, go for whole-grain products, like stone-ground whole-wheat tortillas.

3. **Serve casual, home-style meals.** Aim to prep, cook, and serve in the same pans or bowls (like Le Crueset stoneware) when it's logical—so you'll have less washing to do. When you need, wipe food from rims with a half sheet of unbleached paper towel or clean kitchen towel for a prettier presentation.

4. **Green grillin'.** When using a hot grill with on/off controls, cook food partway and then turn it off to save gas or electricity. The food will continue to "green grill" in the off position with the remaining heat. Be sure foods are properly cooked before serving.

5. **Turn it off; keep on stirring.** When using a hot skillet for sautéing, first use the right size burner for the pan so you don't waste energy. Then, cook food partway and turn the heat off to save gas or electricity. Keep stirring ("green sautéing") the food over the off burner with the residual heat. Be sure foods are properly cooked before serving.

6. **Say hello to "hypercooking."** Heard of hypermiling, where you take any advantage you can to conserve gas while driving? Well, you can do the same with cooking. "Hyperbake" by placing foods, like cookies, into a non-preheated oven, then turn on the heat and bake partway, then turn off the heat and continue to bake until done. Generally, you can turn off the oven 5 minutes before the end of cooking. Hyperfry by placing foods, like chicken nuggets, into room temperature oil, then turn on the heat and fry until done

7. **Residual value.** Even if not fully hyperbaking, you can still take advantage of residual heat to save a little cooking gas or electricity. Finish baking or roasting in the off oven or toaster oven with the remaining heat. Just keep the door closed to keep the heat trapped.

8. **Put a lid on it.** This is one of my favorite green cooking techniques— even if it goes against how I was trained to properly cook. Let the lid do the cooking. When food on the

stovetop is being simmered, sautéed, or boiled (like pasta), finish the cooking by covering it with a tight-fitting lid (to trap the heat), turning off the burner, then allowing to gently finish cooking with the trapped heat. No peeking—or it won't work properly! Try this for pasta: Bring water to a boil; add pasta; bring back to a boil; cover and turn off the heat; "lid cook" for the time (or 1 minute less) that the package recommends. Voilà . . . lid cooked pasta!

9. **Micro-matters.** Since the microwave oven can reduce energy use by roughly two-thirds compared to a conventional oven, use it to do more than just re-heating and making popcorn. Try

"micro-roasting" or "micro-baking": cooking in the microwave oven; "micro-steaming": steaming in the microwave oven; and "micro-stewing": stewing in the microwave oven. Also, make sure to use only materials that are designed for microwave use. (See A Note about Microwaves below.)

10. **Drink—and eat—eco-beer.** Add a friendly neighborhood taste by spiking chilis or stews with locally brewed (if possible, go organic, too) beer. Then simply stew—or, eco-brew.

11. **Cook by season.** The recipes in *Big Green Cookbook* are already planned seasonally (based on North American seasons) for you based on the produce that's generally available

a note about microwaves

The microwave oven is used in several of the recipes in *Big Green Cookbook* due to its significant energy efficiency over a conventional oven. Though minor questions about safety exist and research is ongoing, here's the bottom line: There is currently no significant scientific or health research to suggest avoiding the use of the microwave oven. Here's some additional helpful information:

1. Microwaves cause the vibrations of water molecules in food. That produces the heat that cooks the food.

2. Microwave cooking doesn't reduce the nutritional value of foods any more than conventional cooking—and may retain more of their nutrients due to quicker cooking and cooking without the addition of water.

3. According to the Food and Drug Administration, there's little cause for concern about excess microwaves leaking from microwave ovens unless the door hinges, latch, or seals are damaged.

4. If you believe your oven might be leaking excessive microwaves, contact the oven manufacturer, your state health department, or the nearest FDA office.

5. Follow the manufacturer's instruction manual. Some common microwave oven guidelines:

   • Do not heat water or other liquids in it for excessive amounts of time.

   • Don't operate if the door doesn't close firmly or is warped, bent, or damaged.

   • Never operate if you have reason to believe it'll keep operating with the door open.

   • As an added precaution, don't stand directly against it for long periods while in use.

in most of the country. The United States is a big place, so aim to mostly use produce that's in season in your own local area (or, better yet, your own garden!) for the greenest fruit and veggie experience. If a fruit or vegetable is available at your local farmers' market, that's a good sign of seasonality. And use the Seasonal Produce Guide (page 361) to help you find seasonal ingredients.

12. **Get skinny.** You don't need to be skinny! Rather, choose foods that are thin to start with, like angel hair or capellini pasta instead of fettuccine. And before cooking a food, consider making it thinner. For instance, slice a boneless, skinless organic chicken breast into thin cutlets or pound it into a super-thin fillet (that's called a "paillard") with a kitchen mallet. The slimmer the food, the faster it'll cook— saving you and the planet energy.

13. **Cut more, cook less.** By spending more time cutting, you'll be spending less time cooking—ultimately using less energy. Small dices are greener than large dices. That's because smaller foods cook faster, of course. What if you're clumsy at cutting? This is when having good knife skills will come in handy. So do consider taking a knife skills cooking class to perfect this low-carbon cooking technique.

14. **Go for green doneness.** If it's steak, don't go "medium"; go "medium rare" instead. If it's a hamburger, don't go "well done"; go "medium" instead. If it's poultry, go "well done"; it's the only recommendation. But "well done" doesn't mean overly done and dry. Basically, for green doneness, prepare a food until cooked just to the level required for safe eating—but no longer. The food will generally be juicier. And you'll be using less cooking energy in the process. This tip is useful when ordering at restaurants, too! (See Safe Cooking Temps = Green Cooking Temps on page 19 for more information.)

15. **Make sides the new entrées.** Instead of having entrées and sides in separate recipe categories, I've combined them in *Big Green Cookbook*. That's to encourage you to consider some side dishes (mainly veggie sides) as entrées. It's a green goal to be more of a plant-based eater than a meat-based eater. That includes what's at the center of your plate.

16. **Be at least a part-time vegetarian.** If you're a vegetarian, keep it up! But if you love meat, don't worry—you can still make an eco-difference. Aim to be a flexitarian—or someone who's often a vegetarian, but who'll eat chicken, fish, or possibly meat on occasion. Better yet, be an ecotarian— someone who eats foods based on environmental sustainability. That's a plant-based diet that may or may not contain small amounts of organic animal products. (I'm an ecotarian, by the way!) So, if you choose to eat meat, try going for at least one meatless meal a week. Then keep working at it until you're eating meatless most of the week. (See Meaty Issues on page 28 for more information.)

17. **Green-size me.** A lot of resources and energy goes into meat production. So green-size it! That means to enjoy petite meat portions to make the environmental impact more petite. It's one way to have your meat and eat it, too—even if only slightly more greenly. The same green-sizing idea can be beneficial for any foods that require cooking. For instance, make mini organic meatloaves, meatballs, or mini burgers instead of their hefty counterparts. Indulge in organic chicken nuggets instead of oversized fried chicken breasts. And bake mini cupcakes instead of not-so-mini ones— or instead of a full-size cake—to shrink-size the cooking energy required.

18. **Be decisive with the doors closed.** Ever just hang out with the refrigerator doors open trying to decide what to eat? Try to make most decisions in advance. Minimize the time the fridge or freezer doors are open. If you have one, switch the alarm to the on position. (I have one of these in my refrigerator and it's so annoying when it goes off! But that's the whole point. It means I've been hanging out too long—letting too much of the cold air out. Then it takes more energy to properly cool foods again.) Arrange things logically in your refrigerator and freezer so you always know where to find foods. And keep it nicely stocked with food for optimal energy efficiency. It actually takes more energy to cool air than it does to cool food! So here's something to consider: If you live alone or don't usually keep much in your fridge, it

may not make sense to have a monstrous one—even if it looks cool.

19. **Be a better greener baker.** Are you a swinger? Every time you swing open a hot oven, it may lose 25° to 50°F. That means you'll need to use more energy for reheating—and possibly more energy to cool down the kitchen. So resist the urge to peek and instead use the oven's window when you're baking. And if it's summer, consider doing any big-oven baking really early or really late in the day when it's cooler.

20. **It's on tap.** Bottled water used to have a pure image, but we now know there are issues with it. One is the fact that it's not as tightly regulated for safety as tap water. Another is all of those bottles, period—from the chemicals in the plastic to the landfills that are, literally, all bottled up. So kick the bottled water habit, if you haven't already. Though tap water isn't perfect, it's the greenest choice. (And it's the cheapest choice!) I call for fresh water in the recipes; in other words, fresh cold water from the tap. And if you have any concerns with your tap water, filter it accordingly.

21. **Caramelize without cooking.** You won't find many baked recipes in *Big Green Cookbook*. You will find that something that's traditionally baked may be "micro-baked" instead! When following this technique in a microwave oven, it will speed up cooking time and reduce the amount of energy used. But if you're looking for oven-baked brownness or caramelization,

safe cooking temps = green cooking temps

The best way to know for sure if something is cooked properly (and potentially harmful bacteria is destroyed) is to use a food thermometer. Use these temperatures, recommended by the Partnership for Food Safety, as a guide to safety for *Big Green Cookbook* recipes. For instance, a chicken breast is done at an internal temperature of 165°F. So there's no need to keep cooking until it's 170°F or 175°F; it'll be overcooked—plus, you'll be using excess cooking energy in the process.

EGGS AND EGG DISHES

Eggs.. Cook until yolk and white are firm
Egg dishes .... 160°F

SEAFOOD

Fish... 145°F, or flesh is opaque and separates easily with a fork
Crabs, Shrimp .... Flesh is opaque and pearl-like
Clams..................................... Shells open during cooking
Scallops .... Milky white or opaque and firm

POULTRY

Parts and whole poultry ..... 165°F

PORK

Medium .... 160°F

BEEF

Medium Rare .... 145°F

GROUND MEAT AND MEAT MIXTURES

Beef....................................... 160°F
Turkey .... 165°F

the microwave won't do that. So, if caramelization is key for you, try these ideas. Use stone-ground whole-wheat in place of white flour or use turbinado sugar instead of white sugar to create a richer browner color in a dessert. Sprinkle with nuts to add crunchiness and the texture of a crisp baked coating. You can also lightly brown the top of a savory or sweet "micro-baked" delight by using a small (refillable) butane torch—like chefs use for crème brûlée—for a few seconds.

22. **Room temp = eco-temp.** Unless a recipe calls specifically for a cold or chilled ingredient, most recipes will cook faster when starting with ingredients that are at room temperature. It'll shave off extra minutes of cooking energy, too. However, use cold tap water and let it sit for a bit so it reaches room temperature before it's time to cook. And remember the rules of food safety . . . perishable foods should not sit at room temperature for more than two hours.

23. **Put it on ice.** When making pasta salad, the pasta is cooked and then often continually rinsed under cold water until it's cooled down. But using

so much of this precious resource (water) is not an eco-conscious practice. So instead of all of that rinsing, try this: Drain the cooked pasta, add several ice cubes, toss until the ice melts, then drain again. The pasta should be sufficiently cooled off and ready for pasta salad–making. (By the way, I don't have an automatic ice maker installed in my freezer. So I make ice the old-fashioned way, in a tray. I actually use a covered tray meant for a dozen eggs. I love my half egg-shaped ice cubes. I call them "artisanal ice cubes" to make them seem more glamorous—and green.)

24. **Preserve it!** Over-purchased? Over-picked? Or overgrown? When you have too much produce—or any food—on your hands, look for ways to utilize it. Home canning is one way. Fresh homemade jam can be used in many of the recipes! Use your own favorite jam recipe or find one in the book *Canning & Preserving for Dummies* by Karen Ward. Cook produce in dishes that can be frozen and reheated for another day. Or simply get a little bit creative in your cooking. Just about any veggie can be sautéed with extra-virgin olive oil and tossed with pasta. And most fruits can be whirled into a smoothie. Remember this catch phrase: use it, don't lose it.

25. **Stay in the 20 mpm (minutes per meal) cooking zone.** In *Big Green Cookbook* recipes, every single one has no more than 20 minutes of "on" cooking time. But what if you want to cook in bulk to be even greener?

You'll likely have longer cooking times, but you'll probably still fit into that 20 mpm zone if you calculate how many meals you'll be getting out of your big batch. Do a little math: total cooking time divided by total meals = the actual amount of cooking time per meal. So if you make a casserole in 60 minutes, but it serves 6 separate meals, that means its 10 mpm . . . and it's a winner. A goal of no more 20 mpm is an eco-friendly zone!

26. **If you bulk up, pack it properly.** Cooking double or triple batches is a way to be greener since you'll only be doing the actual cooking once, not twice, or three times. However, you'll want to store the extras properly. Store them in containers that can go into the microwave or toaster oven for a quick reheat, like stoneware or glass. Leftover plastic food containers, like margarine tubs for instance, don't fit into that category; they're not microwave oven–safe. When possible, store in the portions that you plan to later serve. And keep in containers that can be washed and reused.

27. **Waste not, want not.** Be eco-conscious before you plan to cook, not just when you're cooking. If you know you can't eat the whole recipe and you don't want to plan for leftovers, consider halving a recipe. Having less trash and less landfill waste is always a good goal. And even if you compost, it's always a green idea not to be an over-consumer.

eco-friendly shopping guide

Far too much of our food needs to travel long distances to make it to a store shelf. In fact, the average food item travels about 1,500 miles from farm to fork. Shrinking that mileage marker by choosing food less traveled is one important goal for our planet's health—and your own. And there's more than just food miles to think about when it comes to shopping. Below is a guide for helping you make greener choices when you go to the market.

Start using this guide by focusing on just one tip; apply it regularly for a few weeks, and then move on to the next. Taking small realistic steps, rather than making many changes all at once is the best way to become green. After all, the ultimate goal is to be green for good, not just green for now.

- **Shop in a rush, if you must— but steer clear of rush hour.** With the economic concerns of today, many are looking for ways to save money at the pump. If you properly time your grocery shopping trip, you may be able to do just that. And you'll be reducing carbon emissions in the process. So what's the best time to shop? Anytime, except rush hour. If you're sitting in traffic, wasting gas, then it's not the time to be shopping. Consider going after lunch or after dinner, not on your way home from work. You'll likely be full then, so all of the yummy-sounding, but not-so-green foods won't find a way into your shopping basket or cart. Also, consider combining your food shopping outing with other errands—just buy the groceries last to keep them fresh.

- **Plan a green grocery shopping list.** Creating a shopping list is the best way to stick to a budget and a healthful eating plan. It can also be the best way to be an eco-savvy shopper. Plan lists according to how foods are arranged at your favorite shopping locales. Make sure the last foods on your list are those that need to remain chilled or frozen. If necessary, go one day not to shop, but to create a list template to use on your next trip. This will help make shopping easier—and help assure that favorite eco-friendly foods make it into your cart. Plus, it'll make shopping go faster. That means you'll get your perishables home in a timely way— so they'll stay at their freshest the longest, which will prevent waste. And after shopping, remember to arrange alike foods by date—so that the oldest is in front and will get used first. Put the foods that need to go into the freezer or refrigerator away first, too.

- **Just say no to plastic *and* paper.** You've likely gotten the message on this already. By saying no to plastic bags at the checkout, you'll help reduce waste, lower carbon emissions, and more. And since so many of those plastic grocery bags end up in waterways and are potentially swallowed by marine animals, it'll help save our oceans and sea life. Paper bags aren't much better. Even if recycled, they still take a significant amount of energy to manufacture. So take your own reusable bags or tote when food shopping. There are very cool ones available now, even reusable bags and totes made from recycled bottles or old sails from actual sailboats. Keep an eye out for more. It's the hottest trend in shopping accessories. Visit www.reusablebags.com for more ideas.

- **Green-size your shopping.** Consider ways that you can prevent having excess food waste. One way is by green-sizing your shopping. Buy just the foods that you need—and in the sizes or amounts that you can use before they spoil. (That's where that shopping list comes in handy!) By reducing the amount of food that you might potentially waste, you'll be saving money and valuable resources. And watch out for those "buy one, get one free" offers; they may just result in more food waste. (See Waste Not on page 30 for more information.)

- **Go with a fresh date.** Sure, take a date with you to the market, if you like. But the date that's most important is what's stamped on the food. To help prevent food waste, spend a few extra minutes checking expiration dates to make sure you'll be using the food before the dates. Remember, the freshest foods are usually in the back of the shelves, not the front.

- **Join a community supported agriculture (CSA) program or frequent a local farmers' market.** Not all of your shopping needs to be done at a grocery store. In fact, the greenest way to shop can be by hitting a few places, especially if those places include a local farmers' market or a community supported agriculture (CSA) location. (See Find a Farmers' Market on page 366.) However, if you shop at more than one location, map out the shortest, most logical route and the best time of day so you don't use excess gas. Better yet, take public transportation, bike, or walk when you can. Biking with a backpack or rolling a nifty cart on your walk-to-shop excursion is good exercise, too.

- **Buy by number.** When making green purchasing decisions, it is important to know and use the numbers you'll find on the bottom of plastic bottles and containers. Not all plastics are safe, as there are toxic concerns with some. Biodegradability is an issue and not all plastics are recyclable. Even if a plastic is recyclable, it doesn't mean it is in your area. So check with your local municipality about recycling options. All of this should go into your eco-conscious decision making to make sure only the eco-friendliest containers make it into your shopping cart. The general run-down can be seen in the chart on page 23.

   Basically, nix the numbers 3 and 6. And gather more info about the number 7 item you choose, since material varies. Today, much is changing in food packaging. For instance, what

PLASTIC, BY THE NUMBERS

	SAFEST	RECYCLABLE
1 = polyethylene terephthalate (PET) or (PETE)	X*	
2 = high density polyethylene (HDPE)	X	X
3 = polyvinyl chloride (PVC)		
4 = low density plyethylene (LDPE)	X	X
5 = polypropylene (PP)	X	X
6 = polystyrene (PS)		X
7 = polycarbonate or other	Varies	Varies

*Do not reuse

may not be recyclable today may be tomorrow. Look for greener packaging in the future in a market near you.

- **Choose organically produced foods as often as you can.** Going organic is an investment in your health—and the health of the planet. That includes reasonably priced generic or store brands that are organic! It means fewer pesticides and other possibly toxic chemicals will end up in the food you eat—and in the environment as a whole. Organic production helps protect farm workers, too. In terms of meat, it means an animal was given organic feed, and not given hormones or antibiotics. For produce, it means that a farmer is rotating their crops, protecting sources of water, in addition to not using most conventional pesticides and fertilizers. So choose organic foods when available—and you can afford them! And if you can't go organic, go local. It's still an eco-friendly option—especially since food is fresher and little transport is involved. (See Go Organic on page 26 for more information.)

- **Choose locally produced ingredients when logical.** To get to your table, foods use fossil fuels, contributing to global warming pollution. That includes organic foods, too. Cutting down your food miles can ultimately mean fewer carbon emissions. So eating locally produced foods, even if not organically produced, can and should be part of the whole global green picture. (If the foods are from your very own garden, that's even better . . . zero food miles!) What's more, locally produced foods are fresh and seasonal and can play a role in boosting local economies. (See Food Miles: Do They Matter? on page 5 for more information.)

- **Go eco-fishin'.** Fish provide health benefits but unfortunately many of the waters the fish come from are contaminated with polychlorinated biphenyls (PCBs) and mercury; both chemicals raise significant health concerns. And many of the world's waters are currently being overfished. (See Be an Eco-Smart Seafood Connoisseur on page 28 for more

farmers' market miles

The average distance a food needs to travel to get to a farmers' market is less than 60 miles. That's quite a difference from what the average food travels from farm to plate . . . about 1,500 miles!

information.) There's no seafood organic certification in the U.S., but, you can look for Marine Stewardship Council certification, which will help you pinpoint what's not being over-fished. And do ask the fishmonger at your local market what fish is in sea-son in your area. Like fruits and veg-gies, it can vary depending on where you live.

- **Sip smarter beer, wine, and spir-its.** There's a way to enjoy alcoholic beverages (in moderation, of course) while being eco-smart. Alcoholic beverages, including beer, wine, and spirits, produced the conventional way may contain a small amount of harmful contaminants. And a signifi-cant amount of fossil fuels are used to make them. So go organic, if you can. And buy locally when logical. (See Drink Green on page 27 for more information.)

- **Bulk up!** Buy in bulk, when it's ap-propriate for the food—and for you. You'll need to make fewer trips to the market, which saves you time, en-ergy, and money. Additionally, you'll often find that less overall packaging is used in one large item rather than several smaller ones. That's good for the planet as it ultimately means less waste. In fact, the Environmental Protection Agency estimates that

packaging materials account for more than 30 percent of overall post-consumer waste. But remember to watch out for bulk items that are just lots of small packages sold together in more packaging. And only buy in bulk if you know you can use the food before it expires. Otherwise the food waste defeats the environmental pur-pose of buying in bulk.

- **Buy from bulk bins, too.** Help-yourself bins are prevalent in many markets today. When you know the food is fresh in the bins (ask the store manager), it can be a helpful part of low-carbon cooking if you buy just what you need. Items like whole grains, nuts, seeds, rolls, and much more are available. So if you're mak-ing a recipe that calls for four whole grain rolls, you won't need to buy a package of eight if you can buy from bulk bins.

- **Choose the greener picker-upper.** We can save the trees one paper towel roll at a time! The Natural Re-sources Defense Council suggests that if every U.S. household simply replaced one seventy-sheet roll of virgin fiber paper towels with its 100 percent recycled counterpart, we could save 544,000 trees. Using these recycled-paper towels conscien-tiously is an eco-step in the right direction, one sheet (or one-half sheet) at a time. But even before reaching for these green picker uppers, reach for a washable kitchen towel or eco-friendly sponge or cloth.

- **Get the bleach out.** In addition to paper towels, choosing other recycled kitchen material products is important, such as 100 percent recycled aluminum foil. For paper products, selecting unbleached products is also important. That includes baking cups, cheesecloth, coffee filters, waxed paper, and parchment paper. By using them instead of their bleached versions, it can mean less chlorine is dumped into streams and lakes. I like using unbleached, recycled parchment paper because it's so versatile for low-carbon cooking. It goes in the oven and the microwave. It makes an environmentally safe food wrap, too.

- **Bag it up—plastic-free.** So what's better for bagging up leftovers and extra food scraps to store for later use? Some may argue that a good-quality zipper-type plastic storage bag that uses food-safe (#4) plastic is best, as these bags can be washed and reused and then recycled. But I don't know too many people who take the time to wash them. Plus, you can wind up wasting water, one of our planet's most precious resources. And, though recyclable, they may not be in your community. So my suggestion is to toss unbleached thinly coated wax paper bags into your shopping cart. Some companies use vegetable wax now, which is biodegradable. There are environmental question marks, such as where the paper is sourced, but the bags are compostable. Still need other options? Well, forgo plastic wraps, as they're generally made with not-so-safe plastic #3 and chemicals which may make their way into your food. Surprisingly, plastic containers can be an eco-solution. (Though stoneware or glass is better since they're reheatable.) Just make sure they're washable and reusable. Before you buy, check to see what type of plastic they are by reading the number on the bottom. (See Buy by Number, page 22, for more information.)

produce picks

Whenever possible, buy organic when choosing these fruits and veggies: peaches, apples, nectarines, strawberries, cherries, grapes (if imported), pears, bell peppers, celery, lettuce, spinach, potatoes, carrots, and green beans. According to the Environmental Working Group, these produce ranked the highest of forty-three fruits and vegetables researched in terms of pesticide levels. However, that decision is yours and I haven't listed them as "organic" in *Big Green Cookbook* **recipes. I believe it's important to choose locally, too. Local produce is fresh and doesn't require much transportation to get to your table. Plus, I realize that organic produce is not readily available or affordable to all. But even if not certified organic, many small local farmers still grow eco-friendly produce. And that's something to take a bite out of. Just make sure to wash all your produce picks. Above all, make sure to eat your fruits and veggies, period!**

go organic

In a nutshell, going organic means that fewer pesticides and other possibly toxic chemicals end up in the food that you eat—and in the environment as a whole. More specifically, organic crops are grown without most conventional pesticides or sewage- or petroleum-based fertilizers. Animals raised organically must be fed organic feed, given access to the outdoors, and never given growth hormones or antibiotics.

While some people eat mostly organically produced foods, it may not be realistic, readily available, or affordable for others, although organic foods are becoming more available than ever before. And though often higher priced, the cost can be similar in some cases to their conventional counterparts. Nonetheless, I suggest you simply go organic whenever you can. I help you do so in *Big Green Cookbook* by listing at least some of the ingredients as organic. Look for "certified organic" labels (check for the USDA seal) on foods when shopping. (See Know Your Organic Food below for more information.) Here are some of my suggestions:

choose "certified organic" as much as possible.

These foods I've listed as "organic" when they are used in *Big Green Cookbook* recipes.

- **Meat, poultry, and eggs.** Meat production is resource intensive. One green choice people make is to become vegetarians—or at least give up red meat. But there are other eco-conscientious ways to enjoy it, without forgoing it. First, choose organic meat. Look for grass-fed, too. And when you can, purchase from area farmers—you might find them at your local farmers' market. Poultry is viewed as an eco-friendlier alternative to red meats. It's eco-friendliest to choose chicken, turkey, and eggs labeled "100 percent organic." (See Meaty Issues on page 28 for more information.)

- **Milk and yogurt.** Dairy production is resource intensive. But the larger concern may be a hormone used in pro-

---

know your organic food

The USDA's National labeling standards represent the percentage of organic ingredients used in products. How do you know if a food is really organic? Look for these government-regulated label terms:

- **100 percent organic:** A product that contains only organically produced ingredients.*
- **Organic:** A product that contains at least 95 percent organically produced ingredients.*
- **Made with organic ingredients:** A processed product that contains at least 70 percent organic ingredients.

*These products are able to display the USDA Organic seal.

drink green

When drinking beer, look for organic varieties. The grains used to produce organic beer have to be organic and not involve potentially harmful insecticides and fungicides. The beer will also be produced in a way that can emit less carbon and conserve water. However, since organic beer is not readily available throughout the country and the price tag may be high, at least aim to go local when selecting beer. Since local beer requires less transport, it means fewer carbon emissions, too. Plus, it supports your local community.

The same applies to wine production, where the insecticides, fungicides, and other chemicals used are eco-unfriendly. Then, of course, the transport of the wine is another environmental concern. So, go organic as your first choice when choosing wine for that sophisticated palate of yours. It's more readily available than ever before, but be a sophisticated label reader. Only domestic wines labeled "100 percent organic wine" are made with organic ingredients and without *added* sulfites. Another key word to consider is *biodynamic*. It means organic practices are followed in a way that uses the rhythm of the sun, moon, stars, and planets to create a naturally harmonious, self-supporting ecosystem. But do note that the shelf life of organic wine isn't as long as conventionally produced wine. If organic is not your pick, then go as local as possible. If you're looking for a place to find local wine, check your farmers' market.

If vodka, rum, or other spirits are your drink of pleasure, organic choices are not as prevalent as organic wine, although more and more environmentally friendly choices are coming into the marketplace. For instance, distillation may be done in an energy efficient way and use recycled glass bottles and recycled packaging. Keep your eye out for them. Otherwise, do choose locally produced options when available.

duction: recombinant bovine growth hormone (rBGH). It's used to increase milk production, but it may lead to greater need for antibiotics for the dairy cow. Still, the FDA deems products from hormone-treated cows safe. To play it safest, choose milk, cream, yogurt, sour cream, and butter that are rBGH-free. The easiest way to do that: choose "100 percent organic." That means they're produced without antibiotics or harmful pesticides, too.

choose "certified organic" selectively; be sure to choose locally as much as possible.

Many other ingredients are grown or prepared with organic methods and I encourage

that you use them when possible. In some cases, you'll find growers use a Certified Naturally Grown label, which smaller local farmers may opt to use. Choose these options, too. In most cases, I did not call specifcally for organic options for these foods in the recipe ingredient list in *Big Green Cookbook* to allow you to choose the option right for you:

- **Cooking oils.** The grains and seeds that are used to produce cooking oils, such as corn oil, may be genetically modified, so choose organic varieties of cooking oil, when possible.

- **Tea, cocoa, and chocolate.** Certified organic tea, cocoa, and chocolate are becoming widely available now. So choose them most often since it means less synthetic fertilizers and

be an eco-smart seafood connoisseur

It's important that sustainability goes into your fish selection. According to the Environmental Defense Fund in conjunction with the Monterey Bay Aquarium, there are over a couple dozen listings for eco-unfriendly seafood—which means it's not advised to eat those fish due to significant ecological concerns. Those concerns may be related to overfishing, high habitat impacts or bycatch, poor management, or farms that allow significant pollution and use a lot of chemicals.

To find out which fish are currently listed as eco-unfriendly, eco-friendly, or somewhere in between, check out the Environmental Defense Fund's Seafood Selector, at www.edf.org/page.cfm?tagID=1521. Or go to the Monterey Bay Aquarium's Seafood Watch, at www.montereybayaquarium.org/cr/seafoodwatch.asp; you can download a pocket guide for your region there, too. (Download a sustainable sushi wallet card from their Web site, too.)

The seafood selected for the recipes in *Big Green Cookbook* were chosen based on their combined recommendations at the time of writing. They include wild Alaskan salmon, Pacific (U.S.) sardines, Atlantic yellowfin tuna, among others. So enjoy . . . while doing your best to be a sustainable seafood connoisseur.

meaty issues

The meat industry is responsible for a significant amount of air and water pollution. Meat production itself can put a strain on our environment. And there are concerns that the use of antibiotics in meat production may be leading to the development of antibiotic resistance in humans. Going the vegetarian route is an option if these are concerns of yours. But it's important to know that there are greener ways to enjoy meat. First, go organic. That means the animals were given organic feed and were not given antibiotics. Go grass-fed, too. By raising animals on pasture, there is an overall benefit to the environment—and a nutritional benefit to the individual who consumes it. Buy from a local family farm when you can, too. When raised on small family farms, the meat you eat may have required less fossil fuels for its production. Green-sizing your meat is another option—which means eating smaller, or petite-sized portions.

Chicken and turkey are viewed as eco-friendlier options to red meat. But there are still some issues to consider related to antibiotic resistance and pollution. So what's the greenest way to enjoy it? Just like with meat, go organic. That means the birds were given organic feed and were not given antibiotics. In the U.S., no hormones are allowed in poultry (and hog) farming! So don't worry about looking for "hormone-free" on a label. As for "free range," that just suggests that the birds were allowed some outdoor access.

There's one additional eco-step to take, thanks to the American Humane Certified farm animal program, which certifies meat, poultry, milk, and eggs. If a product is American Humane Certified, it's a guarantee to consumers that it is from humanely raised and treated animals.

pesticides were used to produce them. When possible, choose Fair Trade certified tea, cocoa, and chocolate, too. It means they were produced using environmentally sustainable practices and the farmers were paid fairly. And if you want to go one more step, look for those that are Rainforest Alliance certified; it ensures they were produced in a way that protects the environment and wildlife.

- **Sugar.** Commercial sugar production can lead to tropical forest destruction and soil erosion, so choose organic sugars when you can. And instead of organic white sugar, choose turbinado or Demerara; it's less processed.

- **Wine.** Produced the conventional way, wine may contain a small amount of harmful contaminants. So go organic when you can. And buy locally when logical. (See Drink Green on page 27 for more information.)

- **Produce.** Select organic produce when possible, especially when eating skins or peels. But if not, choose locally grown produce. And, of course, buy seasonally. (See Produce Picks on page 25 for more information.)

- **Cheese.** Organic cheeses are not yet widely available. If you find them, choose them. But in general, enjoy locally made cheeses, which are often hand-crafted or "artisanal." Some of the best bets might be found at your local farmers' market. Otherwise,

look at these links

To find sources of organic or locally raised, grass-fed meat and dairy products, start by asking the butcher at your local market. Check out these three Web sites, too:

www.eatwild.com/products

www.heritagefoodsusa.com

www.localharvest.org

enlist the help of a cheesemonger at your favorite food market or local cheese shop and try to find out the story behind the cheese you choose.

- **Frozen, canned, bottled, or packaged foods.** Choose organic processed products when possible. (Do always buy organic canned beans, however, since I suggest no rinsing to prevent loss of nutrients and excess water waste.) When not going organic, compare labels to see where the product was manufactured; go with the more local product. Choose minimally processed choices, or those considered to be natural. And always choose those without excess packaging.

If a food you use isn't in the list above, just remember: choose organic when you can. It's an investment into your health—and the health of the planet. And while thinking globally, go local when logical. Finally, be realistic. If you have to drive one hundred miles to complete your shopping for organic ingredients, the greener option may be to stick closer to home and just do the best you can with what's available.

waste not

You can save valuable resources (and money, too!) by reducing the amount of food you waste. So first, consider all of the ways that you can prevent waste to start with. Here are some of my top tips:

- Create a shopping list and stick to it—buying just the amounts needed.

- Set your fridge temp properly (see The Green Kitchen Checklist, page 8).

- Practice "first in, first out"—FIFO—with foods in your fridge, freezer, and pantry.

- Consider uses for produce about to become overripe, like one of my fruit smoothies.

- Green-size your food—cook and serve just-right amounts.

- Freeze what you can—and in proper portions—to preserve foods to later enjoy as leftovers.

- Give composting a try.

And, if after all of that, you still have leftovers . . . love them!

bites about the bits

Check out these very quick tips for using leftover bits during cooking.

EXTRA EGG YOLKS (WHEN A RECIPE CALLS FOR ONLY WHITES)? Do this: Add them to lean ground organic meat or poultry along with an equal portion of oats to create extra-moist, extra-nutritious burgers. Or use yolks to make a classic hollandaise sauce, zabaglione, or crème brûlée. But what if there's no need for yolks right away? No worries. For a sweet recipe, add ½ tablespoon mild honey per 1 cup yolks; for a savory recipe, add ½ teaspoon sea salt per 1 cup yolks. Pour in an ice cube tray and freeze. Remove the frozen yolk cubes and store in the freezer in an air-tight container. Thaw in the fridge when ready to use.

EXTRA FRESH VEGGIE SCRAPS? Do this: Toss them into the recipe in which you need the rest of the veggie. It's okay if things don't look perfect. Or if you prefer, dice up the veggies and sprinkle onto the finished dish as an edible garnish.

REMAINING COOKING LIQUID FROM STEAMING VEGGIES? Do this: Use it as part of the cooking liquid for whole-wheat couscous or quinoa.

REMAINING COOKING LIQUID FROM COOKING PASTA? Do this: If mixing pasta with a thick sauce, stir in some of the pasta cooking liquid to help thin the sauce to desired consistency.

RESERVED JUICES FROM DRAINED CANNED FRUITS OR REMAINING FRUIT JUICES AFTER PREPPING FRESH FRUITS? Do this: Whisk fruit juices with extra-virgin olive oil and a touch of white wine vinegar to make fruity vinaigrette.

RESERVED LIQUIDS FROM DRAINED CANNED BEANS? Do this: Add interest to organic turkey or other burgers by mixing the liquid from organic canned beans into the mixture before cooking. Or simmer it into ordinary pasta sauce for added body and flavor.

seven ways to love your leftovers

The environment is fed up, literally. Food waste in the United States is not just a waste; it's filling up our landfills. Then, as the food waste in those landfills decomposes, it releases methane, a greenhouse gas, into the atmosphere. Even healthful foods like fruits and veggies that wind up in the landfill instead of in a composter (or in your tummy) do this.

In fact, according to the EPA, landfills are the biggest human-related source of methane in the U.S. They represent one-third of all methane emissions. That's more than those from manure management, coal mining, or natural gas systems! Who knew?

So having less food waste is a vital goal in the quest for a healthier planet. One way to do that is to start loving those leftovers. It's eco-friendly to eat your spare savories.

Though there are quite a few devotees of cold leftover pizza, most leftovers just don't seem appealing. But by enjoying these eats there will be less waste in landfills, less need to buy and prepare something else (adding more global warming pollution to our atmosphere), and more time on your hands to do other good environmental deeds—maybe plant a tree! The dilemma: What if you don't want last night's dinner the next day? Well, problem solved. Sample my luscious, inspired recipe ideas below using common leftovers that will have you saying, "I love leftovers!"

1. leftover: pizza slice

**Serve it in style later:
OMELET DU JOUR**

You'll be at a loss for what to fix for breakfast no more. You can add nearly any leftover to an omelet—from plain veggies or chicken to not-so-plain burritos or pizza. Pizza is definitely a winner! Just chop up into bite-sized pieces and add to the omelet—or, simpler yet, scramble into organic eggs. And add flair by sprinkling extra oregano on the pizza omelet and topping the burrito omelet with salsa or guacamole. You'll be amazed at all the new breakfast options you'll want to regularly add to your repertoire.

2. leftover: cooked veggies

**Serve it in style later:
VEGGIE HUMMUS**

Don't worry if you didn't eat all of your veggies. They might be better the next day. Puree any chilled leftover roasted, grilled, or steamed veggies into a traditional hummus recipe—or even the store-bought variety. Serve with raw veggies or whole-grain pita. It's actually tastier than the original!

savories safety

Follow these four guidelines to make sure your leftovers are safe:

1. **Refrigerate cooked perishable foods within two hours.**
2. **Label and date leftovers.**
3. **When appropriate, reheat solids to 165°F and bring soups to a full boil.**
4. **When reheating in the microwave oven, loosely cover (with environmentally safe wrap) and let food stand for five minutes to let the heat distribute.**

3. leftover: steak dinner ingredients

Serve it in style later:
STEAK DINNER CANAPÉS

Had some no-shows for dinner? No problem. You can have so much fun the next day with a steak dinner. Grass-fed organic steak with all of the accompaniments can be turned into finger food. Thinly slice steak and day-old dinner rolls. Then mash leftover veggies and potatoes—adding a little sour cream, mayo, or yogurt if needed to make a puree. Then spread each bread slice with puree, add a steak slice, top with a leftover salad veggie, and insert a reusable pick or bamboo toothpick.

4. leftover: salad with dressing

Serve it in style later:
"PESTO" PASTA SALAD

Once salad is dressed, the extras are usually a wilted mess. But don't toss it, whirl it instead. Puree all the droopy goodness in an electric blender and use it kind of like a pesto. Try it on chilled whole-wheat noodles for a perky pasta salad.

what vintage is it?

Leftovers! **That word just doesn't have a luscious ring to it. So try one of these trendier names on for size: "spare savories" or "vintage cuisine." I'm sure either name will make any leftover more appealing. Hey, that vintage trick worked for used clothing and jewelry!**

5. leftover: cooked rice or other grain pilaf

Serve it in style later:
A BETTER BURGER

If you choose to eat meat, stretch it. That's where leftover cooked rice, couscous, or quinoa comes in. Mix leftover grains into ground organic poultry or ground grass-fed organic meat along with seasonings of choice and shape into burgers. (Form them flatter than usual so they cook faster.) Just cook and serve. You might decide you like this burger better!

6. leftover: roasted holiday turkey

Serve it in style later:
TURKEY TACOS

Go international with All-American organic turkey. Shred or chop the leftover poultry and simply stir in salsa as needed. It'll be the easiest way ever to create a taco filling. Quickly reheat the turkey-salsa mixture and use along with lettuce, tomato, scallion, guacamole, and cilantro in soft corn tortillas or crisp tacos. Olé!

7. leftover: chinese stir-fry

Serve it in style later:
CHINESE STIR-FRY SALAD

Filled up on egg rolls and left with extra stir-fry? For your next meal, dice up the leftovers, like shrimp and broccoli, toss with mixed salad greens and sliced fresh scallions, then dress with an Asian-style vinaigrette—or with rice vinegar (preferably brown rice) and a mixture of peanut and sesame oil. For added crunch, sprinkle with raw almonds, pine nuts, or cashews. Enjoy with reusable chopsticks.

planet-pleasing party tips

When having your next shindig, choose green as the theme. Or simply make any friendly get-together you toss a bit more environmentally friendly. While I could probably write an entire book (or at least a half a book!) of eco-savvy soiree suggestions, below is a simple, straightforward checklist of my personal quick tips to reduce environmental impact while having fun with flair.

- **The Invite:** Send your invites as Evites—that is, electronically. It saves time and paper. (Plus, you can easily keep track of head counts for your party. That has always come in handy for me!) If you do choose paper, the way to go is 100 percent post-consumer recycled. Or for added panache and planet-friendliness, send "seeded" invitations. It's paper that actually sprouts in water! And there's always that old-fashioned way . . . invite by phone—or even a knock on the door. (A novel idea, huh?)

- **The Guests:** Knowing the head count on your guest list is of eco-importance so you know how much food and beverage will be required. Though parties are all about fun, having excess waste is not. But if you are planning-challenged, make sure you arrange to have your guests take home doggie bags—in eco-friendly packaging, of course. What's more, once you know who's coming, you'll be able to plan for offsetting their travel. Purchase carbon offsets (see Carbon Offsets, right) if guests have to travel far to help counteract the

CO_2 pollution created from their transportation. If coming locally, try to team up partygoers into carpools. (Since I live in New York City, I give directions by subway and by foot, though I hope to add biking directions for my next gathering.)

- **The Question:** What to bring? It's helpful when guests bring something—when it's actually something helpful, that is. Provide them with suggestions so you don't wind up with "stuff." I usually prefer that guests bring their beverages of choice, so I know they'll stay quenched and happy. (Most of my frequent party guests just know to automatically do this.) Then if there are too many drinks, most can usually be stored without chilling. If a guest insists that they want to bring something gift-like, suggest plants or potted herbs. They're good for the environment and make the atmosphere lovely. Another option that has worked for me . . .

carbon offsets

Carbon offsets generally represent CO_2 reduction from one location to offset CO_2 produced somewhere else. Do the best you can to reduce your carbon footprint through realistic energy reductions. But also consider coupling your steps toward energy efficiency with carbon offsets to shrink your overall environmental footprint. See www.carbonfund.org for more.

provide links on Evites to hunger or environmental organizations to make donations in lieu of gifts.

- **The Location:** Your apartment or home may be the usual party venue of choice. But also consider other locations—like a local park. It can be a casual affair that encourages walking, biking, hiking, and other eco-conscious activities. Take advantage of the environment, too. If it's wintertime, beverages can be chilled outdoors instead of using the fridge. If at night, a candlelit event is more dramatic and uses less electricity than a bright-lit living room.

- **The Decorations:** This is where gifts of plants and potted herbs by your party guests can come in handy. Think about other eco-friendly party accessorizing, too. Find clever ways to repurpose used food containers, bottles, or cans from pre-party prep into party decor. Tie ribbon around a washed, clean-cut can (recycle paper labels), then use as a candle holder. Use bottles as whimsical flower vases. Fill a glass bowl with a bountiful array of seasonal fruit and enjoy as a beautiful, edible centerpiece. Cover tables with coverings you already have rather than buying new tablecloths: turn sheets into lovely tablecloths.

for an eco-bbq bash . . .

I love the scent of a good barbecue, but that scent can be polluting. So is there such thing as green-style grilling?

It appears that gas (propane) grills may be one of the greenest way to go. Gas grills, in general, will emit less carbon into the atmosphere than traditional charcoal grills. Tristam West, a researcher with the Department of Energy's Oak Ridge National Laboratory, compared carbon output of grills when producing 35,000 BTu (that means British thermal units) per hour. West's calculations showed that gas produced 5.6 pounds of CO_2 in an hour, compared to about 11 pounds for charcoal. (Electric grills produced even more.) Also, when choosing a propane-fueled grill, go with the size that's right for you. If it's just two of you, go with the lower BTu found in a smaller grill; it'll be better for the environment since it won't require as much fuel for cooking.

However, if you're a fan of charcoal, be sure to go natural so the charcoal won't have harmful chemical additives. Lump coal is basically better than briquettes as it tends not to have additives. Look for recycled wood or anything harvested sustainably, too. Do forgo the smog-creating lighter fluid; use a chimney starter instead. And cut off air supply to the charcoal right after you use it, so you can reuse the unburned coals.

Also, be on the lookout for newer, greener grilling choices—more readily available than ever before. For grills, a solar oven is one option. Hybrid grills are available, too. They use gas or electric, but also use a small amount of wood or charcoal for that memorable flavor. For fuel, try burning eco-friendlier briquettes made from coconut shells or other alternative materials. One very cool alternative developed by mechanical engineer and MIT professor Amy Smith (along with her students) is corn cob briquettes! Watch this video featuring Amy Smith for more: www.ted.com/index.php/talks/amy_smith_shares_simple_lifesaving_design.html.

(For my most recent party, I used my old—but clean—curtains as a cool tablecloth; no one figured it out!)

- **The Table Setting:** Show off your ceramics! Forget about flimsy paper or Styrofoam plates and cheap plastic utensils. The planet will thank you because they don't break down after they're thrown out. Your guests will thank you, too. They don't impress anyone—and they don't work that well anyway. So go reusable—use stainless steel utensils and ceramic plates. Even regular everyday dishes are more impressive than the throwaway kind. But if you'd rather not get sudsy after your soiree, new-fangled, biodegradable (that means compostable, too) options are now available. These are made from corn, bamboo, sugar cane, or recycled fiber paper.

- **The Eats and Drinks:** Well that's easy: just use recipes from *Big Green Cookbook*! (Or give some of your party favorites an eco-friendly makeover—or "greenover.") Try your best to pick recipes that will be seasonal on the party date. Bookmark them. Double or triple what you need. Go ahead, write in this cookbook; it's meant to be used. This is not one of those coffee table books meant for looking, but not touching. Plan which recipes you'll prepare in advance and keep chilled or frozen. (Some recipes, like dips and grain-based salads, are often better prepared a day or two in advance and stored in the refrigerator; the flavors will marry.) Then plan your shopping list accordingly. Buy nonperishable food ingredients and most beverages, including wine, beer, and spirits, well in advance; if you can—so there's less to worry about close to the party date. And buy your produce last so it's fresh—preferably from a farmers' market or a market specializing in local produce. You're ready for cookin' now! Invite a couple of your guests to come in advance to help. If you're able to, hire a caterer—or at least a catering assistant. Check to make sure they're aware of your desire to be planet pleasing, not just people pleasing. (See For an Eco-BBQ Bash . . . on page 34 for more information.)

- **The Green Cleaning:** This is the part no one likes. (Well, no one except my friend Amy . . . a rare friend indeed!) First, make sure that you have bins for trash and for recyclables, so at least that part is done by your party guests. If you compost, it might be difficult to have guests determine which leftover food scraps go into a composter, so do your best with the leftovers from the serving platters. Remember to give still-edible leftovers to guests to take home. There's less waste and less to clean up! A dishwasher does come in handy, of course. Make sure it's fully loaded and set on an energy-efficient cycle. And do enlist the help of some guests to pitch in with the cleaning. Even washing dishes by hand (fill the sink instead of constantly running water) can be pleasurable when everyone chips in . . . while telling party stories and drinking the remnants from the bottom of the wine bottles so they're ready to recycle!

luscious, low-carbon menus

Enjoying a *Big Green Cookbook* recipe or cooking tip here and there is the most practical way to enjoy becoming an eco-friendlier cook. But for those occasions that you want to go all out green, try any of these fifteen menus for delicious deep-green dining.

spring

Casually Green Breakfast
Curly Egg Muffin (page 78)
Fiery Fingerlings (page 88)
Tea or fresh-squeezed orange juice

Eco-Elegant Dinner
French Kissed Cress (page 67)
Pretty in Purple (page 94)
Steamed quinoa or Looks Like Greek to
    Me Salad (page 69)*
Real Lemonade (page 96)

*For vegetarians, serve Looks Like Greek to Me
  Salad as the entrée.

Planet-Friendly Family Fun Meal
Turkey Poppers (page 48) or
    Red Red "Ribs" (page 86)
Green "Quiche" (page 46)
Green Green Salsa (page 54) with
    tortilla chips
Cheesecake Smoothie (page 99)

summer

Casually Green Breakfast
Aztec Frittata (page 142)
Grapacho (page 120), if desired
Berry Good Micro-Bars (page 171)*
*Prepare in advance.

Eco-Elegant Dinner
Figgy Salad (page 130)
Citrus Cream of Capellini (page 151)
Green Shoestrings (page 145)
Key Lime Pie-tini (page 164)

Planet-Friendly Family Fun Meal
Baked Peachy Bites (page 168)
Cheesy Zucchini Macaroni (page 150)
A Better BLT (page 160)*
Summer Lassi (page 166)

*For vegetarians, serve without bacon or
  with soy "bacon" strips.

autumn

Casually Green Breakfast
Don't Cry for Me Omelet (page 216)
Favorite Fall Fruit Smoothie
    (page 238)

Eco-Elegant Dinner
Bartlettuce (page 205)
Zoom Shroom Soup (page 197)
Star Chicken Stir-Fry (page 232) or
    Hot Beans (page 210) with
    steamed quinoa
Mangotini (page 240)

Planet-Friendly Family Fun Meal

Speckled Carrot Salad (page 202)
Chili con Turkey under Pressure (page
    228) or TLC Panini (page 214)
My Own Private Idaho Sticks
    (page 179)
Apple of My Eye (page 243)

winter

Casually Green Breakfast
Granny Cakes (page 273)
Breakfast (soy) sausage links
Freshly-squeezed orange or grapefruit
    juice

Eco-Elegant Dinner
Fall into Winter Salad (page 259)
Golden Gravy—and Turkey, Too*
    (page 284)
Squash-Studded Orzo (page 280)
Mojit-OJ (page 290)

*For vegetarians, serve Squash-Studded Orzo as
  the entrée.

Planet-Friendly Family Fun Meal
Southwestern Sweet Potato "Sushi"
    (page 249)
Guacamole Rápido (page 253) with
    organic tortilla chips
Flash Dancin' Chickenwich (page 285)
Broccoli Trifle (page 263)

all-year-round

Casually Green Breakfast
Very Berry Cup (page 352)
Granola cereal with plain, unsweetened
    soy milk

Eco-Elegant Dinner
Spin-Stir Caesar Salad (page 323)
Cod with Kick (page 343) or
    Brew and Bean Chili (page 320)
    served in fancy bowls
Green Gratin (page 337)
Made-in-NY Cheesecake (page 356)

Planet-Friendly Family Fun Meal
Not-Your-Fast-Food Burgers (page 309)
    or raw veggies with Garlic Breath Dip
    (page 316)
Little Green Pizza (page 334) or Petite
    Turkey Pâté (page 306)
Almost Dessert Squash (page 341)
Happy Planet Cookies (page 358)

in this cookbook . . .

For recipes that require cooking in *Big Green Cookbook*, pay closer attention to the cooking instructions than the cooking times. That's because eco-friendly cooking methods are different from those in typical recipes. And because of that, you'll need to personalize cooking times based on how fast or slow your specific appliance cooks. There are variations based on wattages and whether cooking by gas or electricity, among other factors. So really use this cookbook: *write* in it. Change timing when you need to and note it in the recipe. If a recipe doesn't work perfectly the first time using my cooking times, adjust the timing the next time and personalize it for your green kitchen!

On the right is a list of some of the appliances and equipment that I used when testing recipes for this book. This is not a recommendation or an endorsement of eco-friendliness. It's for your information so you'll know if you might need to adjust cooking times or techniques. These are appliances that I already had before beginning *Big Green Cookbook*; they're not specialty green appliances. So you don't have to replace what you have with something new to make the recipes. Whatever brands you use, be sure to pay close attention to cooking descriptions in recipe instructions—and follow my tips. Then I'm sure you'll be pleased with your luscious, low-carbon cuisine to come!

Saucepans. I didn't use super-fancy pans. I used All-Clad Stainless saucepans whenever a recipe required a saucepan. That means whatever standard stainless pans you have will likely cook in similar fashion. But if you use pans that retain heat well, like copper-lined pans, then you may be able to slightly reduce cooking times—especially "lid cooking" times. (See definition, page 367.)

Range. I used a Wolf thirty-inch gas range to prepare the stovetop and oven-baked recipes in *Big Green Cookbook*, so you may need to add a little more time at the beginning of the cooking process if using an electric stove. On the flip side, when turning off a gas burner, it will be off; whereas an electric burner tends to stay hot for a while. That means if you use electric, you may need to reduce the amount of time at the end of a cooking process—or when something is being "lid cooked."

Microwave oven and toaster oven. Specific details for cooking with various microwave and toaster ovens are listed on page 39. It will help you determine if adjustments need to be made in preparing the recipes in *Big Green Cookbook*.

Microwave Oven. *Recipes tested with:* Sharp Carousel microwave oven (1,200 watts)

Other appliance variability: range from 600 to 1,300 watts (800 and 1,200 watts are common; if unsure, use 800 watts information as your guide). How to adjust:

High Power

1,200 WATTS (used in cookbook)	800 WATTS
1 minute (60 seconds)	1½ minutes
3 minutes	4½ minutes
5 minutes	7½ minutes
10 minutes	15 minutes
15 minutes	20 minutes

(Note: These are approximate guidelines. Use food doneness descriptions, when available, as the primary judge of cooking time.)

50 Percent Power

1,200 WATTS (used in cookbook)	800 WATTS (use high power, not 50 percent power)
1 minute (60 seconds)	45 seconds
3 minutes	2½ minutes
5 minutes	4 minutes
10 minutes	7½ minutes
15 minutes	11 minutes

(Note: These are approximate guidelines. Use food doneness descriptions, when available, as the primary judge of cooking time.)

Toaster Oven. *Recipes tested with:* Krups FBC2 6-slice digital convection toaster oven (1,600 watts; 2 racks)

Other appliance variability: range from 1,200 to 1,800 watts (1,200, 1,400, and 1,600 watts are all common). How to adjust for "bake" function:

1,600 WATTS (used in cookbook)	1,400 WATTS	1,200 WATTS
1 minute (60 seconds)	1¼ minutes (75 seconds)	1½ minutes
3 minutes	3½ minutes	4 minutes
5 minutes	5½ minutes	6½ minutes
10 minutes	11 minutes	13 minutes
15 minutes	17 minutes	18 minutes

(Note: These are approximate guidelines based on the regular baking function, not convection baking. If you choose to use convection baking, reduce cooking times. Use food doneness descriptions, when available, as the primary judge of cooking time. Also note: If you choose to use your conventional oven instead of a toaster oven, more cooking time may be required as it takes time for a large oven to reach suggested temperatures.)

SPRING

BITES & SNACKS

zucchini panini

STUFFED PANINI-GRILLED ZUCCHINI MINI "SANDWICH"

Makes 12 servings: 1 mini "sandwich" each

Have fun being a friend to the environment and be inventive with in-season veggies. Here, zucchini is the "bread" of the panini, making it look kind of like a green party sub. I enjoy eating this by taking off the top zucchini "bun" and eating it, then nibbling on the bottom "sandwich" open-face-style. Go ahead, play with your veggies.

little **green** cooking tip

"Green grill" it! Grill partway, turn off the grill (panini grill or any outdoor grill with an on/off switch), then let the food continue grilling in the off position with the remaining heat. You'll still get succulent results using less gas or electricity.

4 large zucchini, sliced in half lengthwise

2 tablespoons extra-virgin olive oil

2 teaspoons aged balsamic vinegar

½ teaspoon sea salt, or to taste

8 ounces fresh salted organic or locally produced mozzarella cheese, very thinly sliced

12 large leaves fresh basil

1 plum tomato, very thinly sliced

1 cup baby arugula leaves

1. Rub the zucchini halves with 1 tablespoon of the oil. Place zucchini in a panini grill, then set the heat to medium-high (do not preheat). Cook for 8 minutes. Turn off the grill and allow to "green grill" (grill in the off position with residual heat) until just cooked through but slightly crisp, about 5 minutes.

2. Remove the zucchini from the grill and drizzle the cut surfaces with the remaining 1 tablespoon oil and the vinegar. Add salt.

3. On top of the cut sides of four of the zucchini halves, arrange half of the cheese. Top with the basil, tomato, arugula, and the remaining cheese. Top with the remaining zucchini halves, cut side down, to make 4 "sandwiches."

4. Insert 3 bamboo toothpicks or reusable picks into each sandwich and then cut into 3 mini ones. Enjoy like a mini baguette sandwich, or, if you prefer, eat with a fork and knife.

PER SERVING: 90 calories, 7g total fat, 3g saturated fat, 0g trans fat, 15mg cholesterol, 160mg sodium, 4g total carbohydrate, 1g dietary fiber, 5g protein

a planet-friendly bite

Bamboo is a fast-growing, truly renewable resource. In fact, it's one of the fastest growing plants on Earth. Since it has a uniquely short growth cycle, it can be harvested in less than five years versus the twenty that is typical for many hardwoods. And it doesn't need replanting because of its large root network.

farmers' market quesadilla

SWEET ONION QUESADILLA WITH STRAWBERRY-SERRANO SALSA

Makes 6 servings: 2 wedges with ¼ cup salsa each

Juicy ripe strawberries are simply divine as is when fresh and in season. And they can add their divineness when cooked in savory dishes. Pair them with cheese and springtime sweet onion to intrigue the taste buds in this popular appetizer. Just skip the commercially processed salsa that may have been shipped cross-country. Prepare this fresh, luscious, fruity version that requires only your own energy using a chef's knife.

1 medium Vidalia or other sweet onion
8 large strawberries, hulled and diced
1 serrano pepper with some seeds, minced
1 tablespoon plus ¼ cup chopped fresh cilantro
Juice of ½ lime (about 1 tablespoon)
¼ teaspoon plus ⅛ teaspoon sea salt, or to taste
6 (8-inch) stone-ground whole-wheat or sprouted-grain tortillas
2 tablespoons peanut oil
8 ounces shredded organic or locally produced Monterey Jack cheese
   (about 2 cups)

1. Finely dice ⅓ of the onion. Gently combine the diced onion, strawberries, pepper, 1 tablespoon of the cilantro, and the lime juice in a medium bowl. Add ¼ teaspoon salt. Set aside.

2. Very thinly slice the remaining ⅔ onion. Arrange in a single layer on a large microwave-safe plate. "Micro-roast" (cook in the microwave oven*) on high until the onion is just softened, about 1 minute. Add remaining salt.

3. Rub 3 tortillas on one side with 1 tablespoon of the oil (no need to dirty a brush—use your fingers!) and put oiled side down on a bamboo or Paperstone cutting board. Divide the micro-roasted onion, cheese, and remaining ¼ cup cilantro among the tortillas and cover with the remaining 3 tortillas. Rub the tops of the quesadillas with the remaining oil.

4. Heat a large skillet over medium-high heat. Cook the quesadillas one at a time until lightly toasted, about 2 minutes per side, using a lid during the first 2 minutes of cooking time for each. Transfer quesadillas to the cutting board and cut each into 4 wedges. Serve warm with the strawberry-serrano salsa.

PER SERVING: 280 calories, 17g total fat, 8g saturated fat, 0g trans fat, 35mg cholesterol, 520mg sodium, 27g total carbohydrate, 3g dietary fiber, 13g protein

*Microwave oven cooking times will vary. See page 39.

a planet-friendly bite

Unfortunately, dairy foods, including cheese, are responsible for some of our greenhouse gas emissions. Of course, every food or beverage category has some impact on the environment. But there's no need to give up cheese. Just enjoy "real" cheese, not the processed stuff. Choose organic, local, or artisanal cheese varieties that are handmade in small batches, whenever possible. And then savor them like fine wine.

green "quiche"

CRUSTLESS EARTH-STYLE POTATO AND ZUCCHINI "QUICHE"

Makes 6 servings: ⅙ of recipe each

Traditional quiche features a pastry crust usually made with shortening—basically, a chemically-altered fat—or lard. That's not so appealing or artery- or eco-friendly. So rather than a crust, this quiche-like bite is loaded with earth-style veggies to give it body. *Earth-style* means that you'll be using every produce part—skin, seeds, and all. And together with the farm fresh eggs and fragrant tarragon, the earth-style zucchini and potatoes make a memorable mouthful. Serve with an organic Italian herb vinaigrette–dressed salad.

2 tablespoons extra-virgin olive oil

1 medium or ½ large white onion, finely chopped

1 pound baby creamer potatoes, any color/variety, scrubbed unpeeled, and very thinly sliced

2 medium zucchini, thinly sliced

1 large clove garlic, minced

1 teaspoon sea salt, or to taste

¼ teaspoon freshly ground black pepper, or to taste

6 large organic eggs

2 tablespoons chopped fresh tarragon or 2 teaspoons chopped fresh oregano

2 ounces shredded organic or locally produced Monterey Jack cheese (about ¼ cup; optional)

1. Combine the oil and onion in a large, 2-quart, microwave-safe dish. Stir to coat. Cover well with unbleached parchment paper and "micro-roast" (cook in the microwave oven*) on high for 2 minutes.

2. Stir in the potatoes, zucchini, and garlic; cover again with parchment paper and "micro-roast" on high for 8 minutes, stirring once during cooking. Let sit covered in the off microwave to allow for carryover cooking until the vegetables are just cooked through, about 5 minutes. Add ½ teaspoon of the salt and ⅛ teaspoon of the pepper.

3. Stir together the eggs and tarragon with a fork in a medium bowl. Add the remaining salt and pepper. Gently stir the egg mixture into the veggies. Sprinkle with the cheese (if using). Cover with unbleached parchment paper and "micro-roast" on high until the eggs are about set, 4 minutes, rotating the dish once, if necessary. Let sit, covered, in the off microwave until completely set, about 5 minutes.

4. If desired, caramelize the top using a small, refillable butane torch—like chefs use for crème brûlée—for several seconds, or until the top is lightly browned. Serve.

PER SERVING: 200 calories, 10g total fat, 2.5g saturated fat, 0g trans fat, 210mg cholesterol, 460mg sodium, 19g total carbohydrate, 3g dietary fiber, 9g protein

*Microwave oven cooking times will vary. See page 39.

use it, don't lose it

Rather than tossing eggshells into the trash, use them to start growing plants or herbs, like the tarragon used in Green "Quiche." Poke a tiny drainage hole in the bottom of an eggshell half and use it as a miniature planter with a bit of soil and seed. Kids (and adults!) will love this planet-pleasing project. The more plants you grow, the smaller your carbon footprint.

turkey poppers

SPINACH-STUFFED TURKEY BURGER MEATBALLS

Makes 6 servings: 6 meatballs each

It is possible for meat eaters to eat in low-carbon fashion—and have fun doing it. Meatballs might just be the answer! Going mini, not biggie, with meat can help you make a planet-friendlier impact since you'll be eating smaller portions. Using poultry in place of beef will help, too, since it can be less resource intensive to produce. Of course, choosing organically produced poultry when you can is yet another eco-friendly approach. These meatballs will help in all of these cases . . . tastily. Simply pop 'em into your mouth and enjoy.

1 pound ground organic turkey*
1 cup finely chopped fresh baby or regular spinach leaves
½ large Vidalia or other sweet onion, grated
⅔ cup old-fashioned oats
1 large organic egg, lightly beaten
2 tablespoons spicy barbecue sauce
1 large clove garlic, minced
½ teaspoon grated lemon zest
¾ teaspoon sea salt, or to taste
½ teaspoon freshly ground black pepper, or to taste
⅛ teaspoon ground nutmeg (optional)

1. Mix all ingredients together in a large bowl until combined. (Use your hands instead of dirtying a utensil.)

2. Form into 36 meatballs, using 1 tablespoon meatball mixture each. Arrange on an unbleached parchment paper–lined 9½ × 11-inch toaster oven tray. (If using a smaller toaster oven tray, prepare in two batches.)

little **green** cooking tip

Get the same satisfaction, but with less meat. Mix grains and fresh veggies, like oats and onions, into burger, meatloaf, or meatball mixtures, and you'll be getting full satisfaction without as much resource-intensive meat.

3. Place the tray in the toaster oven** (do not preheat). Turn the heat to 450°F and bake for 8 minutes. Turn off the toaster oven. Let the meatballs cook with the residual heat in the off toaster oven until well done, about 5 minutes. Remove from the oven and let sit at least 2 minutes.

4. Insert bamboo toothpicks or reusable picks into each meatball and serve.

PER SERVING: 180 calories, 6g total fat, 1.5g saturated fat, 0g trans fat, 80mg cholesterol, 420mg sodium, 13g total carbohydrate, 2g dietary fiber, 18g protein

* Choose ground turkey with at least 7 percent fat for best culinary results.
**Toaster oven sizes and cooking times will vary. See page 39.

a planet-friendly bite

 There's no need to use energy-guzzling major appliances to make mini-size foods. You'll still get the same succulent results with a toaster oven instead of a conventional oven, using only about half the energy.

quack-n-kumquat rolls

DUCK AND KUMQUAT SPRING LETTUCE ROLLS WITH SPICY HOISIN SAUCE

Makes 6 servings: 1 roll each

This veggie-loaded recipe is versatile. Try it with chicken thigh instead of duck. For veggie lovers, make it exactly the same, but with tempeh instead—or simply without the meat. Fruit lovers will be pleased, too. The kumquats (which you don't peel) add a unique sweet-tartness. The wrapping, though, is the coolest part. These rolls are wrapped in an eco-conscious way—in fresh lettuce. Now that's green, literally!

little **green** cooking tip

"Eco-wrap" it. Rice paper and some other edible wrappers need to be processed—and possibly shipped from overseas—to get to your plate. Use locally grown lettuce leaves as edible, no-cook wraps—or eco-wraps.

1 tablespoon sesame oil

6 ounces boneless, skinless organic duck breast fillet or
    chicken thigh, cut into 1 × ¼-inch strips

¼ teaspoon sea salt, or to taste

¼ teaspoon freshly ground black pepper, or to taste

1 small or ½ large red onion, diced

5 kumquats, very thinly sliced

½ cup hoisin sauce

1 teaspoon chili-garlic paste, or to taste

1½ cups mung bean sprouts

¼ cup chopped fresh basil

¼ cup chopped fresh mint

8 large iceberg lettuce leaves

1. Heat the oil in a large stick-resistant skillet over medium-high heat. Sprinkle the duck with salt and pepper. Add the duck and onion to the skillet and sauté until the duck is cooked through and onions are softened, about 4 minutes. Turn off the heat. Stir in the kumquats and "green sauté" (sauté in a hot skillet with the burner off) for 1 more minute. Remove from the burner and set aside to cool.

2. Meanwhile, whisk together the hoisin sauce and chili-garlic paste in a small serving bowl.

3. Stir the bean sprouts, basil, and mint into the cooled duck mixture.

4. Spoon about ½ cup of the duck mixture into each lettuce leaf. Serve the sauce on the side or drizzle over the filling before rolling. Roll or wrap the leaves over the filling and serve.

PER SERVING: 140 calories, 4.5g total fat, 1g saturated fat, 0g trans fat, 25mg cholesterol, 500mg sodium, 17g total carbohydrate, 3g dietary fiber, 9g protein

go local

If you can only find hoisin sauce that's imported or not-so-natural (or perhaps you can't find it at all), then make your own "local," preservative-free, hoisin-like sauce with mainly organic ingredients. Mix together ¼ cup naturally brewed soy sauce, 2 tablespoons peanut or almond butter, 1 tablespoon mild floral honey, 1 tablespoon rice vinegar (preferably brown rice), 2 teaspoons sesame oil, and a few drops of hot pepper sauce.

eco-paccio

BEEF CARPACCIO WITH PARMESAN AND SPRING FRUIT RELISH

Makes 8 servings: 2 oz carpaccio with ¼ cup relish and arugula each

Not willing to give up beef? No problem. Indulge in petite portions of organic beef and cook it a little, not a lot. So gather up your ingredients for this modern, mouthwatering version of carpaccio. More environmentally conscious meat cuisine is only minutes away.

1 large navel orange, peeled, diced
½ cup red seedless grapes, thinly sliced
½ medium red onion, diced
6 large black or green olives (preferably tree-ripened),
    pitted and diced
1 teaspoon finely chopped fresh thyme
½ teaspoon ground cumin, or to taste
2 teaspoon canola or peanut oil
1 pound well-trimmed lean grass-fed organic beef tenderloin
½ teaspoon sea salt
1 teaspoon freshly ground black pepper
⅛ teaspoon ground cinnamon
2 cups arugula leaves
1 tablespoon extra-virgin olive oil
1 (2-ounce) wedge organic or locally produced Parmesan or
    aged Gouda cheese

1. Combine the orange, grapes, onion, olives, thyme, and cumin in a medium bowl. Set aside

2. Heat the oil in a large skillet over high heat. Sprinkle the beef with the salt, pepper, and cinnamon. Add the beef to the skillet and sear on all sides for 6 minutes total, turning every 1½ minutes (beef will still be rare).* Chill in the refrigerator until cold.

3. Arrange the arugula on a serving platter. Mound the fruit relish in the center of the platter or in 8 small mounds.

little *green* cooking tip

Go for green doneness, not well doneness. If you're a lover of well-done meats, wean your way to medium hamburgers and medium-rare steaks (or rare, if serving carpaccio). Less cooking time means less cooking energy is used. Remember, rarer is greener. (And the meat is often more tender, juicier, and flavorful that way, too.)

4. Slice meat as thin as possible (or pound slices between two sheets of unbleached parchment paper until paper thin, if desired). Arrange the beef slices around the platter. Or serve beef on a separate platter so non-meat eaters can partake in Ecopaccio enjoyment. Drizzle with the olive oil. Then, using a vegetable peeler, shave the cheese over the carpaccio and serve.

PER SERVING: 230 calories, 16g total fat, 6g saturated fat, 0g trans fat, 45mg cholesterol, 310mg sodium, 6g total carbohydrate, 1g dietary fiber, 15g protein

---

*It is not advised to consume rare beef if you're very young, very old, have a compromised immune system, or are pregnant.

use it, don't lose it

 Have leftover olive juice in the can, container, or jar? Add more interest to your meal: use the olive juice to make a dirty—or extra dirty—martini. Then sip while enjoying your appetizer!

DIPS, SALSAS, & SAUCES

green green salsa

RAW TOMATILLO SALSA

Makes 8 servings: 2 tablespoons each

This salsa is really green (the color!) as it's made with fresh tomatillos, not tomatoes. Though tomatillos are often cooked, they're raw
here. What's more, since this salsa is fresh, not processed, packed,
and shipped to get to your table, you'll enjoy its greenness from
start to finish. Try it in Bean Green (page 63)—or with organic tortilla chips.

6 tomatillos, husks removed, rinsed, and quartered
½ large Vidalia or other sweet onion, chopped
¼ cup loosely packed fresh cilantro leaves
1 large clove garlic
Juice of ½ lime (about 1 tablespoon)
¼ teaspoon sea salt, or as needed

Place the tomatillos, onion, cilantro, garlic, and lime juice in a
blender container and puree, about 15 seconds. (It's okay if there
are still some lumps.) Add salt and serve.

PER SERVING: 15 calories, 0g total fat, 0g saturated fat, 0g trans fat, 0mg cholesterol,
75mg sodium, 4g total carbohydrate, 1g dietary fiber, 1g protein

You'll need a little salt to help balance tomatillos' tartness. But don't use just any salt; sprinkle with sea salt. Sea salt typically refers to solar evaporated (sundried), unrefined salt that comes from the oceans and seas of the world, such as the Mediterranean Sea. But if you live in North America, choose one from the coastal ocean closest to you. If fine sea salt is not available, grind the larger crystals in a salt grinder like the ones used for pepper.

fruity fennel salsa

FENNEL, ORANGE, AND PINE NUT SALSA

Makes 6 servings: ⅔ cup each

This looks kind of like coleslaw, but it's to be enjoyed like a salsa. One of the secrets to this salsa's delicious flavor is the fresh gingerroot. It's super-tasty with grilled fish. Just top fish with this salsa, then drizzle the remaining flavorful vinaigrette over the fish or the rest of the meal. Refreshing!

3 tablespoons aged red or white wine vinegar

3 tablespoons extra-virgin olive oil

2 tablespoons chopped fresh cilantro or flat-leaf parsley

2 teaspoons naturally brewed soy sauce

1 tablespoon local fruit spread or homemade jam or
   2 teaspoons mild floral honey

1½ teaspoons grated scrubbed unpeeled gingerroot

3 medium navel oranges

1 medium fennel bulb, trimmed, cored, cut into
   matchstick-size strips (reserve fronds)

½ medium red onion, thinly sliced

¼ teaspoon sea salt, or to taste

⅛ teaspoon freshly ground black pepper, or to taste

¼ cup raw pine nuts

(continued)

Gingerroot on the ingredient list? Always try it "earth-style"; there's no need to peel it, just scrub it first. It still works well and saves time and waste.

1. Whisk the vinegar, oil, cilantro, soy sauce, fruit spread, and gingerroot in a large serving bowl.

2. Cut the peel and white pith from the oranges. Holding the oranges over a bowl to catch juices (save for a beverage), cut between membranes to release segments. Add to the vinaigrette.

3. Add the fennel and onion. Stir gently to combine. Add salt and pepper.

4. Stir in the pine nuts just before serving. Sprinkle with some of the reserved fronds and serve.

PER SERVING: 160 calories, 11g total fat, 1.5g saturated fat, 0g trans fat, 0mg cholesterol, 220mg sodium, 14g total carbohydrate, 3g dietary fiber, 2g protein

use it, don't lose it

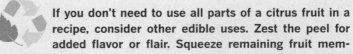

If you don't need to use all parts of a citrus fruit in a recipe, consider other edible uses. Zest the peel for added flavor or flair. Squeeze remaining fruit membranes after segmenting for fresh juice to drink or for making citrus vinaigrette.

not-for-faint-of-heart dip

BAKED ARTICHOKE HEART DIP WITH ALMONDS

Makes 15 servings: ⅓ cup each

This spicy recipe will be a sure palate-pleaser at any planet-friendly party. Rather than baking this gorgeously gooey dip in an energy-inefficient oven, you'll be cooking it in the more energy-efficient microwave. It'll only take a few minutes of "micro-roasting." Ready? Set? Dig in.

10 ounces fresh micro-steamed or thawed frozen artichoke hearts, chopped (about 3 large fresh artichokes; see page 58)
2 tablespoons extra-virgin olive oil
½ teaspoon sea salt
8 ounces shredded organic or locally produced mozzarella cheese (about 2 cups)
2½ oz freshly grated organic or locally produced Parmesan cheese (about ½ cup)
1 cup mayonnaise
⅓ cup finely chopped chives
¼ teaspoon freshly ground black pepper, or to taste
¼ teaspoon cayenne pepper, or to taste
½ cup sliced raw (natural) almonds
Whole-grain crackers

1. Combine the artichoke hearts, oil, and salt in a large, 2-quart, microwave-safe dish. Let marinate for 15 minutes.

2. Stir the cheeses, mayonnaise, and half the chives into the artichoke mixture. Add the black pepper and cayenne.

3. "Micro-roast" (cook in the microwave oven*) uncovered on high until the dip is hot, cheeses are fully melted, and edges are bubbly, about 4 minutes, stirring once halfway through. Sprinkle with the almonds and the remaining chives.

4. Serve warm with whole-grain crackers.

PER SERVING: 200 calories, 19g total fat, 4.5g saturated fat, 0g trans fat, 20mg cholesterol, 230mg sodium, 3g total carbohydrate, 2g dietary fiber, 5g protein

(continued)

little *green* cooking tip

Dips meant to be served warm can be kept warm and ready for dipping for up to 4 hours in a slow cooker. Although they cook for a long time, slow cookers use little energy. So try it. After you're finished "micro-roasting" Not-for-Faint-of-Heart Dip, transfer it to a slow cooker crock and set on low.

for preparing fresh micro-steamed artichokes:

1. Wash the artichokes. Pull off the small or discolored lower petals. Cut the stems close to base. Cut off the top quarter. Plunge into acidulated water (1 tablespoon lemon juice per 4 cups fresh water) to preserve color. The trimmed artichoke stems are edible. Cut the brown end about ½ inch. Peel the fibrous outer layer to reach the tender green of the stem. The stem may be steamed whole with the artichoke. Cut the stem into rounds or julienne for salads or pastas.

2. To "micro-steam" (steam in the microwave) the artichokes, set the 3 prepared artichokes upside down in a microwave-safe dish with ½ cup fresh water and 1 teaspoon each lemon juice and organic extra-virgin olive oil. Cover well with unbleached parchment paper. Cook on high until just tender, about 8 minutes. Let stand covered 5 minutes. Then remove the fuzzy choke before using.

*Microwave oven cooking times will vary. See page 39.

use it, don't lose it

 What do you do when you get to the bottom of a package of nuts, crackers, tortilla chips, or cereal and find everything in small bits and crumbles? Save them (at least for a few days)! They can provide the essence of oven-baked crunchiness on dips and casseroles that are cooked in the microwave oven. Sprinkle the bits and crumbles of anything crunchy on top of the just-cooked food.

shall i dip

SHALLOT-SPIKED VEGGIE DIP

Makes 12 servings: ¼ rounded cup each

Looking for a perfect party dip? Look no further. This is like a glorified ranch dressing—except this one doesn't have a label on it that reads like a strange science experiment. Serve it with seasonal crudités, such as red bell pepper strips, snow peas, and yellow summer squash—1 cup veggies per person.

1 cup organic cottage cheese

1 cup mayonnaise

½ cup organic sour cream

1 large shallot, minced

½ large red bell pepper, minced

3 tablespoons finely chopped chives

2 large cloves garlic, minced

1 small jalapeño with some seeds, minced

½ teaspoon vegetarian Worcestershire sauce*

½ teaspoon sea salt, or to taste

¼ teaspoon freshly ground black pepper, or to taste

Stir together all the ingredients in a medium serving bowl. Refrigerate for at least 1 hour before serving. If desired, sprinkle with additional minced shallot or chives before serving.

PER SERVING: 170 calories, 17g total fat, 3.5g saturated fat, 0g trans fat, 15mg cholesterol, 270mg sodium, 2g total carbohydrate, 0g dietary fiber, 3g protein

*Choose a vegetarian Worcestershire sauce since the regular version contains anchovies.

use it, don't lose it

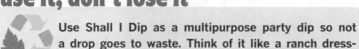

Use Shall I Dip as a multipurpose party dip so not a drop goes to waste. Think of it like a ranch dressing. It's ideal to use for dunking veggies, but also consider serving it with chips or organic chicken nuggets. Try it as a creamy salad dressing or sandwich spread, too.

snappy tzatziki

SUGAR SNAP PEA TZATZIKI SAUCE

Makes 5 servings: ⅓ cup each

If it's spring, it's time for sugar snap peas. But don't try to cook them until they're mushy and olive green. They're meant to be snappy. In fact, save energy; you don't need to cook them at all. Indulge in them raw in this Mediterranean-style sauce that's super-loaded with the crunchy peas to make it extra-snappy-licious!

2 tablespoons extra-virgin olive oil
Juice of ½ small lemon (about 1 tablespoon)
2 large cloves garlic, minced
1¼ cups plain organic Greek yogurt
½ teaspoon sea salt, or to taste
⅛ teaspoon freshly ground black pepper, or to taste
3 ounces sugar snap peas (about 18)
¼ cup finely chopped fresh herbs, such as a mixture of
    mint, dill, and chives

1. Whisk together the olive oil, lemon juice, garlic, and yogurt in a medium serving bowl. Add salt and pepper.

2. Snip the stem ends off the sugar snap peas. Very thinly cut each pea crosswise into paper-thin slices. Stir the sliced peas and herbs into the yogurt mixture. Chill in the refrigerator until ready to serve

3. Serve as a dip with pita or as a condiment to add Mediterranean flair to any dish. Tastes great for several days!

PER SERVING: 130 calories, 11g total fat, 5g saturated fat, 0g trans fat, 10mg cholesterol, 250mg sodium, 4g total carbohydrate, 1g dietary fiber, 5g protein

little **green** cooking tip

Grow your own herbs—indoors or out—so when a recipe calls for a small amount, you won't need to buy big bunches that may go to waste. Besides, herbs, like other living plants and trees, may help offset adverse effects of excess carbon (as carbon dioxide—CO_2) in the atmosphere.

use it, don't lose it

Small yogurt containers are often not made with recyclable material. And when they are, they may not be readily recyclable. Repurpose the leftover containers, such as for holding arts and crafts supplies.

SOUPS & SALADS

the greenest broccoli soup ever

CREAM OF BROCCOLI SOUP

Makes 4 servings: 1½ cups each

To make a traditional creamy broccoli soup from scratch, it can take 30 or more minutes of stewing time. But it's no longer necessary to use that much gas or electricity—as long as you follow some green preparation tricks of the trade. One trick: Use a lid to trap all of the heat in the pot. This will allow the soup to continue cooking even after you turn off the burner. And it'll help you decrease your carbon footprint—deliciously.

4 cups finely chopped or very thinly sliced broccoli florets
    and tender stems
1 medium yellow onion, thinly sliced
8 ounces white, gold, or red baby creamer potatoes, scrubbed
    unpeeled, and thinly sliced
4 cups low-sodium vegetable broth
2 tablespoons unsalted organic butter
1½ teaspoons fresh lemon juice
½ cup organic heavy cream (optional)
1¼ teaspoons sea salt, or to taste
¼ teaspoon freshly ground white or black pepper, or to taste
⅛ teaspoon freshly grated or ground nutmeg, or to taste

(continued)

little **green** cooking tip

Skinny is in. For a quicker-cooking soup, slice any of its veggies as skinny as you can to start with. The thinner the veggies, such as onions and broccoli stems, the faster they'll cook. And that'll leave a skinnier carbon footprint.

1. Add the broccoli, onion, potatoes, broth, butter, and lemon juice to a large saucepan. Cover, place over high heat, and cook for 6 minutes. Reduce the heat to medium-high and cook until the vegetables are just tender, 6 to 8 more minutes. Turn off the burner and keep covered. Let "lid cook" (cook covered while the burner is off) until the vegetables are very tender, about 10 minutes.

2. Use an immersion blender to puree the soup in the saucepan. Or puree the soup in batches in a blender and return to the pot.

3. Stir the cream (if using) into the soup. Add salt, pepper, and nutmeg. Reheat the soup slightly, if necessary, before serving.

PER SERVING: 150 calories, 6g total fat, 4g saturated fat, 0g trans fat, 15mg cholesterol, 890mg sodium, 21g total carbohydrate, 4g dietary fiber, 4g protein

use it, don't lose it

 Have some spare, savory, thick broccoli stems? They're pungent, yet perfectly edible. Grate them and use raw for a broccoli slaw, like coleslaw. Or very thinly slice the stems for a quick sauté or stir-fry.

bean green

HASS AVOCADO AND BLACK BEAN SALAD

Makes 4 servings: 1¼ cups each

I love beans. I especially love how easy they are to cook with. You can buy them in a can and you won't need to soak or cook them. Buy organic varieties and you won't need to rinse them, either. That means you won't waste one of our most precious resources: water. Then pair the beans with velvety avocado in this recipe for a sure winner of a salad.

little
green
cooking
tip

Trying to kick the canned habit? It's not necessary if you buy organic beans and you recycle or repurpose the can. But if you choose, prepare your own dried beans. See soaking and cooking directions on the back of the bag or, if you buy beans from bulk bins, at the California Dry Bean Board Web site: www.calbeans.com/ beanbasics.html.

1 (15-ounce) can organic black beans, drained (do not rinse)
½ large Vidalia or other sweet onion, diced
1 medium red or yellow bell pepper, diced
1 large jalapeño with some seeds, minced
⅔ cup Green Green Salsa (page 54) or prepared tomatillo salsa (salsa verde)
1 Hass avocado, pitted, peeled, and diced
¼ cup chopped fresh cilantro, or to taste
½ teaspoon sea salt, or to taste

1. Combine the beans, onion, bell pepper, and jalapeño in a large serving bowl.

2. Stir in the salsa until evenly combined.

3. Gently stir in the avocado, cilantro, and salt. Serve at room temperature.

PER SERVING: 180 calories, 6g total fat, 1g saturated fat, 0g trans fat, 0mg cholesterol, 470mg sodium, 27g total carbohydrate, 8g dietary fiber, 7g protein

use it, don't lose it

Don't toss out or compost those avocado peels just yet. For a groovy green touch, serve the salad or extra tomatillo sauce in avocado "peel-ups" (peels used as serving cups or bowls). Be sure to scrub the avocado peel—or the peel or skin of any produce—well before preparation, especially if you plan to use it.

singapore slaw

ASIAN-INSPIRED CABBAGE SLAW

Makes 4 servings: 1 cup each

You don't need to travel to Asia to be inspired by Asian foods. And Asian foods no longer need to travel thousands of miles to get to your table. All of the ingredients in this intriguing, delightfully textured slaw are now born in the U.S.A. But go ahead, enjoy it with chopsticks—reusable ones.

3 tablespoons mild floral honey
1 tablespoon rice vinegar (preferably brown rice)
1 tablespoon stone-ground mustard
1 tablespoon naturally brewed soy sauce
2 teaspoons peanut or flaxseed oil
1 teaspoon grated scrubbed unpeeled gingerroot
¼ teaspoon freshly ground black pepper
½ head green cabbage, shredded
1 cup mung bean sprouts
2 scallions, green and white parts, thinly sliced on diagonal
¼ cup shredded radicchio
2 tablespoons chopped fresh cilantro
⅓ cup sliced raw (natural) almonds

1. In a large serving bowl, whisk together the honey, vinegar, mustard, soy sauce, oil, gingerroot, and pepper.

2. Add the cabbage, bean sprouts, scallions, radicchio, and cilantro; toss to coat.

3. Sprinkle with almonds. Serve immediately in the bowl, or, if desired, serve in radicchio leaves.

PER SERVING: 140 calories, 6g total fat, 1g saturated fat, 0g trans fat, 0mg cholesterol, 290mg sodium, 20g total carbohydrate, 3g dietary fiber, 4g protein

use it, don't lose it

Before you shred the radicchio remove four of the leaves to use as serving cups.

bog (black-n-orange-n-green) salad

SPINACH SALAD WITH BLACKBERRIES AND NAVEL ORANGE SEGMENTS

Makes 4 servings: ¼ of salad each

With the arrival of spring, look for the arrival of the beloved blackberry. As soon as you see locally grown berries available, pop the fruity gems into your mouth and enjoy them as is. But they're equally enjoyable in recipes, like this lovely spinach salad with oranges and a tarragon-laced vinaigrette.

2 navel oranges

3 tablespoons safflower, flaxseed, or canola oil

1 tablespoon white wine vinegar

1 teaspoon finely chopped fresh tarragon

¼ teaspoon sea salt, or to taste

¼ teaspoon freshly ground black pepper

4 cups fresh baby spinach or coarsely chopped fresh spinach

10 fresh blackberries, sliced crosswise

2 scallions, green and white parts, thinly sliced

1. Grate ¼ teaspoon of zest from the oranges and reserve. Cut the peel and white pith from the oranges. Holding oranges over a bowl to catch juices (reserve 3 tablespoons juice), cut between membranes to release segments into bowl. Squeeze the remaining orange membranes after segmenting for additional juice. (Nibble on the rest!)

2. Whisk together the oil, reserved orange juice, vinegar, tarragon, salt, pepper, and reserved zest in a small bowl or liquid measuring cup.

3. Arrange the spinach, blackberries, and orange segments on a serving platter. Sprinkle with the scallions. Drizzle with the orange vinaigrette or serve it on the side. Garnish with additional zest, if desired, and serve.

PER SERVING: 150 calories, 11g total fat, 1g saturated fat, 0g trans fat, 0mg cholesterol, 190mg sodium, 14g total carbohydrate, 4g dietary fiber, 2g protein

little
green
cooking
tip

Build your menus around local, in-season produce, when fruits and vegetables are at their nutritious and flavorful best, such as blackberries in spring time. This way you can eat produce that hasn't traveled from another country—which helps to keep "food miles" in check.

Spring

65

go local

Sourcing locally grown produce, like blackberries and spinach, could get easier for city dwellers if a concept developed by professor Dickson Despommier becomes reality. Despommier (along with his graduate students) developed the concept of "vertical farms." The hope is that these "farms" would fit right in with all of the other city high-rises. A very cool idea that would require a very small amount of land compared to traditional farms.

french kissed cress

WATERCRESS SALAD WITH WHITE FRENCH SALAD DRESSING

Makes 4 servings: 1½ cups each

Sure, you can open up a bottle of chemical-laden salad dressing and dump it on some lettuce. (Sorry, I'll pass on that!) But there's a fresher, tastier way in this very simple, elegant salad made with dark, peppery greens and a homemade dressing that's pure decadence. (Please, invite me to that dinner!) It gets even simpler because you can make and serve the dressing and salad all in one bowl.

⅓ cup soybean or canola oil
3 tablespoons white wine vinegar
3 tablespoons mild floral honey
1 small shallot, minced
1 large clove garlic, minced
1 teaspoon Dijon mustard
1 teaspoon sea salt
2 large bunches watercress, thick stems trimmed
½ cup thinly sliced red onion

1. Whisk together the oil, vinegar, honey, shallot, garlic, mustard, and salt in a large serving bowl.

2. Add the watercress and onion. Gently toss and serve.

PER SERVING: 220 calories, 18g total fat, 3g saturated fat, 0g trans fat, 0mg cholesterol, 620mg sodium, 16g total carbohydrate, 1g dietary fiber, 1g protein

---

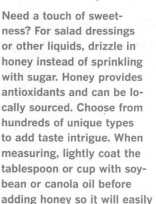

little *green* cooking tip

Need a touch of sweetness? For salad dressings or other liquids, drizzle in honey instead of sprinkling with sugar. Honey provides antioxidants and can be locally sourced. Choose from hundreds of unique types to add taste intrigue. When measuring, lightly coat the tablespoon or cup with soybean or canola oil before adding honey so it will easily drizzle out. Visit www.honey.com for more tips.

use it, don't lose it

Instead of tossing some parsley onto a plate for a garnish, finely chop leftover watercress stems and sprinkle onto other dishes served at the same meal as a watercress salad.

beet carpaccio salad

THINLY SLICED BEET AND GOAT CHEESE SALAD WITH FRESH APRICOT

Makes 4 servings: ¼ of recipe each

A tasty way to enjoy beets is to roast them. Unfortunately, that usually means over an hour of oven-roasting time! Mother Nature will be none too pleased. Fortunately, you can still get fresh-roasted goodness in a planet-friendlier way . . . using the microwave oven. You'll save so much time that this tantalizing salad with "micro-roasted" beets will be a pleasure to prepare.

3 medium beets with greens
1 fresh apricot or small nectarine, pitted, diced
2 tablespoons extra-virgin olive oil
2 tablespoons aged balsamic or red wine vinegar
5 ounces organic or locally produced soft goat cheese, crumbled
⅓ cup coarsely chopped raw walnuts
¼ teaspoon freshly ground black pepper, or to taste

1. Trim off the beet greens about 1 inch above the root. (Reserve leaves for another use.)

2. Place the scrubbed beets into a large microwave-safe dish. Cover well with unbleached parchment paper. "Micro-roast" (cook in the microwave oven*) on high until beets are easily pierced with a knife, about 10 minutes. Keep covered and set aside until cool enough to handle. Peel the skins with a paring knife. Cut the beets into about 8 slices each.

3. Arrange the beet slices on a platter. Line the platter with some of the beet greens, if desired. Sprinkle with the apricot. Drizzle with the oil and vinegar. Sprinkle with the cheese and walnuts. Add pepper. Serve warm or chilled.

PER SERVING: 240 calories, 20g total fat, 7g saturated fat, 0g trans fat, 15mg cholesterol, 160mg sodium, 7g total carbohydrate, 2g dietary fiber, 9g protein

*Microwave oven cooking times will vary. See page 39.

little *green* cooking tip

Put that microwave oven to work. Beets, potatoes, and sweet potatoes can be "micro-roasted" just as tastily as they can be oven-roasted or baked. And due to faster cooking times, the microwave oven can reduce energy use by about two-thirds compared with the conventional oven.

If you have the option, go with smaller beets. It'll allow you to "micro-roast" faster (in 6 to 8 minutes), which saves even more electricity. Smaller produce tends to be more nutritious, too. Research suggests that as produce gets bigger, its vitamins, minerals, and other beneficial compounds can significantly diminish—along with aroma and taste. Good things do come in small packages after all!

looks like greek to me salad

BABY ARUGULA ORZO SALAD

Makes 6 servings: 1½ cups each

Orzo looks like rice, but cooks much faster since it is pasta. It cooks even quicker using my green "lid cooking" approach, too. In fact, it'll help you save several minutes of cooking time—and the accompanying cooking gas or electricity. The end result: a beautiful, full-flavored, perfectly cooked orzo salad that will become a favorite for picnics or your everyday menu.

1 cup whole-wheat orzo

3 tablespoons extra-virgin olive oil

Juice and zest of ½ large lemon, or to taste (about 2 tablespoons juice)

¾ teaspoon sea salt, or to taste

2 cups baby arugula or fresh baby spinach leaves

6 ounces organic or locally produced feta or soft goat cheese, crumbled (about 1½ cups; optional)

2 scallions, green and white parts, thinly sliced

1 cup grape tomatoes, halved lengthwise

½ cup chopped fresh herbs, such as a mixture of basil, flat-leaf parsley, and mint

⅓ cup finely diced unpeeled hothouse cucumber or celery

¼ cup raw pine nuts

little green cooking tip

Grated lemon peel (zest) adds an interesting flavor element to dishes. So much so, that if a recipe also calls for a touch of cheese, you can reduce the amount of cheese, or not use any at all, without losing taste satisfaction.

(continued)

Spring

69

1. Add the orzo and 3 cups fresh water to a small saucepan. Bring to a boil over high heat. Cover and turn off the heat. Let "lid cook" (cook covered while the burner is off) until the orzo is al dente, about 7 minutes. Drain well. (Do not rinse.)

2. Meanwhile, whisk together the oil, lemon juice, and salt in a large bowl.

3. Add the hot, drained orzo to the lemon dressing and toss. Set aside to cool slightly, about 30 minutes, stirring occasionally to help prevent sticking. Then chill in the refrigerator.

4. When the orzo is at room temperature or cooler, add the arugula, cheese (if using), scallions, tomatoes, herbs, and cucumber and gently toss. Stir in the lemon zest. Taste and adjust seasoning, if necessary.

5. Sprinkle with pine nuts. Serve at room temperature.

PER SERVING: 280 calories, 17g total fat, 6g saturated fat, 0g trans fat, 25mg cholesterol, 610mg sodium, 23g total carbohydrate, 3g dietary fiber, 9g protein

---

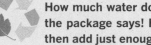

use it, don't lose it

How much water do you need to cook orzo? Less than the package says! First, fill the pan with the orzo and then add just enough water to boil, about 3 cups water to 1 cup orzo. And by using only the amount of water that is necessary, you won't be wasting energy to bring extra water to a boil. Once the water with the orzo boils, cover it with a lid and turn off the heat. The orzo will keep cooking in the hot water while the burner is off.

red sea salad

GINGERY RED GRAPEFRUIT SHRIMP SALAD

Makes 4 servings: ¼ of recipe each

Not all shrimp are created equal and not all are ecologically sound selections. Luckily, U.S. farmed shrimp is one of the more environmentally friendlier choices (see Go Local, page 72). They'll delight you in this refreshing, gorgeous salad.

2 large red or pink grapefruits
2 tablespoons mild floral honey or 3 tablespoons local fruit spread
    or homemade jam
2 tablespoons sunflower, grapeseed, or canola oil
Juice of ½ lime (about 1 tablespoon)
1 teaspoon grated scrubbed unpeeled gingerroot
¼ teaspoon sea salt, or to taste
¼ teaspoon freshly ground black pepper, or to taste
12 large shrimp, shelled and deveined (about ½ pound)
4 packed cups mixed baby greens
1 Hass avocado, pitted and peeled
¼ cup raw pine nuts or chopped pistachios

little **green** cooking tip

Sautéing in a skillet over medium-high or high heat? The skillet will remain hot enough to continue to sauté for at least another minute (perhaps several), even after the burner is off. Take advantage of the hot skillet by "green sautéing" to use less cooking energy.

1. Cut the peel and white pith from the grapefruits. Holding grapefruits over a bowl to catch juices (reserve ¼ cup juice), cut between membranes to release segments. (Squeeze the remaining grapefruit membranes after segmenting for additional juice.)

2. Whisk together ¼ cup of the grapefruit juice, honey, 1 tablespoon of the oil, 2 teaspoons of the lime juice, and gingerroot in a liquid measuring cup. Add salt and pepper. Set aside.

3. Heat the remaining tablespoon oil in a medium skillet over medium-high heat until hot but not smoking. Sauté shrimp for 2 minutes total. Turn off the burner. "Green sauté" (sauté in hot skillet while the burner is off) for 1 minute to fully cook the shrimp. Set aside to cool slightly.

4. Meanwhile, arrange the greens on a platter. Slice the avocado and place on top of the greens. Drizzle with the remaining lime juice. Arrange the grapefruit on top of the greens.

(continued)

5. Toss the cooled shrimp with ½ of the vinaigrette in the skillet. Taste and adjust seasoning, if necessary. Serve the shrimp in avocado "peel-ups" (avocado peels used as shrimp "boats") on the platter.

6. Drizzle the remaining vinaigrette over the salad, sprinkle with the pine nuts, and serve.

PER SERVING: 310 calories, 19g total fat, 2g saturated fat, 0g trans fat, 85mg cholesterol, 250mg sodium, 27g total carbohydrate, 5g dietary fiber, 12g protein

go local

 According to the Environmental Defense Fund, about 9 out of 10 shrimp eaten in the U.S. are imported from Latin America or Southeast Asia. Instead look for U.S. farmed shrimp, Oregon pink shrimp (bite-sized "cocktail" shrimp), and spot prawns from Canada to lessen your environmental impact.

strip salad

ORGANIC NEW YORK STRIP STEAK ON FRESH SPINACH—RED ONION BED

Makes 4 servings: 1 sliced steak with 1¼ cups salad each

If you're a meat eater, choose a "green-sized" (just right–sized portion) grass-fed organic strip steak; it'll be free of antibiotics. Prepare it on a panini grill where both sides cook at once—which will help you use less energy. To serve, cut the steak thinly on a bias and fan it out on top of the salad. It'll look like so much more than one petite portion. And the taste will excite you so much that you may actually want to strip!

4 (4-ounce) grass-fed organic New York strip steaks (top loin),
    1-inch thick
2 teaspoons canola or peanut oil
1 teaspoon finely chopped fresh thyme
½ teaspoon sea salt, or to taste
½ teaspoon freshly ground black pepper, or to taste
6 cups fresh baby spinach or coarsely chopped regular spinach
1 small red onion, thinly sliced
3 tablespoons extra-virgin olive oil
2 tablespoons aged balsamic vinegar
2 ounces organic or locally produced blue cheese, crumbled
    (about ½ cup; optional)

1. Lightly rub steaks with the oil and sprinkle with the thyme.

2. Cook in a panini grill on medium-high heat until medium-rare,
   about 3 minutes. (Alternatively, cook in a skillet over medium-
   high heat for about 3 minutes per side for medium-rare.) If you
   desire a more well-done steak, turn off the panini grill and let
   "green grill" (cook in the off panini grill with residual heat until
   desired doneness). Add salt and pepper immediately after cooking. Let steaks sit at least 5 minutes before slicing.

3. Meanwhile, toss the spinach and onion with oil and vinegar. Arrange salad evenly on 4 plates. Slice each steak into 8 pieces.
   Divide steak evenly among the salads, sprinkle with the cheese
   (if using), and serve.

PER SERVING: 280 calories, 17g total fat, 3.5g saturated fat, 0g trans fat, 40mg cholesterol, 410mg sodium, 8g total carbohydrate, 2g dietary fiber, 24g protein

go local

Befriend your local butcher! He or she can help you
with your planet-pleasing portioning. In this recipe,
for instance, I purchased a 1-pound New York strip
steak that was 7 × 2¼ × 2 inches thick. I then had it cut into
4 steaks, 3½ × 2¼ × 1 inch thick, to make this dish. (You can do
this step on your own, if you choose.) Remember, the thinner the
steak, the quicker it'll cook.

little
green
cooking
tip

Green-size it! If you're a meat
eater, consider reducing your
portion size to lessen the
overall environmental impact.
If you're used to a 10-ounce
steak, try 8 ounces next time.
A good green goal: Wean
your way down to 4 ounces
or smaller.

VEGETARIAN DISHES

soba sesame

SESAME SOBA NOODLE BOWL WITH BELL PEPPERS AND CUCUMBER

Makes 4 servings: 1½ cups each

Soba is a Japanese-style noodle that's usually made from buckwheat. It's cooked very quickly with little energy by use of "lid cooking." Then, unlike many pasta salads, the noodles aren't rinsed; they're tossed with dressing and cooled at room temperature. Soba is a little gooey when prepared in this eco-friendly manner, but it adds a nice creaminess to the finished dressed noodles. And it's a cool entrée filled with vivid colors and textures that'll please persnickety people—and their palates.

8 ounces soba noodles or whole-wheat angel hair pasta*
¼ cup rice vinegar (preferably brown rice)
2 scallions, green and white parts, thinly sliced
2 tablespoons mild floral honey or 3 tablespoons local fruit spread
   or homemade jam
1½ tablespoons naturally brewed soy sauce
1 tablespoon grated scrubbed unpeeled gingerroot
1½ teaspoons Asian garlic-chili sauce
2 tablespoons sesame oil
1 large orange or red bell pepper, thinly sliced
½ cup very thinly sliced unpeeled hothouse cucumber
3 tablespoons chopped fresh cilantro (optional)
1 tablespoon raw sesame seeds

1. Bring 4 cups fresh water to a boil in a large saucepan over high heat. Stir in the noodles and return to a boil. Cover and turn off the heat. Let "lid cook" (cook covered while the burner is off) until the noodles are just cooked through, about 6 minutes. Drain well. (Do not rinse.)

2. Meanwhile, whisk together the vinegar, scallions, honey, soy sauce, gingerroot, and garlic-chili sauce in a liquid measuring cup.

3. Place the noodles in a large serving bowl. Drizzle with the oil and toss to coat. Add the dressing and toss again, separating noodles while tossing.

4. Let sit at room temperature to cool slightly, about 30 minutes, stirring occasionally to help prevent sticking. Then chill in the refrigerator.

5. Just before serving, stir in the bell pepper, cucumber, and cilantro (if using). Sprinkle with sesame seeds. Serve chilled or at room temperature with reusable chopsticks.

PER SERVING: 320 calories, 8g total fat, 1g saturated fat, 0g trans fat, 0mg cholesterol, 860mg sodium, 56g total carbohydrate, 1g dietary fiber, 10g protein

---

*If using angel hair pasta, "lid cook" for 3 minutes, not 6.

little **green** cooking tip

Which part of the scallion are you supposed to use: the green or the white part? Both—for great flavor and to avoid waste.

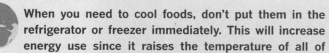

a planet-friendly bite

When you need to cool foods, don't put them in the refrigerator or freezer immediately. This will increase energy use since it raises the temperature of all of the items in the fridge or freezer—which then need to be cooled back down. Rather, let foods cool slightly at room temperature for about 30 minutes before chilling. But do remember that perishable foods should never be left at room temperature longer than 2 hours.

peachy b&b pancakes

BUCKWHEAT BLUEBERRY-PEACH PANCAKES

Makes 3 servings: 2 pancakes each

When fresh blueberries are available, it's prime time for pancakes. These have a thicker, gooier batter than a regular, runny boxed-mix pancake batter because they're made with 100 percent buckwheat flour, which gives them an earthier texture when cooked. But perhaps my favorite part of these pancakes is the topping. I love to drizzle mine with a mixture of pure maple syrup and a mango-strawberry fruit spread. I'm hooked! Now it's your turn.

½ cup plus 1 tablespoon buckwheat flour

1 teaspoon double-acting baking powder

¼ teaspoon sea salt

1 tablespoon cold unsalted organic butter, cut into pieces

2 tablespoons local apricot or other fruit spread or
    homemade jam or 1 tablespoon mild floral honey

⅓ cup vanilla soymilk

1 large organic egg

½ cup fresh blueberries

1 medium white or yellow peach, pitted and diced

¼ cup pure maple syrup or mixture of 2 tablespoons each
    pure maple syrup and local fruit spread or homemade jam,
    at room temperature

1. Combine the ½ cup flour, baking powder, salt, butter, and fruit spread with a pastry blender in a medium bowl until a fine crumbly mixture.

2. Whisk together the soymilk and egg in a liquid measuring cup. Add to the flour mixture. Whisk until the batter is well combined and let stand for 5 minutes.

3. Toss the blueberries with the remaining 1 tablespoon buckwheat flour. Stir into the batter. Stir in the peach.

little *green* cooking tip

How do you like your peaches? I'm a "leaner"— I like my peaches extra-juicy, so I have to lean over to prevent getting dripped on. That type of peach is delicious for eating out of hand—and will be best in baking and in pancake making, too.

4. Spoon the batter, about ¼ cup per pancake (to make 6 pancakes total), onto a hot flat griddle over medium heat. Spread batter out with a spatula to about 4-inches in diameter. Cook until brown and crisp and cooked through, about 3 minutes per side. (Alternatively, cook the pancakes in two batches [3 pancakes each] in a large stick-resistant skillet over medium heat.)

5. Transfer the pancakes to a platter. Keep warm by covering with recycled aluminum foil, if necessary. Serve with the maple syrup.

PER SERVING: 280 calories, 7g total fat, 3.5g saturated fat, 0g trans fat, 80mg cholesterol, 420mg sodium, 48g total carbohydrate, 5g dietary fiber, 6g protein

go local

I love supporting local companies—especially those that put an emphasis on high-quality, natural, and fresh ingredients. It helps to keep food miles down, too. One product I enjoy from such a company is Sarabeth's fruit spread. (Though if you make homemade jam from homegrown fruit, that's an even eco-friendlier choice!) I used it in this pancake recipe—and many other *Big Green Cookbook* recipes.

curly egg muffin

EGG MUFFIN WITH SMOKED GOUDA AND CURLY ENDIVE

Makes 4 servings: 1 muffin each

Have a hankering for a fast-food breakfast sandwich? Move over Egg McMuffin! You'll be tickled green by this mouthwatering muffin. It's my favorite breakfast sandwich of all time. The smoked Gouda gives the essence of real bacon. But you won't find any pork here. What you will find is that this muffin is delectable . . . for lunch and dinner, not just breakfast.

1½ tablespoons unsalted organic butter
4 large organic eggs
¼ teaspoon sea salt, or to taste
¼ teaspoon freshly ground black pepper, or to taste
4 whole-grain English muffins
4 (1-ounce) slices organic or locally produced naturally smoked
   Gouda cheese
12 leaves curly endive
Juice of ½ small lemon (about 1 tablespoon)

1. Melt the butter in a large stick-resistant skillet over medium heat. Break the eggs into the skillet. Puncture the yolks and add salt and pepper. Cover and cook for 1 minute. Turn off the heat and let "lid cook" (cook covered while the burner is off) until the eggs are cooked and softly set on top, about 5 minutes. (The eggs may not look cooked, so judge doneness with your fingers, too. The eggs should be slightly firm with no runniness.)

2. Meanwhile, split and lightly toast the English muffins. Immediately top four of the halves with a cheese slice.

3. Place one egg on top of each of the remaining English muffin halves. Top with the endive. Drizzle with any of the remaining butter in the skillet. Splash with the lemon juice. Then place the Gouda-topped muffin on the endive, cheese side down. Serve.

PER SERVING: 380 calories, 20g total fat, 10g saturated fat, 0g trans fat, 255mg cholesterol, 830mg sodium, 32g total carbohydrate, 7g dietary fiber, 20g protein

tip o' the mornin'

ASPARAGUS TIP AND MUSHROOM OMELET WITH SHAVED PARMESAN

Makes 4 servings: 1 wedge each

No, this isn't an Irish omelet. I just like the name. But the highlight of this open-face omelet isn't its name; it's the asparagus, which is plentiful in the spring. And the highlight of its greenness is the way it's cooked, using my "lid cooking" technique.

8 large organic eggs

1½ ounces freshly grated or shaved organic or locally produced
    Parmesan cheese (about ½ cup)

2 scallions, green and white parts, minced

½ teaspoon sea salt, or to taste

¼ teaspoon freshly ground black pepper, or to taste

1 pound thin asparagus spears (about 24)

2 tablespoons unsalted organic butter

5 large chanterelle mushrooms, stemmed, or morels, thinly sliced

Juice of ½ small lemon (about 1 tablespoon)

1. Whisk together the eggs, cheese, green portion of the scallions, 1 tablespoon of cold fresh water, salt, and pepper in a large bowl. Set aside.

(continued)

little
green
cooking
tip

One essential piece of equipment for an environmentally friendly kitchen is a large, 12-inch, stick-resistant skillet with a tight-fitting lid. *Tight-fitting* is the key. When a lid fits a skillet snuggly, it traps the heat, which means you can turn off the burner and keep cooking with the residual heat.

2. Cut off the top four inches of the asparagus (save ends for another use). Then cut the 4-inch tips in half.

3. Heat the butter in a large, stick-resistant skillet over medium-high heat. Add the lower 2 inches of the tips. Cover and cook for 1 minute. Remove the cover, add the top 2 inches of the tips, the white portion of the scallions, and mushrooms and sauté until all the asparagus is crisp-tender and the scallion is caramelized, about 2 minutes. Stir in the lemon juice. Taste and adjust seasoning, if necessary.

4. Evenly pour the egg mixture over the asparagus in the skillet. Cover and cook for 1½ minutes. Turn off the heat and let "lid cook" (cook covered while the burner is off) until the eggs are softly set on top, about 12 minutes.*

5. Slide the omelet onto a plate. Invert another plate on top, flip over, and serve open-face style. Cut omelet into 4 wedges to serve. Serve with additional shaved Parmesan cheese, if desired.

PER SERVING: 270 calories, 20g total fat, 9g saturated fat, 0g trans fat, 450mg cholesterol, 590mg sodium, 5g total carbohydrate, 1g dietary fiber, 19g protein

*If your omelet isn't fully set on top, slide it out onto a plate. Invert another plate on top. Flip over. Then slide back into the skillet and cook for 1 minute over medium-high heat.

a planet-friendly bite

Do you celebrate Easter? Then decorate eggs green for that Easter basket. Dye locally-produced hard-cooked eggs with an array of colorful, natural foods from your pantry or fridge, like blueberries, orange peels, beets, fresh herbs, or coffee. Just think about the foods that you don't want to get on your clothing because they can stain; those are the ideal foods for coloring eggs.

mediterranean morning canapés

SCRAMBLED ORGANIC EGGS WITH SPINACH AND FETA ON TOMATO ROUNDS

Makes 4 servings: 2 topped tomato slices each

Trying to make an impression on someone (or just yourself!) with breakfast in bed? These scrambled egg canapés look glamorous, but they're quick and easy to create. Plus, you don't need to toast anything. You'll simply slice up some vine-ripened tomatoes to use in place of toast.

little **green** cooking tip

Go bowl-less; pan-scramble your eggs. Crack eggs right into the hot skillet and stir vigorously right in the pan to scramble them. Don't worry if they're not perfect. The fact that you won't need to use or wash an extra bowl just for that step will make it worth it.

1 tablespoon extra-virgin olive oil

1 tablespoon unsalted organic butter

1 large clove garlic, minced

Juice of 1 small or ½ large lemon (about 2 tablespoons)

9 packed cups fresh baby spinach

8 large organic eggs

2 teaspoons finely chopped fresh oregano

½ teaspoon sea salt, or to taste

¼ teaspoon freshly ground black pepper, or to taste

2 medium vine-ripened tomatoes, cut into 6 slices each

2 ounces crumbled organic or locally produced
   feta cheese (about ½ cup)

1. Heat the oil and butter in a large stick-resistant skillet over medium-high heat. Add the garlic and sauté for 30 seconds. Add the lemon juice and spinach and sauté until the spinach is wilted, about 2 minutes.

2. Crack the eggs directly into the skillet as quickly as possible; stir vigorously with each addition. Add the oregano, salt, and pepper as needed. Cover, turn off the heat, and let "lid cook" (cook covered while the burner is off) until the eggs are fully cooked through and softly set on top, about 2 minutes.

(continued)

3. Onto 8 of the thickest tomato slices, place a scoop (about ½ cup) of the eggs. (To easily do this, measure eggs into a ½-cup dry measuring cup; place a tomato slice on top; then invert onto plate.) Sprinkle each egg-topped tomato slice with 1 tablespoon of the cheese. Finely dice the remaining 4 tomato slices and use as an edible garnish. Serve.

PER SERVING: 300 calories, 21g total fat, 9g saturated fat, 0g trans fat, 450mg cholesterol, 730mg sodium, 12g total carbohydrate, 4g dietary fiber, 17g protein

use it, don't lose it

Use functional garnishes that you can actually eat. Don't just plop a parsley sprig—or worse, an inedible garnish—onto a plate if you can't or don't plan on eating it. The best garnish is an ingredient that's already incorporated into the dish. It's a great way to use excess food left over from prep, like bits of tomatoes or other veggies.

sweet beets

AGED BALSAMIC MICRO-ROASTED BEETS AND CITRUS FRUIT WITH MINT

Makes 4 servings: 1 cup each

Beets usually take an hour or more to roast, but not if you "micro-roast" them! In this recipe, "micro-roasted" beets are tossed with oranges, fennel, mint, and freshly made balsamic vinaigrette—you'll be mesmerized by all of the flavors and textures. And though you might be tempted to simply serve this like a salsa, give it a starring role alongside couscous, organic poultry, or fish. Or simply pick up a fork and savor it as a brilliant entrée.

3 medium red beets with greens
3 medium golden beets with greens
2 large navel oranges
1 small fennel bulb, trimmed, quartered, cored, and cut into matchstick-
    size strips (reserve fronds)
¼ cup finely chopped fresh mint
1 small shallot, minced
2 tablespoons extra-virgin olive oil
1 tablespoon aged balsamic vinegar
¾ teaspoon sea salt, or to taste
¼ teaspoon freshly ground black pepper, or to taste
¼ cup raw shelled pistachios, coarsely chopped

1. Trim off the beet greens about 1 inch above the root. (Reserve leaves for another use.)

2. Place the scrubbed beets into a large microwave-safe dish. Cover well with unbleached parchment paper. "Micro-roast" (cook in the microwave oven*) on high until the beets are easily pierced with a knife, about 10 minutes. Keep covered and set aside until cool enough to handle. Peel the skins with a paring knife. Cut the beets into ⅓-inch dice, separating the yellow and red beets.

3. Cut the peel and white pith from the oranges. (Reserve the peel for another use.) Cut the peeled oranges across into 4 or 5 slices, then cut the slices into ⅓-inch dice.

(continued)

Green things come in small packages. The smaller a veggie, the less cooking energy will be required to prepare it. For beets, use a 3-inch or less diameter rule. (Small ones are more tender than larger ones, too.)

4. Add the yellow beets, oranges, fennel, mint, and shallot to a medium serving bowl.

5. Whisk together the oil, vinegar, salt, and pepper in a small bowl. Gently stir the vinaigrette and the red beets into the yellow beet mixture. Taste and adjust seasoning.

6. If desired, sprinkle with some of the reserved fronds. Sprinkle with the pistachios and serve. Serve each portion on beet greens on individual plates, if desired.

PER SERVING: 210 calories, 11g total fat, 1.5g saturated fat, 0g trans fat, 0mg cholesterol, 540mg sodium, 28g total carbohydrate, 7g dietary fiber, 5g protein

---

*Microwave oven cooking times will vary. See page 39.

use it, don't lose it

When a recipe calls for just the beets and not the beet greens, find a use for the greens in the recipe—or elsewhere in the meal. For instance, arrange beet greens on a platter and use as a colorful, edible bed for serving a recipe, like Sweet Beets. However, if you have no desire to use beet greens, then buy beets without them.

fava of love

FRESH FAVA BEANS WITH LEMON VINAIGRETTE

Makes 3 servings: ½ cup each

I was inspired to create this recipe from one of my favorite menu items at my local teahouse, Blackbird Parlour. So when fava beans were in season, I picked up a few pounds of them and got to work in my kitchen to come up with a fresh version. It does take time to shuck the beans and remove their waxy covering, but it's worth it—especially since it only takes minutes to cook them.

2 pounds fresh fava beans, shelled (2½ cups shelled)*

2 tablespoons extra-virgin olive oil

Juice of ½ lemon (about 1½ tablespoons)

½ teaspoon sea salt, or to taste

⅛ teaspoon freshly ground black pepper, or to taste

⅛ teaspoon ground cumin, or to taste

2 tablespoons finely diced red onion

1 small clove garlic, minced

1 tablespoon finely chopped fresh flat-leaf parsley

1 teaspoon finely chopped fresh dill

1. Fill a medium bowl with ice and water. Set aside.

2. Bring a small saucepan of salted water (2 cups fresh water and 1 teaspoon sea salt) to a boil. (Note: The water should just cover the beans.) Add the shelled fava beans. Cover and turn off the heat. Let "lid cook" (cook covered while the burner is off) until the beans are just tender, about 5 minutes. Drain, then shock in the bowl of ice water, to stop cooking. Drain again and remove the skins (waxy outer coverings) of the beans by holding a bean with both thumbs and index fingers. Tear into the waxy covering of each bean with your left thumbnail, then pinch out the edible fava with your right thumb and index finger. (Makes about 1¼ cups.)

little *green* cooking tip

When you need to boil beans or other veggies use just enough water to cover the food. That means you'll waste less water and you'll be able to bring it to a boil faster—saving earthly resources in both cases.

(continued)

3. Whisk together the oil, lemon juice, salt, pepper, and cumin. Stir in the fava beans, onion, garlic, parsley, and dill. Taste and adjust seasoning, if necessary.

4. Serve at room temperature with whole-wheat pita bread on the side.

PER SERVING: 140 calories, 10g total fat, 1.5g saturated fat, 0g trans fat, 0mg cholesterol, 420mg sodium, 10g total carbohydrate, 3g dietary fiber, 4g protein

---

*To shell (or shuck) the beans, snip off or pull on the stem of the pod and unzip them on one or both sides. If need, use your clean fingernails to help fully open the "zipper." Push beans loose from the pods into a bowl using your thumbs.

go local

 If you don't grow your own fresh herbs and you prefer not to buy a bunch when you only need a tiny bit, it's okay to adjust recipes to your liking using other locally available herbs. For instance, fresh basil or chives both work deliciously in place of dill in this recipe. But, if you still want that dilly goodness, go ahead and use about ½ teaspoon dried dill instead of fresh.

red red "ribs"

STACK OF HOT RED BELL PEPPER STRIPS

Makes 3 servings: 9 strips each

These "ribs" have nothing to do with barbecued pork or beef. They have everything to do with finger-licking, stick-to-your ribs veggie madness. They're best enjoyed as a side dish, though if a pepper fan, you might just find yourself making this your appetizer, entrée, and side dish. And if you're a green fan, you'll appreciate that this vivid red finger food is grilled in minutes, rather than barbecued for hours like traditional ribs.

3 large red bell peppers, cut into about 9 long slices each*

2 tablespoons extra-virgin olive oil

2 teaspoons aged red wine vinegar

1 teaspoon crushed red pepper flakes

½ teaspoon sea salt, or to taste

2 tablespoons thinly sliced fresh basil (optional)

1. Toss together bell peppers, oil, vinegar, crushed red pepper, and salt in a stainless-steel bowl.

2. Place the pepper strips, skin side down, over direct high heat on an outdoor or indoor grill. Grill until lightly charred, about 3 minutes.

3. Remove the peppers from the grill and place back into the same bowl. Cover to allow to steam until cooked through with an al dente texture, about 6 minutes.

4. To serve, stack the bell pepper "ribs" onto a platter. Drizzle with any remaining red wine vinaigrette. Sprinkle with basil (if using). Pick up and eat with your fingers, just like real ribs. Serve hot, at room temperature, or chilled.

PER SERVING: 140 calories, 10g total fat, 1.5g saturated fat, 0g trans fat, 0mg cholesterol, 400mg sodium, 10g total carbohydrate, 3g dietary fiber, 2g protein

*Use three different colors of bell peppers for added eye appeal.

little **green** cooking tip

Finger licking is proper eco-friendly etiquette! Some things are better eaten with your fingers, like organic chicken nuggets, asparagus spears, or riblets of veggies. So skip the utensils when you don't really need them. Then you won't need to wash anything—other than your sticky fingers.

use it, don't lose it

No worries if you're cooking for one. There are so many delectable ideas for enjoying "vintage" (left over) veggies—even when dining solo. Spare savory grilled bell peppers blended into hummus or tossed with whole-wheat pasta turn the simple into the sensational.

fiery fingerlings

SERRANO FINGERLING HASH BROWNS

Makes 4 servings: 1 cup each

There's a "hot" new potato in town: fingerling potatoes are it. The Russian Banana (readily grown in America) is the superstar of the fingerlings—and they're the perfect choice in this full-flavored dish. The best part is that because of their petite size, they cook quickly. By slicing them into slender coins, it'll only take minutes to fix these heavenly hash browns. Of course, the shorter the cooking time, the better for the environment.

2 tablespoons unsalted organic butter
1 tablespoon extra-virgin olive oil
1½ pounds fingerling or baby red creamer potatoes, scrubbed unpeeled, and very thinly sliced
1 small or ½ large red onion, chopped
1 serrano pepper with some seeds, minced
2 large cloves garlic, minced
¾ teaspoon sea salt, or to taste
¼ cup chopped fresh flat-leaf parsley

1. Heat 1 tablespoon of the butter with the oil in a large stick-resistant skillet over medium-high heat. Add the potatoes, onion, and serrano pepper. Stir to combine. Cover and cook for 7 minutes, stirring once.

2. Remove the lid and sauté until the potatoes are cooked through yet al dente, 2 to 3 minutes. Add the garlic and sauté for 1 minute.

3. Turn off the heat, stir in the remaining butter, and cover. Let "lid cook" (cook covered while the burner is off) until the potatoes are tender and slightly browned, about 5 minutes.

4. Remove the lid. Add salt. Stir in the parsley and serve immediately.

PER SERVING: 230 calories, 9g total fat, 4.5g saturated fat, 0g trans fat, 15mg cholesterol, 450mg sodium, 34g total carbohydrate, 4g dietary fiber, 4g protein

little *green* cooking tip

A sharp knife is a key to a low-carbon kitchen. It'll help you slice foods thin. Using a mandoline is another option; it's especially helpful for slicing potatoes. The thinner you slice foods, like potatoes when preparing Fiery Fingerlings, the faster they'll cook—and the less carbon you'll be adding into the atmosphere.

micro mashers

RUSSET SMASHED POTATOES À LA MICROWAVE

Makes 5 servings: 1 cup each

Comfort food can please your tummy *and* please the planet. And it's just 10 minutes away! By chopping the potatoes into tiny cubes, they'll cook fast. And by "micro-roasting" them instead of baking them, they'll cook even faster. But don't eat these too *fast*. They're so darn delicious that you'll want to slowly relish every rich, velvety bit.

2 pounds russet potatoes scrubbed unpeeled, cut into ½-inch cubes (about 3 large)

4 large garlic cloves, peeled

1 cup fat-free organic milk or plain unsweetened soy milk, at room temperature

2 tablespoons unsalted organic butter

1½ teaspoons sea salt, or to taste

¼ teaspoon freshly ground black pepper, or to taste

2 teaspoons extra-virgin olive oil (optional)

3 tablespoons chopped chives

1. Add the potatoes and garlic to a large microwave-safe dish. Cover well with unbleached parchment paper. "Micro-roast" (cook in the microwave oven*) on high for 4 minutes. Stir and "micro-roast" until the potatoes are just tender, about 4 more minutes. Let sit covered in the off microwave to allow for carry-over cooking until the potatoes further soften, about 5 minutes.

(continued)

Spring

Start a new culinary tradi-
tion. Instead of warming milk
before adding it to the potatoes for mashing, use room-
temperature milk instead.
There's no need to use the
extra energy—just make sure
the milk isn't super-chilled
straight from the fridge.

2. Carefully remove the parchment paper from the bowl. Add the milk, butter,** salt, and pepper. Mash with a potato masher until smooth, adding additional milk, if necessary. Taste and adjust seasoning, if necessary.

3. Transfer to a serving bowl (or serve straight from the microwave dish if you don't care about looks!). Drizzle with the oil (if using) for added richness. Sprinkle with the chives and serve.

PER SERVING: 200 calories, 4.5g total fat, 3.5g saturated fat, 0g trans fat, 15mg cholesterol, 740mg sodium, 35g total carbohydrate, 3g dietary fiber, 6g protein

*Microwave oven cooking times will vary. See page 39.
**Prepare without the butter if serving to a vegan—or to someone on a weight loss diet.

go local

Move over bananas! There's a better way to get heart-friendly potassium—and in a source that can be found closer to home. It's the lovable potato. One medium potato with the peel provides 620 mg of potassium. That makes it a good source of potassium, for sure. Bananas provide about 450 mg per serving. So remember this: Pick the planet-pleasing potato for potassium. (Now try to say that sentence 10 times fast!)

FISH, POULTRY, & MEAT DISHES

avocado à la ahi

FLORIDA AVOCADO AND SEARED AHI TUNA TARTARE WITH FRESH LIME

Makes 4 servings: ¾ cup with 6 endive leaves each

Guacamole is one of my most favorite things. So I'm always trying to find ways to incorporate its flavors into new recipes, like this light, yet luscious dish. It'll tantalize the taste buds of tuna lovers. The tuna only takes a few minutes of cooking to sear. Then, for an extra eco-friendly touch, serve it in an avocado "peel-up" instead of a bowl and enjoy it with Belgian endive leaves—which you don't need to get from Belgium, by the way.

8 ounces sashimi-quality yellowfin tuna fillet

2 tablespoons canola or peanut oil

¾ teaspoon sea salt, or to taste

1 large Florida avocado or 2 medium Hass avocados, pitted, peeled, and diced

1 small jalapeño with some seeds, minced

¼ cup finely chopped red onion

¼ cup finely chopped fresh cilantro

1 large clove garlic, minced

Juice and zest of 2 limes (about ¼ cup juice)

¼ teaspoon ground cumin

3 Belgian endives, leaves separated

1. Rub tuna with 1 tablespoon of the oil and add salt. Cook in a panini grill over high heat for about 1½ minutes. (Alternatively, heat a small skillet over high heat, add the tuna, and sear for 3 minutes total—1½ minutes per side.)* Cool tuna.

(continued)

Don't be fooled by foreign-sounding veggie names. Often a veggie may be named after a country it originated, but can now be locally grown in the States, such as the Belgian endive. It should be enjoyed often in winter and spring. Use it like a green chip, ideal for scooping and dipping.

2. While the tuna is cooling, gently combine the avocado, jalapeño, onion, cilantro, garlic, lime juice, half the zest, cumin, and remaining oil with a fork in a medium bowl.

3. Cut the cooled tuna into small bite-sized cubes or strips and stir into the avocado mixture. Taste and adjust seasoning, if necessary.

4. Serve the tartare in avocado "peel-ups" (peel halves used as serving bowls; about ¾ cup per "peel-up"), surrounded by the endive leaves. Sprinkle with the remaining zest and serve.

PER SERVING: 290 calories, 16g total fat, 2.5g saturated fat, 0g trans fat, 25mg cholesterol, 540mg sodium, 22g total carbohydrate, 17g dietary fiber, 20g protein

---

*Wanna go greener? Skip step 1 and go raw. If using a high-quality sushi-grade tuna, this recipe will still taste divine. Just remember that it's not advised to eat raw or undercooked fish if you're very young, very old, have a compromised immune system, or are pregnant.

a planet-friendly bite

 Yellowfin tuna from the U.S. caught by trolling or pole-and-line gear or albacore tuna from the U.S. or Canada are considered the eco-best fish by the Environmental Defense Fund in collaboration with the Monterey Bay Aquarium.

fruity chicken on fire

GRILLED JALAPEÑO-APRICOT ORGANIC CHICKEN THIGHS

Makes 4 servings: 1 thigh each

The ubiquitous grilled chicken breast needs a makeover. It's time to appreciate the thighs. After all, chickens are more than just breasts. Thighs are usually less expensive, too. To keep grill time to a minimum, you'll pound the chicken thighs with a kitchen mallet so they're very thin. (I wish I could just pound my own thighs to make them thinner!) Finally, the fresh apricots provide a perfect touch of sweetness and add that characteristic caramelization during grilling.

little **green** cooking tip

3 apricots, halved and pitted
¼ cup canola oil
1 small white or yellow onion, coarsely chopped
1 large jalapeño with some seeds
3 tablespoons chopped fresh basil
2 tablespoons local apricot or other fruit spread or homemade jam or 1
　　tablespoon mild floral honey
1 teaspoon sea salt
4 boneless, skinless organic chicken thighs, pounded ⅓-inch thick

1. Add the apricots, oil, onion, jalapeño, basil, fruit spread, and salt to a blender container. Cover and puree for 30 seconds, or just until no lumps remain.

2. Place the chicken in a large bowl or baking pan. Pour the apricot mixture over the chicken. Let marinate at room temperature for 30 minutes, but no more than 1 hour. (If you plan to marinate for 1 hour or more, do so in the refrigerator.)

3. Remove the chicken from the marinade and discard leftover marinade. Cook the chicken in a panini grill on medium-high heat until fully cooked, about 5 minutes total. (Alternatively, cook chicken over direct medium-high heat on an outdoor or indoor grill, about 4 minutes per side.)

(*continued*)

Keep that kitchen mallet in the ready position. It'll be used regularly for low-carbon cooking. For instance, pound boneless, skinless organic chicken breasts or thighs between sheets of unbleached parchment or waxed paper with a kitchen mallet until very thin. It'll keep cooking times to a minimum. Plus, it'll make a small portion seem large.

4. Serve chicken immediately. It's lovely over grilled red bell pepper rings. Garnish with additional basil, if desired.

PER SERVING: 190 calories, 13g total fat, 2.5g saturated fat, 0g trans fat, 50mg cholesterol, 340mg sodium, 5g total carbohydrate, 0g dietary fiber, 14g protein

---

use it, don't lose it

It's usually advised by food safety experts not to reuse a marinade in which raw meat or poultry was marinated. But if you prefer not to lose it, there is a safe way to use it. The USDA suggests it's okay to reuse the marinade from raw meat or poultry if it's boiled first to destroy any harmful bacteria. My suggestion: Bring it to a full rolling boil for at least three minutes before using for basting, dipping, or other culinary uses.

pretty in purple

PAN-SEARED ORGANIC POULTRY BREAST PAILLARD WITH FRESH BLUEBERRY SAUCE

Makes 4 servings: 1 paillard with ⅓ cup sauce each

I found my thrill! If you like your food pretty, this poultry dish takes the cake. It's elegant—and purple. And it'll impress nearly any guest. The portion will sound petite, but because the chicken is flattened into a paillard, it'll look larger. And it'll cook super-fast—about 3 minutes!

2 (6-ounce) boneless, skinless organic chicken or duck breasts, split and pounded into ¼-inch-thick paillards

1 tablespoon canola oil

1 teaspoon sea salt, or to taste

½ teaspoon freshly ground black pepper, or to taste

2 tablespoons extra-virgin olive oil

2 large shallots, finely diced

½ cup local blueberry or other fruit spread or homemade jam or ⅓ cup mild floral honey

¼ cup apple cider vinegar

¾ cup fresh blueberries

1 teaspoon finely chopped fresh tarragon

1. Cut each chicken paillard in half. Rub each with the canola oil. Season with the salt and pepper. Cook in a panini grill on medium-high heat until fully cooked, about 3 minutes. (Alternatively, cook in a skillet over medium-high heat for about 2 minutes per side.) Set aside on a plate.

2. Heat the olive oil in a large stick-resistant skillet over medium-high heat. Add the shallots; cook, stirring frequently until softened and just beginning to caramelize, about 1½ minutes. Carefully stir in the blueberry spread, vinegar, blueberries, and tarragon. Once hot, add the cooked chicken paillards and any chicken juices. Cover and cook for 1 minute. Turn off the heat. Let "lid cook" (cook covered while the burner is off) until the blueberries are soft and chicken has been slightly infused with the essence of blueberry, about 5 minutes.

3. Remove the chicken. Spoon the sauce over the paillards. (If you don't want all the sauce with your poultry, it's delicious over whole grains, too!) If desired, garnish with additional tarragon leaves and serve.

PER SERVING: 290 calories, 13g total fat, 2g saturated fat, 0g trans fat, 45mg cholesterol, 630mg sodium, 27g total carbohydrate, 1g dietary fiber, 18g protein

No kitchen mallet? No problem. Check the toolbox for a rubber mallet or a big hammer! Wash it well. Then use it to flatten boneless, skinless organic chicken, duck, or meat of choice between sheets of unbleached parchment or waxed paper. Whack it good! The flatter the meat, the faster it'll cook.

a planet-friendly bite

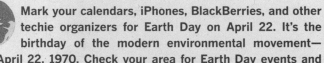

Mark your calendars, iPhones, BlackBerries, and other techie organizers for Earth Day on April 22. It's the birthday of the modern environmental movement—born April 22, 1970. Check your area for Earth Day events and participate in the celebration. Visit www.earthday.net for more.

SIPS & SWEETS

real lemonade

NATURAL LEMONADE WITH FRESH LEMON SLICES

Makes 4 servings: 1½ cups each

Some of my favorite childhood memories revolve around food. And there was one beverage that still warms (or cools) the cockles of my heart and soul: fresh-squeezed lemonade. I'm not referring to that peculiar, packaged, instant-mix concoction. I'm referring to the refreshing type that looks real, tastes real, and *is* real. Once you take a sip, those lemonade-stand moments will seem like yesterday. And the only thing instant will be your grin! If you like pink lemonade, add a splash of tart cherry juice.

4 lemons
½ cup turbinado or Demerara sugar
4 fresh mint sprigs, for garnish (optional)

1. Juice 3 of the lemons to yield about ½ cup juice. Slice the remaining lemon.

2. Stir the lemon juice with the sugar in a 2-quart pitcher until the sugar dissolves, about 1 minute. Stir in 5½ cups cold fresh water until well mixed. Add the lemon slices, reserving 4 of the slices for garnish.

little **green** cooking tip

Though there are always exceptions, I suggest garnishing foods with edible ingredients that are already a part of the dish. But mint sprigs in drinks are one of my exceptions. They add color, fragrance, and fresh flavor. Plus they're edible. So eat the mint; it's an eco-friendly breath freshener.

3. Pour the lemonade over ice in tall glasses. Garnish each glass rim with a lemon slice. Top with mint (if using).

PER SERVING: 100 calories, 0g total fat, 0g saturated fat, 0g trans fat, 0mg cholesterol, 20mg sodium, 27g total carbohydrate, 27g dietary fiber, 0g protein

use it, don't lose it

 Zest the peels before juicing and add extra zing to other parts of a meal in which you serve lemonade. A zestier idea . . . do mini vodka-lemonade shots from the lemon "peel-ups" (halved lemon peels to be used as cups)! First, scoop out any remaining membranes in each lemon "peel-up." Pour about 1 tablespoon each vodka (try Square One or Tru Organic Vodka) and lemonade into each and drink up!

fuzzy mojito

TROPICAL PUREE OF PEACH RUM PUNCH

Makes 2 servings: ¾ cup each

Peaches are at the top of my favorite fruit list. And when they become seasonal, I jump at the chance to use them wherever I can. One of those places is in this cocktail. This tropical-tasting drink is filled with ingredients that luckily don't need to be transported from the tropics, though it may be a transporting experience if you drink too much of this potent punch!

2 medium fully ripe peaches, pitted
⅓ cup light rum
3 tablespoons turbinado or Demerara sugar
Juice of ½ lime (about 1 tablespoon)
4 fresh mint leaves

1. Add 6 ice cubes to a blender container, then add all the ingredients. Cover and puree, about 45 seconds.

2. Pour in fun beverage glasses. Garnish with additional mint sprigs, if desired, and serve.

PER SERVING: 210 calories, 0.5g total fat, 0g saturated fat, 0g trans fat, 0mg cholesterol, 0mg sodium, 34g total carbohydrate, 2g dietary fiber, 1g protein

little *green* cooking tip

Give your blender some green lovin'. If you generally leave your electric blender on your kitchen countertop, unplug it when you're not using it. Even when not in use, having an appliance (even a little one) plugged in can still drain electricity.

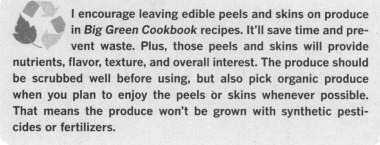

use it, don't lose it

I encourage leaving edible peels and skins on produce in *Big Green Cookbook* recipes. It'll save time and prevent waste. Plus, those peels and skins will provide nutrients, flavor, texture, and overall interest. The produce should be scrubbed well before using, but also pick organic produce when you plan to enjoy the peels or skins whenever possible. That means the produce won't be grown with synthetic pesticides or fertilizers.

cheesecake smoothie

STRAWBERRY CHEESECAKE–INSPIRED SMOOTHIE

Makes 3 servings: 1 cup each

Cheesecake is a comforting crowd pleaser. But it typically takes so much baking time that the carbon footprint it leaves will cause Mother Earth to be none too pleased. So skip the baking and bring out the blender. In seconds you can whirl up a creamy, fruity delight that tastes just like cheesecake in a glass. Cheers, Mother Earth.

Strawberries are yummy any time, but especially in late spring and early summer when they're at their sweetest, juiciest best. Choose locally grown berries when you can. And if they start to get mushy on you, a smoothie is an ideal use for them.

2 cups hulled fresh strawberries, sliced, or small wild strawberries
4 ounces organic cream cheese or cream cheese–style soy spread
1 cup fat-free organic milk or plain unsweetened soymilk
Juice of ½ lemon (about 1½ tablespoons)
3 tablespoons turbinado or Demerara sugar
½ teaspoon pure vanilla extract
2 tablespoons graham cracker crumbs

1. Freeze the sliced strawberries in a single layer on a plate for at least 1 hour (or overnight).

2. Add the frozen strawberry slices to a blender container along with the cream cheese, milk, lemon juice, sugar, and vanilla. Cover and puree, about 30 seconds.

3. Pour into 3 chilled glasses. Sprinkle with graham cracker crumbs and serve.

PER SERVING: 250 calories, 14g total fat, 8g saturated fat, 0g trans fat, 45mg cholesterol, 180mg sodium, 27g total carbohydrate, 2g dietary fiber, 7g protein

use it, don't lose it

Have extra cream cheese but no plans to smear it on a bagel? Check the All-Year-Round Recipes of *Big Green Cookbook*. You'll find you can savor the spare portion in an hors d'oeuvre, Nutty Blue Napoleons (page 296), or in a "real" cheesecake, Made-in-NY Cheesecake (page 356).

drunken berries

SEMISWEET CHOCOLATE-DIPPED COCKTAIL STRAWBERRIES

Makes 6 servings: 3 strawberries each

Chocolate and strawberries is a classic combination. And the liqueur in this recipe takes that combination to another class. So when strawberries are plentiful (or fresh-plucked from the fields), keep this recipe handy. But don't just let berries have all of the fun soaking up the liqueur, try this with any other locally available seasonal produce.

¼ cup chocolate liqueur
18 extra-large strawberries with stems or other
   extra-large fruit pieces
1 pound high-quality semisweet chocolate,
   coarsely chopped

1. Drizzle the liqueur over the strawberries in a small bowl. Set aside.

2. Place the chocolate in a medium-size microwave-safe bowl and cook in the microwave oven* on medium power until the chocolate turns shiny, about 2½ minutes, stirring once after 2 minutes. Remove the bowl from the microwave and stir the chocolate until melted. (Alternatively, place the chocolate in a double boiler over barely simmering water and melt while stirring on occasion. Once the chocolate is melted, remove from the heat.)

3. Meanwhile, line a sheet pan with unbleached parchment paper.

4. Gently pat excess liquid from the strawberries with an unbleached paper towel. Hold the stem of the strawberry and dip into the melted chocolate, twisting while lifting out. Let the excess chocolate drip off. Then place onto the parchment paper. Repeat with the rest of the strawberries. Set them aside to allow the chocolate to harden, about 30 minutes, and serve.

PER SERVING: 330 calories, 16g total fat, 10g saturated fat, 0g trans fat, 25mg cholesterol, 0mg sodium, 42g total carbohydrate, 22g dietary fiber, 5g protein

*Microwave oven cooking times will vary. See page 39.

use it, don't lose it

kissed nects

SLICED NECTARINES WITH WHITE CHOCOLATE–MARSCAPONE DIP

Makes 12 servings: 3 tablespoons dip with slices from 1 nectarine each

Every once in a while it's okay to indulge in something super-rich. I choose to whip up decadent treats for parties—so I don't overindulge all by myself. This dessert dip is designed for a soiree. It's ideal for an elegant dinner gathering or a casual picnic. And it's likely the most luscious way ever to enjoy fresh fruit of the season. Dip into it with slices of just-ripe nectarines. As Robert Palmer might say (or sing), "Simply irresistible!"

6 ounces high-quality white chocolate, coarsely chopped,
   or white chocolate chips
1 cup organic heavy cream
1 (8-ounce) container organic marscapone cheese
1 teaspoon pure vanilla extract
¼ teaspoon pure almond extract
12 large nectarines, pitted and sliced
Fresh mint sprigs, for garnish (optional)

(continued)

little *green* cooking tip

Found a springtime fruit recipe you love but want to keep it interesting? Give other local, springtime fruits their day in the spotlight. Try a nectarine recipe with other fresh seasonal fruit, like white peach or apricot. If it's June, and you don't mind dealing with pits, choose Bing cherries. A cherry pitter comes in handy.

1. Place the white chocolate and ½ cup of the cream in a microwave-safe bowl and cook in the microwave oven* on medium until the chocolate turns shiny, about 1½ minutes. Remove the bowl from the microwave and stir the chocolate until melted. (Alternatively, place the chocolate and cream in a double boiler over barely simmering water and melt while stirring on occasion. Once the chocolate is melted, remove from the heat.)

2. Let the chocolate mixture cool to room temperature.

3. In a medium bowl, whisk the remaining cream, mascarpone cheese, and extracts until smooth. Whisk the melted chocolate mixture into the mascarpone until smooth.

4. Serve the dip in a bowl and place on a platter. Arrange the nectarines slices (try it with other fruit, too) on the platter. Garnish with fresh mint sprigs (if using) and serve.

PER SERVING: 250 calories, 16g total fat, 10g saturated fat, 0g trans fat, 45mg cholesterol, 30mg sodium, 26g total carbohydrate, 3g dietary fiber, 4g protein

*Microwave oven cooking times will vary. See page 39.

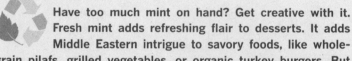

use it, don't lose it

Have too much mint on hand? Get creative with it. Fresh mint adds refreshing flair to desserts. It adds Middle Eastern intrigue to savory foods, like whole-grain pilafs, grilled vegetables, or organic turkey burgers. But even if it's just a garnish, mint can (and should) be eaten along with what it's meant to accent.

pineapple boat

PINEAPPLE HALVES FILLED WITH TROPICAL DESSERT FRUIT SALAD

Makes 6 servings: 1 rounded cup fruit each

Whatever the season, fruit salad can be served. Here you'll enjoy fruits that can all be found in the spring. When ripe and juicy you don't need to dress the salad in any way. Just enjoy the pure goodness of the fruits. And for that special earth-friendly touch, serve it in boats made from the pineapple. For green bonus points, use small papaya "peel-ups" (peels used as serving cups or bowls) for individual servings.

1 pineapple
1 cup cubed papaya
1 large white nectarine, pitted and cubed
2 kiwis, unpeeled, halved lengthwise, then sliced into half-moons
1 cup red or green seedless grapes

1. Cut a fresh pineapple lengthwise. Do not remove the leaves. Remove the inner portion of each pineapple half in sections, creating hollow boatlike shells. Trim the sections and cut into chunks.

2. In a large bowl, gently stir the pineapple chunks with the papaya, nectarine, kiwis, and grapes.

3. Mound the fruit mixture into the pineapple boats and serve.

PER SERVING: 90 calories, 0g total fat, 0g saturated fat, 0g trans fat, 0mg cholesterol, 0mg sodium, 22g total carbohydrate, 3g dietary fiber, 1g protein

use it, don't lose it

Have papaya seeds a-plenty? For added intrigue, sprinkle this fruit salad with some of the peppery (and edible) papaya seeds.

little *green* cooking tip

Kiwi skin is edible, so eat it! Think of it like fuzzy peach skin, only extra-fuzzy. Just be sure to scrub it first. And go organic when possible, especially when eating the skin. You'll find that it holds up better in a fruit salad when the skin is kept on, too.

summer

bites & snacks

chopstick veggie bowls . . . 106
very veggie bowls with Asian peanut vinaigrette

cup of caprese . . . 108
vine-ripened Caprese tomato cups

crispy okra coins . . . 109
whole-wheat panko-crusted fried okra rounds

cool plum turkey . . . 110
tarragon turkey salad in plum "peel-ups"

retro-metro double plum meatballs . . . 112
organic meatballs in plum tomato–purple plum sauce

dips, salsas, & sauces

cherry chutney . . . 114
fresh bing cherry chutney

tropical topper . . . 116
papaya–red onion salsa

just peachy salsa . . . 117
summer fresh peach salsa

bits-o-berry guacamole . . . 118
guacamole studded with fresh strawberries

soups & salads

cool cantaloupe soup . . . 119
fresh cantaloupe soup in cantaloupe bowl

grapacho . . . 120
green grape gazpacho

cress green sips . . . 121
chilled watercress soup

chinese "chicken" salad . . . 122
garlic-ginger tofu salad with veggie confetti

apricot "cheesecake" salad . . . 124
nut-crusted goat cheese salad with apricots and apricot vinaigrette

avant-garde arugula salad . . . 125
watermelon-arugula salad with feta cheese and pine nuts

bibb-n-beets . . . 127
bibb salad with beets, goat cheese, and sunflower seeds

fava of the sea . . . 128
lemon-zested tuna salad with fava beans

figgy salad . . . 130
fig, country ham, and arugula salad with fig-balsamic vinaigrette

vegetarian dishes

panini ab&p . . . 132
almond butter and peach toastie

black beans-n-"rice" . . . 133
spicy black beans and quinoa

eggplant topper on toast . . . 135
Mediterranean skillet-roasted eggplant bruschetta entrée

salad pizza . . . 136
mesclun salad pizzette with peaches and pecans

BITES & SNACKS

chopstick veggie bowls

VERY VEGGIE BOWLS WITH ASIAN PEANUT VINAIGRETTE

Makes 8 servings: 1 lettuce bowl with ¾ cup filling each

Raw veggies never tasted so good! The fresh herbs add delight and the perky peanut sauce adds pizzazz. Though the part I like best about this bite is that you get to eat it with chopsticks from its edible "bowl" of lettuce leaves. Then after you've eaten most of it, you can roll it up like a spring roll and eat the bowl. Guess that's one way to clean your plate!

2 cups mung bean sprouts

1 medium hothouse cucumber, unpeeled, halved lengthwise
   and thinly sliced

2 scallions, green and white parts, thinly sliced

1 large carrot, scrubbed unpeeled, and coarsely grated

2 ounces snow peas, ends snipped, very thinly sliced

¼ cup chopped fresh mint

¼ cup chopped fresh cilantro

8 leaves Boston or iceberg lettuce

1 recipe Chow Peanut Sauce (page 107)

½ cup coarsely chopped raw peanuts (optional)

1. Gently toss together the bean sprouts, cucumber, scallions, carrot, snow peas, mint, and cilantro in a small bowl.

2. Spoon about ¾ cup of the vegetable mixture into each lettuce leaf. Drizzle with the Chow Peanut Sauce or serve sauce on the side. Sprinkle with the peanuts (if using) and serve.

PER SERVING: 70 calories, 3g total fat, 0g saturated fat, 0g trans fat, 0mg cholesterol, 140mg sodium, 9g total carbohydrate, 2g dietary fiber, 3g protein

chow peanut sauce

ASIAN PEANUT VINAIGRETTE

Makes ⅔ cup

⅓ cup rice vinegar (preferably brown rice)
3 tablespoons unsalted natural peanut butter
2 tablespoons turbinado or Demerara sugar
1 tablespoon naturally brewed soy sauce
½ teaspoon chili-garlic paste, or to taste

Place all ingredients in a small lidded bowl; cover and shake vigorously to combine. Alternatively, place all ingredients in a blender container; cover and puree until just blended, about 10 seconds.

little
green
cooking
tip

Go ahead! Use produce varieties that make it easy on you. I'm referring to anything considered seedless. By picking up seedless produce, such as hothouse cucumbers or seedless watermelon, you'll enjoy preparing your low-carbon cuisine more.

a planet-friendly bite

Eating Asian-style food with chopsticks adds that special ethnic flair. Instead of disposable chopsticks, go for reusable ones—and be friendlier to the environment. One planet-pleasing option is reusable, high-tech, portable chopsticks made with a combination of recycled wood from old baseball bats and stainless steel. Very cool! Of course, if you do eat with the disposable ones, consider at least one other use for them before tossing 'em. They make intriguing hair accessories or functional plant stakes. Just rinse them before using them in your hair, please!

cup of caprese

VINE-RIPENED CAPRESE TOMATO CUPS

Makes 4 servings: 1 tomato cup each

I adore Italy. I adore Italian food. Luckily, many of the tastes of Italy can be found nearby. A key to simply prepared, superb Italian cuisine is to make sure all of the ingredients you use are at their freshest, especially the vine-ripened tomatoes.

4 medium vine-ripened tomatoes
8 ounces fresh organic or locally produced buffalo mozzarella, cubed (or plain boccocini)
2 tablespoons extra-virgin olive oil
1 tablespoon aged balsamic vinegar
¼ teaspoon sea salt, or to taste
¼ teaspoon crushed red pepper flakes
2 tablespoons thinly sliced fresh basil leaves

1. Slice ½ inch of the tops off the tomatoes. Dice the tomato tops and set aside.

2. Cut around the inside perimeter and scoop out the inside of each tomato to create cups. (Reserve scooped tomato portion for another purpose.) Pat dry the inside of the cups with a clean kitchen towel or an unbleached paper towel.

3. In a bowl, stir the mozzarella, diced tomato tops, oil, vinegar, salt, and crushed red pepper. Set aside to marinate for 20 minutes.

4. Mound the mozzarella-tomato mixture into each tomato cup. Top with basil and serve.

PER SERVING: 210 calories, 15g total fat, 8g saturated fat, 0g trans fat, 40mg cholesterol, 310mg sodium, 5g total carbohydrate, 2g dietary fiber, 11g protein

---

little **green** cooking tip

Don't refrigerate the tomatoes! Refrigerating them won't allow them to fully ripen and be at their juiciest, nutritional best. Also, make sure they're locally grown, such as fresh from your garden or a farmers' market so you can be assured that the tomatoes haven't been refrigerated by others.

crispy okra coins

WHOLE-WHEAT PANKO-CRUSTED FRIED OKRA ROUNDS

Makes 4 servings: ½ cup each

Though it doesn't sound very green, deep-frying can be surprisingly kind to the environment. When you deep-fry, you cook all sides of a food at once since it is completely immersed in oil. This helps speed up frying time. You also need to wisely choose the food to be fried. Go for baby bites, like these coin-sized pieces of okra. They'll be ready in 90 seconds! Served as a snack or hors d'oeuvre, they might be devoured as quickly, too. Try serving them with organic arrabiatta or marinara sauce.

4 cups canola oil

⅔ cup whole-wheat panko breadcrumbs

⅓ cup stone-ground whole-wheat flour

1 teaspoon sea salt, or to taste

½ teaspoon freshly ground black pepper, or to taste

½ teaspoon garlic powder, or to taste

¼ teaspoon cayenne pepper, or to taste

6 ounces okra, stem removed, sliced into ½-inch-thick coins

½ cup plain unsweetened soymilk or whole organic milk

2 teaspoons white wine vinegar

1. Heat the oil in a large skillet or a mini deep fryer to 350°F. (If using a deep fryer, follow fryer instructions.)

(continued)

little **green** cooking tip

When you need to drain excess grease from foods, use natural unbleached 100 percent recycled paper towels. It won't impart chemicals onto your foods. Plus it keeps chlorine and its associated toxins out of the environment—and your home.

2. Combine the panko, flour, salt, black pepper, garlic powder, and cayenne in a medium bowl. Set aside.

3. Whisk together the soymilk and vinegar in another medium bowl. Dip the pieces of okra in the soymilk-vinegar mixture. Let excess liquid drip off. Then dredge the okra in the panko mixture, coating well.

4. Carefully add okra to the hot oil and cook until golden brown, about 1½ minutes. (Fry the okra in batches, if necessary.) Remove from the oil and drain on unbleached paper towels. Sprinkle with additional salt and serve immediately. If desired, serve with a dipping sauce made by mixing mayonnaise with a pinch each of cayenne pepper and garlic powder.

PER SERVING: 230 calories, 15g total fat, 1g saturated fat, 0g trans fat, 0mg cholesterol, 620mg sodium, 21g total carbohydrate, 4g dietary fiber, 5g protein

go local

 If you're a Northerner like me, then you can enjoy fresh okra mainly in the summer. But if you live in the South, lucky you; fresh okra is available locally all year round.

cool plum turkey

TARRAGON TURKEY SALAD IN PLUM "PEEL-UPS"

Makes 8 servings: 1 stuffed plum "peel-up" each

When roasted for Thanksgiving dinner, turkey can be so comforting. So if you enjoy turkey, it's okay to be comforted by it more than once a year. Try it in this cool, flavor-bursting summertime appetizer salad. The thin turkey cutlets will take just minutes to cook. Paired with plums, it's delightfully refreshing. Served in the plums, it's dazzling.

1 pound boneless, skinless organic turkey breast cutlets
½ cup thinly sliced celery
¼ cup minced Walla Walla or other sweet onion
3 tablespoons organic sour cream
3 tablespoons mayonnaise
1 tablespoon white wine vinegar
1 tablespoon chopped fresh tarragon
½ teaspoon sea salt, or to taste
4 large black or purple plums
¼ cup raw (natural) sliced almonds

little
green
cooking
tip

A panini grill is a green cooking appliance. It allows both sides of a food, like organic turkey or chicken cutlets, to be cooked at the same time.

1. Choose thin-sliced turkey cutlets or pound the cutlets thin with a kitchen mallet (½ inch or thinner). Grill turkey cutlets in a panini grill on medium-high heat until well done, about 4 minutes. (Do this in two batches, if necessary.) Alternatively, place turkey breast cutlets in a large stick-resistant skillet or grill pan over medium-high heat. Cover and cook for 5 minutes. Flip cutlets and cook covered for 2 more minutes, or until cooked through. Cool and cut into cubes.

2. Gently combine the turkey, celery, onion, sour cream, mayonnaise, vinegar, tarragon, and salt in a large bowl. Refrigerate until ready to serve.

3. Cut the plums in half lengthwise and remove the pits. Carefully carve out the inside of the fruit, leaving about ⅛ inch of fruit, to create serving cups—plum "peel-ups." Set the 8 plum "peel-ups" aside. Finely dice the scooped out fruit. Stir the diced plum into the turkey salad.

4. When ready to serve, stir in the almonds. Stuff ⅓ rounded cup turkey salad into each plum "peel-up." Sprinkle with additional almonds, if desired. Serve.

PER SERVING: 150 calories, 7g total fat, 1.5g saturated fat, 0g trans fat, 40mg cholesterol, 200mg sodium, 9g total carbohydrate, 1g dietary fiber, 15g protein

use it, don't lose it

Extra onion can be peeled and chopped, or just peeled, then frozen for later use. It'll lose some of its texture during freezing, but will work well in cooked dishes.

Summer

retro-metro double plum meatballs

ORGANIC MEATBALLS IN PLUM TOMATO–PURPLE PLUM SAUCE

Makes 8 servings: 2 meatballs each

Eating a plant-based diet is the eco-friendliest eating approach there is. However, completely giving up red meat isn't essential, especially if you've loved being a meat eater your entire life. So choose organic meat . . . it's a start. Then, simply enjoy in moderation.

5 plum tomatoes or 3 medium vine-ripened tomatoes, quartered
2 medium purple or black plums, pitted and quartered
⅓ cup brown sugar
¼ cup aged red wine vinegar
1¼ teaspoons sea salt
12 ounces lean grass-fed organic ground beef
3 tablespoons grated white onion
1 large organic egg
¼ cup plain whole-grain breadcrumbs
⅛ teaspoon freshly ground black pepper

1. Add the tomatoes to a blender container. Cover and blend on low until just pureed, about 15 seconds. Add the plums, brown sugar, vinegar, and ½ teaspoon of the salt. Cover and blend on low until just combined, about 15 seconds. Set aside.

2. Combine the ground beef, onion, egg, breadcrumbs, remaining ¾ teaspoon salt, and pepper in a medium bowl. Form the mixture into 16 meatballs, about 2 tablespoons each.

little **green** cooking tip

Green-size your beef! If you choose to eat beef, savor small bites of it, like these meatballs, rather than filling your plate with a steak. Since it's widely believed that beef farming is inefficient, you'll reduce your ecological footprint by choosing less beef.

3. Pour the tomato-plum mixture into a large saucepan. (The saucepan needs to be big enough so that the meatballs fit in a single layer and are covered by the sauce.) Add the meatballs and cover with a lid. Place over high heat and bring to boil. Stir, then reduce heat to medium and cook, covered, until the meatballs are nearly cooked through, about 6 minutes. Turn off heat. Let "lid cook" (cook covered while the burner is off) until the meatballs are well done and have absorbed some of the sauce, about 10 more minutes. Insert bamboo or reusable picks into each and serve warm with the sauce.

PER SERVING: 110 calories, 3g total fat, 1g saturated fat, 0g trans fat, 50mg cholesterol, 400mg sodium, 12g total carbohydrate, 1g dietary fiber, 10g protein

go local

Many people shop at their local farmers' market to purchase local seasonal fruits and veggies. But there is often so much more. Grass-fed organic beef may be available at your farmers' market. So not only will you enjoy one-on-one interaction with the ranchers, you can get beef that's less traveled—which can mean a reduction of fuel emissions.

DIPS, SALSAS, & SAUCES

cherry chutney

FRESH BING CHERRY CHUTNEY

If you enjoy cherries but their pits have always been the pits to deal with, you no longer need to bother. Invest in a cherry pitter—they cost about 12 bucks. (I love mine!) You can then truly love this cheery fruit—just the fruit.

Makes 8 servings: 2 tablespoons each

Fresh cherries are in season for such a short time that I love looking for a variety of ways to enjoy them while I can. So other than just popping them into your mouth and spitting out the pits (though, I admit, that's still my favorite way to eat them), this chutney is a classier way to enjoy sweet cherries. Traditional chutney is a sweet-spicy Indian condiment that is usually cooked, but this version is raw, almost like a salsa. Try it as a tasty topping for roasted or grilled organic pork tenderloin or turkey, a zesty sandwich condiment, or a unique ingredient to add pizzazz to plain cooked quinoa or other whole grain.

2 cups fresh Bing cherries, pitted
1 tablespoon apple cider vinegar
½ teaspoon minced fresh rosemary
¼ teaspoon freshly ground allspice (optional)
⅛ teaspoon cayenne pepper
⅛ teaspoon sea salt, or to taste
1 small shallot, minced

1. Place ½ cup of the cherries, the vinegar, rosemary, allspice (if using), cayenne, and salt into a blender container. Cover and puree until blended, about 30 seconds. Transfer cherry puree to a small serving bowl.

2. Mince the remaining cherries and stir them along with the shallot into the cherry mixture. Taste and adjust seasoning, if necessary, and serve.

PER SERVING: 25 calories, 0g total fat, 0g saturated fat, 0g trans fat, 0mg cholesterol, 35mg sodium, 7g total carbohydrate, 1g dietary fiber, 0g protein

a planet-friendly bite

Every year, hundreds of thousands of tourists head to Washington, D.C., to see the cherry blossoms. Many of the trees were originally a gift to our nation's capital from Tokyo in 1912, given as a symbol of friendship and goodwill. And, not that it was the intent, but planting trees is considered a long-range investment for the environment—and the climate. Want to plant your own trees? Go to www.arborday.org/trees/index.cfm to find out how.

tropical topper

PAPAYA-RED ONION SALSA

Makes 6 servings: ½ cup each

Salsa doesn't need to come from a jar. It doesn't need to have to-matoes in it, either. This fresh papaya version is so zippy that after a few bites you may end up doing a little salsa (or tango or meren-gue)! Then, after you've burned off a few calories, enjoy your salsa recipe with a goat cheese quesadilla or grilled fish. Better yet, mix it into black beans, quinoa, or couscous.

1 large papaya, peeled, seeded, and diced (about 3 cups)
¼ cup finely diced red onion
1 small jalapeño with some seeds, minced
2 tablespoons finely chopped fresh cilantro
Juice of ½ lime or ½ small lemon (about 1 tablespoon)
½ teaspoon sea salt, or to taste
⅛ teaspoon ground cumin, or to taste

Mix together the papaya, onion, jalapeño, cilantro, and lime in a small bowl. Add salt and cumin. Serve in a papaya "peel-up," if desired.

PER SERVING: 30 calories, 0g total fat, 0g saturated fat, 0g trans fat, 0mg cholesterol, 200mg sodium, 8g total carbohydrate, 1g dietary fiber, 1g protein

little *green* cooking tip

Get a little crazy. Sprinkle a few of the papaya seeds (yes, they're edible) into the salsa for extra pep. Go peppier and add all of the jalapeño seeds. Or freeze extra jalapeño seeds to add heat to any dish at a later date.

use it, don't lose it

To make a papaya "peel-up," cut the papaya in half lengthwise. Scoop out the seeds, Carefully carve out the inside of the fruit, leaving about ⅛ inch of fruit on the skin. Dice the fruit. Use the carved out papaya peel—"peel-up"—as a serving bowl for this salsa or other recipe.

Big Green Cookbook

116

just peachy salsa

SUMMER FRESH PEACH SALSA

Makes 4 servings: ½ cup each

The velvety skin of the peach is one of its loveliest attributes and it adds character to this fresh salsa. The rest of the peach adds scrumptiousness. The best time to make this salsa is in summer when peaches are at their juiciest best. And the best time to eat it is . . . well, any time you make it.

2 large or 3 medium peaches, pitted and diced
1 large vine-ripened tomato, diced
¼ cup finely diced red onion
2 tablespoons finely chopped fresh cilantro
Juice and zest of 1 lime, or to taste (about 2 tablespoons juice)
¼ teaspoon sea salt, or to taste

Gently stir together the peaches, tomato, onion, cilantro, and lime juice in a medium serving bowl. Add salt. Sprinkle with some of the zest. Serve with tortilla chips or grilled fish or organic chicken.

PER SERVING: 60 calories, 0g total fat, 0g saturated fat, 0g trans fat, 0mg cholesterol, 150mg sodium, 15g total carbohydrate, 2g dietary fiber, 1g protein

It's summer! It's time for peach picking—even if from a local market, not a tree. Pick organic ones when you can—even though they're not always as pretty as conventionally grown peaches. Then there's virtually no need to peel off the fuzzy skins. Use them whenever you can in recipes. And even if organic, do scrub well first.

a planet-friendly bite

About 60 million Americans will likely be lighting up barbecue grills for Independence Day (July Fourth). When they do so, on that one day they'll be burning the equivalent of 2,300 acres of forest and using enough energy to meet the yearly residential demand of a town about the size of Flagstaff, Arizona. But there's no need to cancel those barbecue plans. Just be eco-conscientious when cooking out. For instance, if charcoal grilling, choose natural lump charcoal from sustainably sourced hardwood; opt for a chimney starter instead of lighter fluid; and grill lots of veggies—even fruits, like the peaches for this salsa.

bits-o-berry guacamole

GUACAMOLE STUDDED WITH FRESH STRAWBERRRIES

Makes 10 servings: ⅓ cup each

It's that time of year to head to your farmers' market—or the farm—and pick up a juicy pint of strawberries. This succulent fruit of the season is paired here with buttery avocados for a refreshing taste twist on traditional guacamole. The avocado itself is refreshing for the environment, too. Now that's doubly refreshing.

2 Hass avocados, pitted, peeled, and cubed
Juice of 1 lime, or to taste (about 2 tablespoons)
⅓ cup finely diced hulled fresh strawberries
⅓ cup diced white onion
2 tablespoons chopped fresh cilantro
1 small jalapeño with seeds, minced
¾ teaspoon ground cumin
¼ teaspoon sea salt, or to taste

1. Gently stir together all ingredients in a medium serving bowl until just combined.

2. Serve as a dip with blue or yellow corn tortilla chips. Or enjoy it as a sandwich condiment, bean soup garnish, omelet filling, or toast spread.

PER SERVING: 50 calories, 4.5g total fat, 0.5g saturated fat, 0g trans fat, 0mg cholesterol, 60mg sodium, 4g total carbohydrate, 2g dietary fiber, 1g protein

little **green** cooking tip

Serve the guacamole in the avocado peels. Then call them guacamole "peel-ups." No extra bowl—or bowl washing—required.

a planet-friendly bite

Are you a tree hugger? Go ahead, hug those trees—we love what they do for the environment . . . clean the air—avocado trees included. According to the California Avocado Commission, one California avocado tree can absorb the same amount of carbon dioxide each year as what's produced by a car driven about 26,000 miles.

SOUPS & SALADS

cool cantaloupe soup

FRESH CANTALOUPE SOUP IN CANTALOUPE BOWL

Makes 8 servings: 1 cup each

A cool thing about cantaloupe is that the rind can be a serving bowl. It turns anything you serve in it into a fabulous fun food. You can make a cool (literally!) soup with the fruit, too. When its über-hot outside, a chilly bowl of soup is the ultimate antidote.

2 cantaloupes, halved, seeded
8 large fresh mint leaves
Juice and zest of 1 lime, or to taste (about 2 tablespoons juice)
1 tablespoon turbinado or Demerara sugar
⅛ teaspoon sea salt

1. Scoop the fruit out of the cantaloupe halves using a melon baller. Add the cantaloupe balls, mint, lime juice, sugar, and salt to a blender container or food processor. Cover and blend until smooth and frothy, about 30 seconds. Stir in a pinch of the zest.

2. Chill in a 2-quart pitcher in the refrigerator, if desired.

3. Pour 1 cup of the soup into each cantaloupe half. Pour the remaining soup into small bowls or chill in the refrigerator for later. Sprinkle with the remaining zest, and serve.

PER SERVING: 50 calories, 0g total fat, 0g saturated fat, 0g trans fat, 0mg cholesterol, 60mg sodium, 13g total carbohydrate, 1g dietary fiber, 1g protein

little
green
cooking
tip

Wash a cantaloupe—or any fruit—even when you're not eating its skin or peel. That's because if there is any dirt or bacteria on the outside, then it won't make its way to the fruit on the inside when cutting into it.

use it, don't lose it

The tough rinds of any melon or pineapple make sturdy earth-friendly bowls after being cut in half and the inside flesh (and seeds) are scooped out. They're great for chilled soups, fruit salads, or tuna or organic chicken salad—if they contain some of the fruit.

Summer

119

grapacho
GREEN GRAPE GAZPACHO

Makes 5 servings: ½ cup each

In need of a light first course on a steamy summer evening? Sip on this subtly sweet gazpacho. It's a sure winner during those times when you're hungry but it feels too hot to eat. It's like sipping on a summer breeze. What's more, it's a smart way to use leftover bread or bagels—adding a little body to this palate pleaser.

1½ cups green seedless grapes
1 cup chopped unpeeled hothouse cucumber
1 small or ½ large green bell pepper, chopped
1 slice day-old bread, any type, chopped (about ¼ cup)
1 small shallot, chopped
2 tablespoons extra-virgin olive oil
2 tablespoons white wine or apple cider vinegar
1 small clove garlic, chopped
¼ teaspoon sea salt, or to taste

1. Add the grapes to a blender container. Cover and puree until just blended, about 15 seconds. Add the remaining ingredients and puree, about 15 seconds. Taste and adjust seasoning, if necessary.

2. Chill at least 30 minutes. Ladle into bowls. If desired, sprinkle with edible flowers or with finely diced red or black grapes.

PER SERVING: 100 calories, 6g total fat, 1g saturated fat, 0g trans fat, 0mg cholesterol, 130mg sodium, 11g total carbohydrate, 1g dietary fiber, 1g protein

little **green** cooking tip

When pureeing ingredients, it's helpful to do some chopping in advance. It means less electricity is required since you're doing some of the work, instead of leaving it all up to a blender or food processor. Plus, it'll help assure everything gets fully pureed.

use it, don't lose it

Day-old bread? No problem. Bread that's not so fresh anymore can actually be preferable to fresh bread for making salad croutons, stuffing, or soup. So don't toss it out; chop it up and toss it into a hot or cold soup recipe, like Grapacho, to add body.

cress green sips

CHILLED WATERCRESS SOUP

Makes 4 servings: 1⅓ cups each

How do you get a creamy soup without cream? Potatoes are the greenest answer. By cooking the potatoes in broth until very tender, they turn into super-creamy mashed potatoes when the soup is pureed. This is the key to the soup's creaminess that's as appetizing hot as it is cool.

2 tablespoons unsalted organic butter or peanut oil

1 extra-large or 2 medium Yukon gold potatoes, scrubbed unpeeled, and finely diced

2 large leeks (white and pale green parts only), very thinly sliced

4 cups low-sodium vegetable broth

1 bunch watercress, thick stems trimmed, coarsely chopped

1¼ teaspoons sea salt, or to taste

¼ tsp freshly ground black pepper, or to taste

1. Melt the butter in a large saucepan over medium-high heat. Add the potatoes and leeks; sauté until the leeks are slightly softened, about 3 minutes. Add the broth and bring to a boil over high heat. Cover, reduce heat to medium, and simmer for 10 minutes.

2. Add the watercress, cover, and turn off the heat. Let "lid cook" (cook covered while the burner is off) until the potatoes are soft, about 20 minutes.

3. Use an immersion blender to puree the soup in the saucepan. Or puree the slightly cooled soup in batches in a blender and return soup to the saucepan. Add salt and pepper.

4. Chill at least 4 hours or overnight. Ladle into small bowls or cups and serve.

PER SERVING: 160 calories, 6g total fat, 3.5g saturated fat, 0g trans fat, 15mg cholesterol, 890mg sodium, 23g total carbohydrate, 3g dietary fiber, 3g protein

little
green
cooking
tip

When a soup recipe calls for pureeing, like a watercress or broccoli soup, it's actually nice to see little flecks of the veggies. So puree until just creamy enough, but not pristinely smooth. Then you won't be spending extra time or, more important, extra energy.

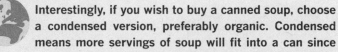
chinese "chicken" salad

GARLIC-GINGER TOFU SALAD WITH VEGGIE CONFETTI

Makes 4 servings: ¾ cup each

If you're a vegetarian, ecotarian, flexitarian, or just trying to eat less chicken, this "chicken" salad is a must-try. The chicken in it is actually tofu! It's a nice change of pace—and packed with flavor. Garlic lovers will find this right up their taste-bud alley, too.

3 tablespoons naturally brewed soy sauce

2 tablespoons rice vinegar (preferably brown rice)

2 large cloves garlic, minced

2 teaspoons grated scrubbed unpeeled gingerroot, or to taste

2 teaspoons mild floral honey or 1 tablespoon local fruit spread or homemade jam

1½ teaspoons sesame oil

½ teaspoon Asian garlic-chili sauce, or to taste

1 (14-ounce) package firm tofu, well-drained

16 snow peas, very thinly sliced crosswise

2 scallions, green and white parts, minced

½ small red bell pepper, finely diced

1 tablespoon chopped fresh cilantro

1 tablespoon chopped fresh flat-leaf parsley

1. Whisk together the soy sauce, vinegar, garlic, gingerroot, honey, oil, and garlic-chili sauce in a large bowl. Taste and adjust seasoning, if necessary.

2. Crumble the drained tofu and stir into the soy sauce mixture.

3. Stir in the snow peas, scallions, red pepper, cilantro, and parsley. Stir well to combine.

4. Serve chilled or at room temperature in a red bell pepper half or enjoy on wide slices of red bell peppers, like crackers. Alternatively, mound the mixture atop small round brown rice crackers, about 1 tablespoon per cracker. Garnish with additional cilantro or parsley, if desired.

PER SERVING: 370 calories, 8g total fat, 1g saturated fat, 0g trans fat, 0mg cholesterol, 740mg sodium, 65g total carbohydrate, 17g dietary fiber, 19g protein

use it, don't lose it

 Before tossing packages out, check to see if they can be recycled. If not, always think twice before tossing into the trash. That's worth repeating: always think twice before tossing into the trash. For instance, if you purchase tofu in a square tub-shaped container and determine that you're unable to recycle that container in your community, repurpose that tub! One idea: Wash, dry, and then use to hold crayons or other art supplies.

little **green** cooking tip

When chopping cilantro or parsley, don't worry about being so precise and picking off leaves and leaving all the stems. You can use both the leaves and the thin, tender stems.

apricot "cheesecake" salad

NUT-CRUSTED GOAT CHEESE SALAD WITH APRICOTS AND APRICOT VINAIGRETTE

little **green** cooking tip

A mortar and pestle is a handy tool in the low-carbon kitchen. It can do the work of a food processor the old-fashioned way—by hand— carbon emission–free! It's more fun, too—you get to pound away the stresses of the day.

Makes 4 servings: 1 cup with 1 cheese round each

Having special dinner guests? This salad will make a lasting impression. And the "cheesecake" topper will titillate. Instead of breading and frying the cheese as is often done in fine restaurants, no cooking is required for the goat cheese round on this salad. It's simply coated with nuts to add taste and texture. And, if all else fails, the name of the salad alone should dazzle your guests.

1 (3-ounce) log soft fresh organic or locally produced goat cheese, at room temperature, cut into 4 equal rounds
3 tablespoons coarsely chopped raw nuts of choice, such as pistachios, hazelnuts, walnuts, or almonds
3 fresh apricots, pitted
2 teaspoons apple cider vinegar or white wine vinegar
3 tablespoons extra-virgin olive oil
1 tablespoon minced shallot
¼ teaspoon sea salt, or to taste
½ teaspoon freshly ground black pepper, or to taste
1 bunch watercress, thick stems trimmed, coarsely chopped
1 large Belgian endive, cored, leaves thinly sliced lengthwise

1. Press both sides of each cheese round into the nuts to adhere. Set aside.

2. Finely dice 1 of the apricots. Then "cream" it using a chef's knife or mash it using a mortar and pestle. Stir together the creamed apricot and vinegar in a small bowl or in the mortar until blended. Whisk in the oil and shallot. Add salt and pepper. Set aside.

3. Thinly slice the remaining apricots. Toss the sliced apricots, watercress, endive, and apricot vinaigrette in a large serving bowl or arrange on a platter. Taste and adjust seasoning, if necessary. Top each serving with a nut-crusted cheese round.

PER SERVING: 210 calories, 19g total fat, 5g saturated fat, 0g trans fat, 10mg cholesterol, 240mg sodium, 5g total carbohydrate, 2g dietary fiber, 6g protein

avant-garde arugula salad

WATERMELON-ARUGULA SALAD WITH FETA CHEESE AND PINE NUTS

Makes 4 servings: 3 cups each

From the middle of June until the end of August watermelon is at its peak. This inventive, sweet-n-savory salad recipe highlights the pretty pink melon and should be enjoyed often. It's an entrée salad, so there's no need to worry about what meat to eat.

3 pounds seedless watermelon with rind
Juice and zest of 1 small or ½ large lemon (about 2 tablespoons juice)
½ teaspoon sea salt, or to taste
½ teaspoon freshly ground black pepper, or to taste
3 tablespoons extra-virgin olive oil
4 cups baby arugula leaves
2 cups mixed baby salad greens or watercress
3 tablespoons chopped fresh mint
⅓ cup crumbled organic or locally produced feta or fresh goat cheese
¼ cup raw pine nuts or chopped pistachios

1. Scoop the flesh of the watermelon from the rind. (Save the rind for another purpose.) Cut the flesh into ½-inch cubes. (You should have about 6 cups.)

2. Whisk together the lemon juice, salt, and pepper in a large serving bowl until combined. Whisk in the oil.

(continued)

little **green** cooking tip

Juice (by hand!) a lemon half or halves. Then, use the lemon "peel-up" (peel used as serving cup) to serve freshly cracked black pepper for each person to pinch and season their salad or other foods to taste. If any pepper is left over, store the lemon "peel-up" with pepper in the refrigerator for later use as a lemon-pepper seasoning.

Summer

3. Drain the watermelon and add to the dressing. Add the arugula, mixed greens, and mint; very gently toss to coat. Taste and adjust seasoning, if necessary.

4. Sprinkle with the cheese and nuts. Serve immediately.

PER SERVING: 260 calories, 19g total fat, 3.5g saturated fat, 0g trans fat, 10mg cholesterol, 440mg sodium, 21g total carbohydrate, 2g dietary fiber, 5g protein

---

use it, don't lose it

What's the easiest way to get 3 pounds of seedless watermelon with rind? It's about half of one whole round baby seedless watermelon. Save the watermelon rind to use as a very green serving bowl for the salad. And don't worry about the teeny white seeds you'll likely find in seedless watermelon; they're soft and edible. But whatever watermelon you use, add the excess liquid drained from the cubed watermelon to a beverage, like fresh watermelon-accented lemonade, or simply sip it straight from a shot glass.

bibb-n-beets

BIBB SALAD WITH BEETS, GOAT CHEESE, AND SUNFLOWER SEEDS

Makes 4 servings: ¼ of recipe each

For the undiscovered (or discovered) artist, this salad recipe is for you. It looks like edible pop art; the lettuce is the canvas for the rest of the ingredients. The vivid beet-red vinaigrette is like the paint. The savory herb-covered goat cheese balls look like candy truffles. When finished with your masterpiece, you then must decide if you want to just look at it or if you prefer to eat it.

2 medium red beets with greens

2 tablespoons white wine vinegar or tarragon vinegar

2 teaspoons local raspberry or other fruit spread or homemade jam or
   1 teaspoon mild floral honey

1 teaspoon stone-ground mustard

½ teaspoon sea salt, or to taste

¼ teaspoon freshly ground black pepper, or to taste

¼ cup sunflower or extra-virgin olive oil

2 tablespoons chopped fresh tarragon

2 tablespoons chopped fresh chervil or dill

6 ounces soft fresh organic or locally produced goat cheese, at room
   temperature

8 ounces Bibb or Boston lettuce, leaves separated

2 tablespoons raw hulled sunflower seeds

1. Trim off the beet greens about 1 inch above the root. Reserve the leaves for other use at the same meal—or use in place of part of the lettuce in this recipe. Place the scrubbed beets into a large microwave-safe dish. Cover well with unbleached parchment paper. "Micro-roast" (cook in the microwave oven*) on high until the beets are easily pierced with a knife, about 10 minutes. Keep covered and set aside until cool enough to handle. Peel the skins with a paring knife. Cut beets into ⅓-inch cubes. Set aside.

2. Whisk together the vinegar, fruit spread, mustard, salt, and pepper. Whisk in the oil. Stir in the diced beets.

little **green** cooking tip

The fewer cooking and eating utensils you use, the less there is to wash. Try forgoing eating utensils when possible. If using Bibb or Boston lettuce, serve all other salad ingredients in each leaf, pick up, fold over, and eat (very carefully!) like a spring roll. The vinaigrette can be served on the side as a dipping sauce.

(continued)

3. Combine the tarragon and chervil in a small bowl. Using a melon baller or measuring spoon, form cheese into 12 to 16 balls, about 2 teaspoons each. Then roll the balls into the herb mixture.

4. Arrange the lettuce on a serving patter. Spoon the beet mixture onto the leaves. Arrange the cheese balls on top of the salad. Sprinkle with the sunflower seeds and serve.

PER SERVING: 290 calories, 25g total fat, 8g saturated fat, 0g trans fat, 20mg cholesterol, 490mg sodium, 7g total carbohydrate, 1g dietary fiber, 10g protein

*Microwave oven cooking times will vary. See page 39.

use it, don't lose it

Tops are tasty, too! Thinly slice raw beet greens and toss them into any salad, especially one that includes beets. Or use them in place of the salad greens already suggested in a recipe. Turn *Bibb-n-Beets* into *Beet Green-n-Beets*, if you like.

fava of the sea

LEMON-ZESTED TUNA SALAD WITH FAVA BEANS

Makes 4 servings: ¾ cup each

The eco-key to this recipe is choosing an eco-friendly canned tuna, like those sourced from well-managed albacore fisheries in the U.S. where they use pole-and-line gear. Once you have that, the rest should go swimmingly.

1 pound fresh fava beans, shelled (1¼ cups shelled)*

1 (6-ounce) can minimal mercury albacore tuna, drained,
 separated into chunks

3 large celery stalks, thinly sliced

8 cherry tomatoes, thinly sliced, or 16 grape tomatoes,
 quartered lengthwise

¼ cup finely diced Vidalia or other sweet onion

¼ cup chopped fresh flat-leaf parsley

2 tablespoons chopped fresh cilantro

Juice and zest of 1 lemon, or to taste (about 3 tablespoons juice)

3 tablespoons mayonnaise

1 tablespoons spicy Dijon or stone-ground mustard

¼ teaspoon sea salt, or to taste

8 slices whole-grain or flaxseed bread (optional)

little
green
cooking
tip

If you sometimes put a
saucepan of water on the
stove to boil and then forget
about it, use a whistling tea
kettle to boil water. The pot
will whistle at you when it's
ready!

1. Fill a medium bowl with ice and water. Set aside.

2. Bring a small saucepan of salted water (1½ cups fresh water
 and ¾ teaspoon sea salt) to a boil. (Note: The water needs to
 just cover the beans.) Add the shelled fava beans. Cover with a
 lid and turn off the heat. Let "lid cook" (cook covered while the
 burner is off) until the beans are just tender, about 5 minutes.
 Drain, then shock in the bowl of ice water to stop cooking. Drain
 again and remove the skins (waxy outer coverings) of the beans
 by holding a bean with both thumbs and index fingers. Tear into
 the waxy covering of each bean with your left thumbnail, then
 pinch out the edible fava with your right thumb and index finger.
 (Makes about ⅔ cups.)

3. In a medium bowl, combine the fava beans, tuna, celery, tomatoes, onion, parsley, cilantro, lemon juice, mayonnaise, and
 mustard. Stir in about ½ teaspoon of the zest. Add salt.

4. Spread the mixture on 4 slices of bread (if using), then top with
 remaining bread slices and cut in half diagonally. Alternatively,
 serve the salad with vegetables cut into "chips." Use any remaining zest for your accompanying beverage.

PER SERVING: 160 calories, 9g total fat, 1.5g saturated fat, 0g trans fat, 15mg cholesterol,
430mg sodium, 8g total carbohydrate, 2g dietary fiber, 13g protein

*To shell (or shuck) the beans, snip off or pull on the stem of the pod and unzip them on
one or both sides. If need, use your clean fingernails to help fully open the "zipper." Push
beans loose from the pods into a bowl using your thumbs.

Summer

figgy salad

FIG, COUNTRY HAM, AND ARUGULA SALAD WITH FIG-BALSAMIC VINAIGRETTE

Makes 4 servings: 1¼ cups salad and 2 slices ham each

When figs are fresh, enjoy them. They're unique fruits that are gorgeous to the eye and divine to the palate. Here you'll be whipping some of the fig into a dressing—with your body power, not electrical power. And you'll be pairing this Italian-inspired salad with ingredients close to home, like prosciutto-like American country ham.

5 fresh Calimyrna or Mission figs
2 tablespoons aged balsamic vinegar
½ teaspoons stone-ground mustard
⅓ cup extra-virgin olive oil
¼ teaspoon freshly ground black pepper, or to taste
5 cups baby arugula leaves
1 small or ½ medium red onion, very thinly sliced
8 thin slices organic American country ham or prosciutto
1½ ounces organic or locally produced Parmesan cheese shavings
(optional)

1. Finely dice 1 fig. Then "cream" it using a chef's knife or mash it using a mortar and pestle. Stir together the creamed fig, vinegar, and mustard in a small bowl or in the mortar until blended. Whisk in the oil. Add pepper. Set aside.

2. Toss the arugula and onion with about half of the vinaigrette and arrange on 4 plates.

3. In the center of each plate, arrange the ham in a circle, so it looks like a blooming flower.

little **green** cooking tip

With some solid knife skills, you can do the work of small kitchen appliances or other fancy gadgetry all with a single chef's knife, while emitting "oohs" and "ahhs" from onlookers.

4. Halve the remaining 4 figs and position in the center of the ham "flower."

5. Sprinkle with the cheese (if using). Drizzle with the remaining vinaigrette—or serve on the side.

PER SERVING: 310 calories, 23g total fat, 4g saturated fat, 0g trans fat, 25mg cholesterol, 930mg sodium, 18g total carbohydrate, 3g dietary fiber, 11g protein

go local

Prosciutto is the word for "ham" in Italy. Italian prosciutto is salt-cured and air-dried. You can find American-style prosciutto, too. It's often called American country ham and you can use it in any recipe that calls for prosciutto. The process of dry-curing with salt helps prevent the growth of bacteria—which helps make the hams safe to eat without cooking. They can generally be stored in a cool place for up to 2 months.

VEGETARIAN DISHES

panini ab&p

ALMOND BUTTER AND PEACH TOASTIE

Makes 4 servings: 1 toastie each

Peanut butter and jelly is something nearly every kid enjoys. (Little do they realize that it's a vegetarian sandwich!) But when you grow up, it's time to take it to the next level—at least some of the time. So make the culinary upgrade to almond butter instead of plain peanut, whole-grain or flaxseed bread instead of mushy white, and fresh seasonal peach instead of super-sweet jelly. It'll bring back school-day memories—and create new ones, too.

½ cup natural almond butter*
8 slices whole-grain or flaxseed bread
1 large peach, pitted and very thinly sliced

1. Spread 1 tablespoon of the almond butter on each bread slice. Top four of the slices with the peach. Top with the remaining bread slices, almond butter side down. Spray the sandwich with homemade cooking spray.**

2. Heat a panini grill to medium-high heat. Place each sandwich in the grill. (Cook in batches, if necessary.) Cook until lightly toasted, about 2½ minutes. (Alternatively, pan-toast each sandwich in a preheated skillet or grill pan over medium-high heat until lightly toasted on the bottom, about 1½ minutes; then flip, turn off the heat, and cook while the burner is off until lightly toasted, about 1½ minutes more.)

little **green** cooking tip

You can go greener with panini by passing on the "panini" part. Turn a panini into a no-cook sandwich and simply eat without grilling.

3. Slice toasties in half diagonally and serve immediately.

PER SERVING: 380 calories, 22g total fat, 2.5g saturated fat, 0g trans fat, 0mg cholesterol, 260mg sodium, 37g total carbohydrate, 6g dietary fiber, 13g protein

---

*Add a pinch of sea salt if using unsalted almond butter to brighten the peach flavor.
**Fill a Misto or similar spray bottle with oil of choice.

a planet-friendly bite

 California's Central Valley provides 100 percent of the U.S. commercial production of almonds and the majority of the world's supply, about 80 percent. Demand for almonds has increased. And that means so have almond tree plantings. That's real almond joy!

black beans-n-"rice"

SPICY BLACK BEANS AND QUINOA

Makes 4 servings: 1 cup beans with ¾ cup quinoa each

Beans and rice are a classic combination. Unfortunately, most whole grains, such as brown rice, take a lot of energy to cook. So taste this new classic with quinoa as a slightly greener alternative to rice. It's a whole grain and cooks super-fast. It's trendy, too.

1 tablespoon extra-virgin olive oil
1 small yellow onion, chopped
4 frozen soy "sausage" links, thawed, very thinly sliced into coins (optional)
3 large cloves garlic, chopped
1 large vine-ripened tomato, diced
1 (15-ounce) can organic black beans, drained (do not rinse)
½ cup low-sodium vegetable or organic chicken broth
¼ cup red or black seedless grapes, thinly sliced
¾ teaspoon cayenne pepper
¾ teaspoon sea salt, or to taste
2 teaspoons finely chopped fresh thyme or oregano
1 tablespoon chopped fresh flat-leaf parsley
3 cups cooked quinoa, warm*

(continued)

When a recipe typically calls for rice, quinoa usually works nicely in its place. It's a whole grain, but cooks in minutes because of its tiny size.

1. Heat the oil in a large saucepan or deep skillet over medium heat. Add the onion; sauté until soft, about 6 minutes. Add the "sausage" (if using) and garlic; sauté until the garlic is fragrant, about 1 minute.

2. Stir in the tomato, beans, broth, grapes, cayenne, and salt. Cover and cook for 5 minutes. Stir in the thyme, then cover again, and turn off the heat. Let "lid cook" (cook covered with burner off) until the flavors are fully blended and mixture is stewlike, about 10 minutes. Stir in the parsley. Taste and adjust seasoning, if necessary.

3. Serve the bean mixture over the quinoa or on the side. Garnish with additional parsley, if desired.

PER SERVING: 290 calories, 4g total fat, 0g saturated fat, 0g trans fat, 0mg cholesterol, 580mg sodium, 53g total carbohydrate, 9g dietary fiber, 12g protein

*To make low-carbon quinoa: In a small saucepan, combine 1 cup quinoa (rinsed and drained) and 2 cups water. Place over high heat. Bring to a boil. Cover and turn off the heat. Let "lid cook" (cook covered while the burner is off) until the quinoa is tender, fully cooked, and liquid is absorbed, about 20 minutes.

use it, don't lose it

After you've poured out the beans, recycle the can as well as the label. Better yet, recycle the label but re-purpose the can. Use it as a "thing" holder. Or think outside the can and find your own clever use.

eggplant topper on toast

MEDITERRANEAN SKILLET-ROASTED EGGPLANT BRUSCHETTA ENTRÉE

Makes 6 servings: 6 bruschetta each

I love to mix things up—especially when someone tells me I'm not supposed to. This eggplant dish is supposed to be an appetizer but I love it as a vegetarian entrée. Think of it like an open-faced sandwich—replaced by many mini ones. It's more fun to eat that way.

1 (12-ounce) whole-grain baguette, cut diagonally into 36 slices
½ cup plus 1 tablespoon extra-virgin olive oil
1 medium eggplant, unpeeled, cut into ⅓-inch cubes
1 large Walla Walla or other sweet onion, diced
2 large cloves garlic, minced
¾ teaspoon sea salt, or to taste
2 medium vine-ripened tomatoes, cut into ⅓-inch cubes
⅓ cup chopped fresh basil
Juice of 1 lemon, or to taste (about 3 tablespoons)
¼ cup raw pine nuts

1. Lightly rub both sides of the bread slices with ¼ cup of the oil. Arrange in a single layer on large baking sheets. Place sheets in the oven (do not preheat). Turn the heat to 450° F and bake until just beginning to crisp, about 8 minutes. Remove the sheets from the oven and flip slices over. Return to the oven and turn off the heat. Continue to toast with the residual heat in the off oven until lightly toasted, about 8 more minutes. Cool on wire rack.

2. Add ¼ cup of the oil to a large stick-resistant skillet. Add the eggplant, onion, garlic, and salt and sauté over medium-high heat, until the onion is softened and eggplant is slightly softened, but not cooked through, about 5 minutes. Cover and cook for 2 minutes. Stir, cover, and turn off the heat. Let "lid cook" (cook covered while the burner is off) until the eggplant is completely softened, about 10 minutes. Pour into a bowl and let cool slightly.

3. Stir the tomatoes, basil, lemon juice, and the remaining tablespoon of oil into the cooled eggplant mixture. Taste and adjust seasoning, if necessary.

(continued)

little
green
cooking
tip

Try "hyperbaking." A conventional oven is not a green appliance. So when you do need to use it, take advantage of every bit of energy and heat it produces, such as when toasting bread slices for bruschetta or when baking cookies. There's no need to preheat the oven.

Summer

4. Spread about 2 tablespoons of the eggplant mixture on top of each toast. Sprinkle with the pine nuts and serve at room temperature.

PER SERVING: 430 calories, 28g total fat, 4g saturated fat, 0g trans fat, 0mg cholesterol, 250mg sodium, 38g total carbohydrate, 8g dietary fiber, 10g protein

---

a planet-friendly bite

 More than 80 percent of the pine nuts consumed in the U.S. every year are imported. But pine nuts do grow in the United States in Arizona, California, Colorado, New Mexico, and Oregon. It's interesting that these nuts are grown in the Southwest but common in Mediterranean and Asian foods, not Southwestern cuisine. Regardless of the style of cuisine in which you enjoy them, you can freeze pine nuts for about 9 months to keep them fresh until ready to use.

salad pizza

MESCLUN SALAD PIZZETTE WITH PEACHES AND PECANS

Makes 4 servings: ½ pizzette each

Three minutes of cooking time is all that this picture-perfect pizza needs. It's actually a salad and pizza in one—making it a meal in one. What's more, it provides the perfect pairing of crispy and moist, sweet and savory, and hot and cool. So if you're looking for a piece of culinary yin and yang, this earth-friendly pizza is your food find.

2 tablespoons apple cider vinegar
2 tablespoons canola or flaxseed oil
2 medium yellow or white peaches, pitted, thinly sliced
½ cup thinly sliced red onion
½ teaspoon sea salt, or to taste
¼ teaspoon freshly ground black pepper
2 (8-inch) whole-wheat lavash flatbreads or pocketless pita bread
⅓ cup finely crumbled organic or locally produced blue cheese
3 cups mesclun mix or mixed chopped leafy greens
¼ cup raw pecans, chopped

1. Place the vinegar, oil, ¼ of the peach slices (slices from ½ peach), ¼ cup of the onion, salt, and pepper in a blender container. Cover and puree until just combined, about 15 seconds. Set aside.

2. Place one flatbread at a time on a toaster oven tray. Place in the toaster oven* (do not preheat). Broil until lightly toasted, about 1½ minutes per side. Remove from the oven and immediately sprinkle with the cheese.

3. Toss together the mesclun, remaining peaches, and remaining onion with ¼ cup of the vinaigrette in a medium bowl. Taste and adjust seasoning, if necessary.

4. Arrange the salad on the toasted flatbreads. Sprinkle with the pecans. Cut in half and serve immediately with the remaining vinaigrette on the side.

PER SERVING: 310 calories, 17g total fat, 3g saturated fat, 0g trans fat, 10mg cholesterol, 700mg sodium, 37g total carbohydrate, 6g dietary fiber, 9g protein

* Toaster oven sizes and cooking times will vary. See page 39.

little
green
cooking
tip

When broiling in a toaster oven or a conventional oven, just turn on the broiler and you're ready to go. There's no need to preheat!

a planet-friendly bite

Got gas? In the U.S., approximately 22 percent of the energy consumption comes from natural gas. More than 62 percent of homes use natural gas to fuel stoves, water heaters, furnaces, and more. Natural gas burns cleaner than other fossil fuels, such as coal and oil, since it has less sulfur, carbon, and nitrogen emissions. Still, it is a nonrenewable energy source—which means there are environmental issues. Burning natural gas (just like other fossil fuels) produces CO_2. Scientific consensus is that increasing levels of CO_2 and other greenhouse gases in our atmosphere are changing the global climate.

fruity fontina flatbread

MESCLUN SALAD FLATBREAD WITH GRAPES, FONTINA, AND PINE NUTS

Makes 4 servings: ½ flatbread sandwich each

Dairy foods require a variety of earth's precious resources to produce. But there's no need to give up cheese—especially if it's something you adore (I certainly do!). Rather, use just the amount that you need, rather than overindulging in big chunks of it. In this full-flavored flatbread recipe, you'll taste the cheese—and everything else. It's a wonderful balance of cheesiness, nuttiness, fruitiness, and tanginess. Now that's yumminess.

½ cup black or red seedless grapes
¼ cup thinly sliced red onion
2 tablespoons extra-virgin olive oil
1 tablespoon white wine vinegar
½ teaspoon sea salt, or to taste
¼ teaspoon freshly ground black pepper
2 (8-inch) whole-wheat lavash flatbreads or pocketless pita bread
¾ cup shredded organic or locally produced Italian-style Fontina cheese
2 tablespoons raw pine nuts
2 cups mesclun mix or mixed chopped leafy greens
2 tablespoons chopped fresh basil

1. Place ¼ cup of the grapes, half of the onion, the oil, vinegar, salt, and pepper in a blender container. Cover and puree until just combined, about 30 seconds. Set aside.

2. Place one flatbread at a time on a toaster oven tray. Place in the toaster oven* (do not preheat). Broil until lightly toasted, about 1½ minutes per side. Remove from the oven, immediately sprinkle with the cheese and pine nuts and cut in half. Repeat with the remaining flatbread.

3. Thinly slice lengthwise the remaining ¼ cup grapes. Toss with the mesclun, basil, the remaining onion, and half of the dressing in a large bowl. Taste and adjust seasoning, if necessary.

little *green* cooking tip

Go even greener by simply going untoasted. Every little bit of energy savings helps. If you choose the untoasted route with this recipe, pick pita pockets instead. You can stuff and enjoy them a little easier.

4. Arrange the salad on two of the toasted flatbread halves. Top with the remaining flatbread halves. Cut each flatbread sandwich in half again. Serve immediately with the remaining dressing on the side.

PER SERVING: 310 calories, 18g total fat, 5g saturated fat, 0g trans fat, 25mg cholesterol, 690mg sodium, 29g total carbohydrate, 4g dietary fiber, 11g protein

---

*. Toaster oven sizes and cooking times will vary. See page 39.

use it, don't lose it

 When recipes require specific vegetable amounts that result in veggie leftovers, hit the salad bar of your local market instead. There, you can purchase exactly 2 ounces of mesclun or ¼ cup of sliced red onion. And even if the cost of fresh food bars seems high, it might be cheaper in the long run since you won't have any waste.

breakfast bruschetta

POACHED EGG-TOPPED TOASTS WITH FRESH TOMATO-BASIL SALSA

Makes 4 servings: 1 topped toast each

When you want eggs but you don't really want "breakfast food," this bruschetta is the best bet. It's a beautiful dish that will impress guests, too. Equally impressive is how big the flavors are considering how little cooking time is required. In fact, eggs can be considered among the fastest cooking of all protein sources, helping them naturally be green eggs—sans ham. The fresh salsa provides a naturally delicious finishing touch. But if you need to cheat, just replace the salsa with a dollop of organic marinara sauce for an even faster finish.

2 medium vine-ripened tomatoes, diced
1 scallion, green and white parts, thinly sliced
3 tablespoons thinly sliced fresh basil
1 clove garlic, minced
2 teaspoons plus 1 tablespoon extra-virgin olive oil
1 teaspoon sea salt, or to taste
8 large organic eggs
4 large slices bread of choice
1½ tablespoons unsalted organic butter, at room temperature
1 small or ½ large lemon

1. Combine the tomatoes, scallion, 1½ tablespoons of the basil, the garlic, and 2 teaspoons of the oil in a medium bowl. Season with ½ teaspoon of the salt. Set aside.

2. Bring 1 inch of fresh water and ¼ teaspoon of the salt to a boil in a large skillet over high heat. Turn off the heat and add eggs by breaking them directly into the water. Immediately cover the pan. Allow the eggs to "lid cook" (cook covered while the burner is off) undisturbed for 6 minutes, or until done as desired. Remove the eggs with a large slotted spoon to drain on an unbleached paper towel–lined plate.

3. Meanwhile, lightly toast the bread. Spread with mixture of the butter, the remaining 1 tablespoon of oil, and the remaining ¼ teaspoon salt.

little **green** cooking tip

What should you do with the shells after you've cracked all of the eggs? Wash and crush them, then add to your compost bin; they add nutrients to soil. If you don't compost, simply stir the crushed eggshells into soil around a plant.

4. Place 2 poached eggs on top of each slice of toast. Strain the liquids from the salsa and top each with about ⅓ cup of the salsa. Sprinkle with the remaining basil. Squeeze the lemon juice on top of each bruschetta, and serve.

PER SERVING: 380 calories, 27g total fat, 8g saturated fat, 0g trans fat, 435mg cholesterol, 750mg sodium, 17g total carbohydrate, 3g dietary fiber, 17g protein

use it, don't lose it

 Occasionally a recipe will require you to strain off liquids from veggies or fruits. Although the juices are not used in the recipe, it doesn't mean they're not edible. In fact, these strained liquids are usually worthy enough to drink as inspired beverages! For Breakfast Bruschetta, sip the strained tomato-basil salsa liquid from step 4 as a savory shot served along with a lemon wedge. (It'll be about 3 ounces of liquid—two shots worth.) Whoever thought swigging a shot with your eggs would be a good thing?

aztec frittata

CORN, BEAN, AND BELL PEPPER FRITTATA

Makes 4 servings: 1 wedge of frittata each

Frittatas are Italian-style omelets that are fast cooking and filling, so they're ideal as a dinner entrée when you don't have an hour to spend in the kitchen. In fact, they're ideal at any time of the day. Whip up this pie-like frittata if you want a little flavor kick, as it's full of Southwestern flair. You'll love having another way to nibble on your fresh-picked corn.

6 large organic eggs
2 scallions, green and white parts, thinly sliced
1 small clove garlic, minced
1 tablespoon finely chopped fresh cilantro or flat-leaf parsley
¾ teaspoon sea salt, or to taste
1 teaspoon hot pepper sauce
1 tablespoon canola or peanut oil
1 cup fresh corn kernels (about 2 medium cobs)
1 (15-ounce) can organic kidney or pinto beans, drained (do not rinse)
1 medium red bell pepper, diced
¼ cup low-sodium vegetable broth
1 cup shredded organic or locally produced Monterey Jack cheese (optional)
⅓ cup salsa or Green Green Salsa (page 54; optional)

1. Whisk together the eggs, scallions, garlic, cilantro, salt, and hot pepper sauce in a medium bowl until combined. Set aside.

2. Heat the oil in a large stick-resistant skillet over medium-high heat. Stir in the corn, beans, bell pepper, and broth. Cover and cook until the peppers are soft, about 5 minutes.

3. Stir the vegetable mixture, and then spread evenly in the pan. Pour the egg mixture over the vegetable mixture. Shake the pan slightly to allow the egg to fully settle. Sprinkle with the cheese (if using). Cover, reduce the heat to medium, and cook until the eggs are set around the edges, but not the center, about 3 minutes.

little **green** cooking tip

There's no need to rinse canned beans. It's a waste of water. Just choose an organic brand, drain, and enjoy. Choose a variety with no added salt if sodium is a concern for you. And don't be afraid to try an organic store brand from time to time. It's still green—and can save you green.

4. Cover again and turn off the heat. Let "lid cook" (cook covered while the heat is off) until the eggs are completely set, about 10 more minutes.

5. Slide the frittata onto a plate, place another plate on top, then invert so the caramelized (browned) side is up. Cut into wedges with a pizza cutter and serve with salsa (if using).

PER SERVING: 280 calories, 13g total fat, 3g saturated fat, 0g trans fat, 320mg cholesterol, 590mg sodium, 25g total carbohydrate, 6g dietary fiber, 16g protein

a planet-friendly bite

 In addition to going organic, choose canned foods with BPA-free lined cans. BPA, or bisphenol A, is a chemical that some scientists suggest may disrupt regular hormone activity in the body. Eden Foods, for example, is one company that uses BPA-free lined cans.

veggie-studded sticky quinoa

COOL QUINOA WITH EGGPLANT, ARUGULA, AND PINE NUTS

Makes 4 servings: 1¼ cups each

Quinoa is one of the world's greenest whole grains as it can be cooked in such a low-carbon way. To top that, quinoa is considered one of the world's healthiest grains. So get ready to get greener and healthier by indulging in this unique dish. It's a bit unusual as it's meant to be slightly sticky and served as a side dish or entrée, not a salad. Plus it's cool, making it ideal for sizzling-hot summer days.

¼ cup extra-virgin olive oil
1 medium eggplant, unpeeled, cut into ½-inch cubes
½ cup quinoa, rinsed and drained
Juice of 1 lemon (about 3 tablespoons)
¾ teaspoon sea salt, or to taste
2 cups fresh baby arugula
2 scallions, green and white parts, thinly sliced
½ cup grape tomatoes, quartered lengthwise
2 tablespoons chopped fresh mint
2 tablespoons raw pine nuts

1. Heat 2 tablespoons of the oil in a large saucepan over medium heat. Add the eggplant and stir to coat. Cover and cook, stirring once, until the eggplant is soft and nearly cooked through, about 7 minutes.

2. Stir in the quinoa and 1 cup fresh water. Bring to a boil over high heat. Cover and turn off the heat. Let "lid cook" (cook covered while the burner is off) until the quinoa and eggplant are fully cooked, about 25 minutes.

3. Meanwhile, whisk together the remaining 2 tablespoons of oil, the lemon juice, and salt in a medium serving bowl. Add the hot quinoa to the dressing and stir to combine. (The mixture will be souplike.) Set aside to cool for about 30 minutes. Then cool in the refrigerator until fully chilled.

4. Toss the chilled quinoa (it will be a bit sticky) with the arugula, scallions, tomatoes, mint, and pine nuts. Taste and adjust seasoning, if necessary. Serve with lemon wedges, if desired.

PER SERVING: 290 calories, 19g total fat, 2.5g saturated fat, 0g trans fat, 0mg cholesterol, 450mg sodium, 27g total carbohydrate, 7g dietary fiber, 6g protein

use it, don't lose it

 **Mint is one of the easier herbs to grow—as long as it gets several hours of at least partial sunlight each day.**
So if you've never grown a fresh herb in your garden or on a windowsill, consider starting with mint—any variety you desire. Then, when your green thumb succeeds, you can freeze extra fresh mint for use anytime.

green shoestrings

JULIENNE OF GARLIC ZUCCHINI

Makes 2 servings: 1 cup each

If you have summer-lovin' affection for zucchini, you'll appreciate this fast flavor blast that looks like green spaghetti—or shoestrings. (Though shoestrings can't possibly taste as good!) Try it as a straightforward side or entrée—or enjoy it in any way you please.

2 tablespoons extra-virgin olive oil
1 large shallot, thinly sliced
1 large clove garlic, minced
2 medium zucchini, cut into thin, spaghetti-like strips
2 tablespoons chopped fresh basil
½ teaspoon sea salt, or to taste
¼ teaspoon freshly ground black pepper, or to taste

1. Heat the oil in a large stick-resistant skillet over medium heat.

2. Add the shallot and sauté over medium heat until softened, about 3 minutes. Add the garlic and sauté until fragrant, about 30 seconds.

(continued)

little
green
cooking
tip

Cooked sliced veggies aren't supposed to be mushy when they're done. Overcooking veggies causes a loss of nutrients and uses excess cooking energy. Veggies that are cooked through, yet have a bit of a bite, are just right.

Summer

3. Stir in the zucchini and cover. Cook, stirring once, until the zucchini is cooked, yet still firm, about 5 minutes. Cover and turn off the heat. Let "lid cook" (cook covered while the burner is off) until the zucchini is tender and stringlike, about 5 minutes.

4. Stir in the basil, salt, and pepper and serve.

PER SERVING: 170 calories, 14g total fat, 2g saturated fat, 0g trans fat, 0mg cholesterol, 600mg sodium, 11g total carbohydrate, 2g dietary fiber, 3g protein

use it, don't lose it

Even if a recipe seems like a stand-alone side, think outside the side-dish box and enjoy it in a variety of ways. It's a delicious way to use any leftovers—or "spare savories." And it's an opportunity to enjoy something you love in a new way, adding to your recipe repertoire. For example, combine spare Green Shoestrings with whole-wheat linguine and organic tomato-basil sauce for a clever pasta entrée. Or use it as a bed for a grilled portobello mushroom "steak," fish fillet, or organic poultry paillard.

ears of sunlight

CHILE-LIME CORN ON THE COB

Makes 4 servings: 1 cob each

Corn on the cob is so delicious and versatile it should be one of those foods with an entire restaurant devoted to it—like a pancake house. I'd go! But since I don't know of one, this recipe will have to do. Although fresh-picked grilled corn with nothing other than a sprinkling of sea salt is always a winner, this recipe adds extra pizzazz if you want to up the flavor ante.

2 tablespoons local apricot or other fruit spread or homemade jam
    or 1 tablespoons mild floral honey
Juice of ½ lime (about 1 tablespoon)
1 small jalapeño with seeds, minced
4 medium ears fresh corn, shucked
4 (1-teaspoon) pats unsalted organic butter (optional)
½ teaspoon sea salt, or to taste

1. Prepare an outdoor or indoor grill (medium-high heat). In a small bowl, stir the fruit spread, lime juice, and jalapeño until combined.

2. With tongs, place the corn on the grill away from direct heat. Brush the corn with the jalapeño-lime sauce. Rotate frequently until just beginning to caramelize, about 7 minutes.

3. Place the corn on a plate and cover with a lid or recycled aluminum foil and let steam until fully cooked, about 3 minutes.

4. Uncover, rub each ear with butter to coat (if using), and add salt. If desired, insert a corn holder into the stem end of each cob and serve.

PER SERVING: 100 calories, 1g total fat, 0g saturated fat, 0g trans fat, 0mg cholesterol, 300mg sodium, 22g total carbohydrate, 2g dietary fiber, 3g protein

little **green** cooking tip

When cooking food on an indoor electric grill, it's important that all parts of a food touch the cooking surface since that's the only source of heat. If a food isn't flat, slice it so it'll cook evenly, such as cutting corn cobs into smaller "cobbettes."

a planet-friendly bite

July 4 is the most popular day of the year for cookouts as three-quarters of the nation's grill owners use at least one of their grills then, according to a survey conducted by Hearth, Patio & Barbecue Association. That's about 60 million folks! The survey also found that nearly 8 of 10 American households own a grill and that more than 4 in 10 own more than one grill. Based on these numbers, Tristram West of the Department of Energy's Oak Ridge National Laboratory calculated that the grills would emit nearly 225,000 metric tons of carbon dioxide (CO_2). However, all of the grills in use on Independence Day would basically need to stay lit nonstop for three years to be roughly equal to the average annual U.S. CO_2 emissions. So, go ahead, enjoy your Fourth of July barbecue!

stinkin' smashers in skins

GARLIC MASHED YUKON GOLD POTATOES IN POTATO SKINS

Makes 4 servings: 1 stuffed potato half each

You don't need lots of dairy—milk or buttermilk, butter, and cheese—to make a potato delicious. In fact, you don't need *any*! In this smashing potato recipe, soymilk creates creaminess, olive oil adds richness, and garlic makes them stinkin' good. And "micro-roasting" them—rather than baking them in a big oven—and then eating them in the peel makes them green.

2 large Yukon gold potatoes, scrubbed unpeeled
½ cup plain unsweetened soymilk, at room temperature
1 tablespoon extra-virgin olive oil
2 large cloves garlic, minced
⅓ cup minced chives or 2 scallions, green and white parts, minced
½ teaspoon sea salt, or to taste
¼ teaspoon freshly ground black pepper, or to taste

1. Poke holes in the potatoes with a fork to vent steam. Place potatoes in a large microwave-safe dish. Cover well with unbleached
   parchment paper. "Micro-roast" (cook in the microwave oven*)
   on high until nearly fork tender, yet still slightly firm in the center,
   about 6 minutes. Let sit covered in the off microwave or set aside to
   cook by carryover cooking until the potatoes further soften, about
   6 minutes.

2. Slice the potatoes in half lengthwise. Scoop the potato from the
   skins into a medium bowl, leaving about ¼ inch potato on the
   skin. Reserve skins.

3. Mash the potato filling with a potato masher. Then add the
   soymilk, oil, and garlic and mash until smooth yet still thick.
   Add additional soymilk if too thick. Stir in most of the chives.
   Add salt and pepper.

4. Season the skins with salt and pepper and spoon the mashed potato filling into the skins (about ⅓ rounded cup each). Place filled skins back onto the microwave-safe dish. Heat in the microwave oven for 30 seconds on high, or until heated through. Sprinkle with the remaining chives and serve.

PER SERVING: 150 calories, 4.5g total fat, 0.5g saturated fat, 0g trans fat, 0mg cholesterol, 320mg sodium, 25g total carbohydrate, 3g dietary fiber, 4g protein

---

*Microwave oven cooking times will vary. See page 39.

go local

 There are so many colorful shapes, sizes, and varieties of potatoes—hundreds of varieties, in fact. All of them have subtly different flavors and textures. Even when a recipe calls for a specific type, such as Yukon gold potatoes, you can play with your potato pick. Visit your farmers' market (see page 366) and use any local potato that's similar in size. Blue potatoes are always an eye opener—and mouth opener!

cheesy zucchini macaroni

THREE-CHEESE WHOLE-WHEAT MACARONI AND CHEESE WITH ZUCCHINI

Makes 10 servings: ²⁄₃ cup each

Cheesy macaroni. Zucchini. How do I love thee? I don't have enough room on this page to count the ways. When these two foods marry in this ultra-healthy looking recipe, it will wow your taste buds. It's as rich, creamy, and delicious as it is easy to fix. It's much tastier than anything you can find in a box. And it's much greener—in two ways.

1½ teaspoons sea salt, or to taste

8 ounces (2 cups) whole-wheat elbow macaroni

1 medium zucchini, halved lengthwise and thinly sliced

3 tablespoons unsalted organic butter

3 tablespoons buckwheat flour

2¼ cups whole or reduced-fat (2 percent) organic milk or plain unsweetened soymilk

2 scallions, green and white parts, minced

¼ teaspoon freshly ground white or black pepper, or to taste

⅛ teaspoon freshly grated nutmeg

1 cup shredded organic or locally produced Swiss cheese

1 cup shredded organic or locally produced extra-sharp Cheddar cheese

1 cup shredded organic or locally produced Muenster or provolone cheese

1. Bring 4 cups fresh water and 1 teaspoon of the salt to a boil in a medium saucepan. Stir in the macaroni and zucchini. Bring back to a boil. Cover and turn off the heat. Let "lid cook" (cook covered while the burner is off) until the macaroni is al dente, about 5 minutes. Drain well and set aside.

2. Meanwhile, melt the butter in a large saucepan over medium-low heat. Whisk in the flour until combined. Very gradually whisk in the milk until smooth. Increase the heat to medium-high. Add the white part of the scallions, pepper, and nutmeg while stirring constantly. Bring just to a boil. Stir in the cheeses until melted, about 1 minute. Turn off the heat. Cover and let "lid cook" (cook covered while the burner is off) until the cheeses are fully melted.

little *green* cooking tip

Whenever a recipe calls for scallions, use both the green and white parts. The white part has a stronger flavor and should be cut smaller than the green part when used raw. Or cook the white part within a recipe and use the uncooked green part as the finishing touch.

3. Stir the cheese mixture into the cooked macaroni and zucchini. Add the remaining salt. Let sit 5 minutes before serving to allow mixture to combine.

4. Serve in individual bowls or pour into a large serving bowl. Sprinkle with the green part of the scallions to serve.

PER SERVING: 280 calories, 16g total fat, 10g saturated fat, 0g trans fat, 50mg cholesterol, 430mg sodium, 22g total carbohydrate, 2g dietary fiber, 14g protein

use it, don't lose it

 Have extras? Skip the plastic containers. Store your "spare savories" (leftovers) in containers that can go straight from the fridge to the microwave or toaster oven, and then to the table—so you'll only need one dish instead of three.

citrus cream of capellini

CREAMY LEMON CAPELLINI PASTA WITH FLAT-LEAF PARSLEY

Makes 6 servings: 1 cup each

"Skinny" pasta will cook faster than chubby noodles. And with "lid cooking," you'll use very little cooking energy. That'll please Mother Nature. And the lovely, light lemony taste of this comforting pasta will please you.

1¾ teaspoons sea salt, or to taste
12 ounces whole-wheat capellini or angel hair pasta
½ cup organic heavy cream
1 tablespoon unsalted organic butter
Juice and zest of 1 lemon (about 3 tablespoons juice)
¼ teaspoon freshly ground black or white pepper, or to taste
⅓ cup freshly grated organic or locally produced Parmesan cheese
¼ cup chopped fresh flat-leaf parsley
⅓ cup raw pine nuts (optional)

(continued)

little *green* cooking tip

Producing dairy foods, like cream, butter, and cheese, leaves a big carbon footprint, but you can still enjoy them. Serve recipes that contain a significant proportion of these luscious ingredients as smaller-portioned entrées or sides, rather than starring-role entrées. It's called "green-sizing"!

1. Bring 6 cups fresh water and ¾ tsp of the salt to a boil in a large saucepan over high heat. Add the pasta and return to a boil. Cover and turn off the heat. Let "lid cook" (cook covered while the burner is off) until the pasta is al dente, about 6 minutes. Drain the pasta, reserving ½ cup of the cooking liquid.

2. Place the drained pasta back into the dried saucepan and set over medium-high heat. Stir in the cream, butter, lemon juice, and zest. Cook while stirring until the pasta is hot, about 1 minute. For a thinner sauce, add the reserved pasta cooking liquid. Add salt and pepper.

3. Pour the pasta into a serving bowl or serve directly from the saucepan. Sprinkle with the cheese and parsley. Top with the pine nuts (if using) and serve.

PER SERVING: 320 calories, 12g total fat, 7g saturated fat, 0g trans fat, 35mg cholesterol, 620mg sodium, 44g total carbohydrate, 5g dietary fiber, 9g protein

a planet-friendly bite

Using a lid when cooking saves wasted energy—and time. However, despite popular belief, it only saves seconds, not minutes, off the time it takes to bring an average amount of water to a boil. I tested this theory. It took me 6 minutes 45 seconds to bring a small lidded saucepan with 4 cups of cool fresh water to a full boil over high heat. It took 7 minutes 15 seconds without the lid. Try your own experiment. My final answer: use a lid to bring water to a boil only if you choose. But also consider that since you can't see water boiling in a lidded pan, you might want to think twice!

FISH, POULTRY, & MEAT DISHES

honeydew of the sea

GRILLED MAHI MAHI ON HONEYDEW-AVOCADO PUREE

Makes 4 servings: 1 fillet with ½ scant cup puree each

Mahi mahi is one of the fastest-growing commercially caught fish. And mahi mahi from the U.S., caught by pole or trolling, is one of the most sustainable, eco-friendliest choices. Though mahi mahi means "strong strong," the fish's flavor is mildly sweet. You'll find the lovely and thin fish in this dish "swimming" in a velvety pool of fruity puree.

½ honeydew melon, cubed

2 tablespoons extra-virgin olive oil

1¼ teaspoons sea salt, or to taste

½ teaspoon cayenne pepper, or to taste

2 (8-ounce) mahi mahi fillets, cut in half to make 4 thin fillets, about ¾-inch thick

1 Hass avocado, pitted, peeled, and diced

½ small white onion, coarsely chopped

¼ cup packed fresh cilantro leaves

Juice and zest of 1 lime, or to taste (about 2 tablespoons juice)

1. Add 1 cup of the melon, the oil, ¾ teaspoon of the salt, and cayenne to a blender container. Cover and puree, about 15 seconds. Place the mahi mahi fillets in a wide-bottomed bowl or a baking pan. Pour the honeydew marinade over the mahi mahi and let marinate for 30 minutes.

(continued)

little *green* cooking tip

Having a cookout—or a cook-in? Slice fish or organic poultry or meat into thin cutlets or fillets before grilling. They'll require less grilling energy—and leave a smaller carbon footprint.

2. Meanwhile, add the remaining melon to the blender container (no need to wash the container after step 1) along with the avocado, onion, cilantro, lime juice, and ¼ teaspoon of the salt. Cover and puree, about 15 seconds. Taste and adjust seasoning, if necessary. Set aside.

3. Prepare an outdoor or indoor grill (medium-high heat) or place a grill pan over medium-high heat. Grill the marinated fish (discard leftover marinade) over direct heat until just opaque in the center, about 4 minutes per side. (Alternatively, cook in a panini grill on medium-high heat until opaque in the center, about 6 minutes.) Add the remaining ¼ teaspoon salt.

4. Spoon a pool of honeydew-avocado puree onto a plate and top with the grilled fish fillets. Sprinkle with the lime zest and, if desired, garnish with additional cilantro sprigs. If there is leftover puree, enjoy it like a soup, stirred into steamed grains, or with organic tortilla chips.

PER SERVING: 260 calories, 13g total fat, 2g saturated fat, 0g trans fat, 85mg cholesterol, 850mg sodium, 13g total carbohydrate, 3g dietary fiber, 22g protein

a planet-friendly bite

 According to the California Avocado Commission, avocado orchards can reduce storm runoff and thus the potential for flooding. And by filtering rainwater, the orchards may improve water quality, too.

scallops with iridescent salsa

SCALLOPS WITH FRESH LYCHEE SALSA

Makes 4 servings: 4 scallops with 1 tablespoon salsa each

There are some things that make living in chilly New England and Canada worth it. And one of those things is the sea scallop. If you love scallops, then do make sure to relish this gem of a recipe. It's a very light entrée that's sweet, savory, and summertime scrumptious. Or if you prefer, turn this into an elegant appetizer that'll serve eight, two scallops each.

1 cup fresh peeled, pitted, and diced lychees*
2 tablespoons finely diced red onion
2 tablespoons finely diced unpeeled hothouse cucumber (optional)
1 tablespoon finely chopped fresh cilantro
1 small jalapeño with some seeds, minced
1 small clove garlic, minced
Juice and zest of ½ lime, or to taste (about 1 tablespoon juice)
16 large fresh sea scallops
1 tablespoon canola or peanut oil
½ teaspoon sea salt, or to taste

1. Combine the lychees, onion, cucumber (if using), cilantro, jalapeño, garlic, and lime juice together in a medium bowl. Set aside.

2. Pat dry the scallops with an unbleached paper towel. Remove the muscle from the scallops.

3. Heat the oil in a large stick-resistant skillet over high heat. Cook scallops until brown on both sides and cooked through, about 1½ minutes per side. Add salt.

(continued)

little *green* cooking tip

Always be sure to cook with fish and shellfish that are considered eco-friendly, like sea scallops are. Farmed bay scallops are even eco-friendlier. So if you choose to use them to go even greener, keep in mind that they're smaller than other varieties, so sauté for a shorter time than sea scallops. And in this recipe, mix the lychee salsa right into them to serve.

4. Arrange 4 scallops on each plate. Top each serving with 1 tablespoon of the lychee salsa. Taste and adjust seasoning, if necessary. Sprinkle with the lime zest.

PER SERVING: 120 calories, 4g total fat, 0g saturated fat, 0g trans fat, 20mg cholesterol, 390mg sodium, 10g total carbohydrate, 1g dietary fiber, 11g protein

---

*Wash fresh lychees. Then, similar to working with an avocado, place the lychee on a cutting board and slice through the skin lengthwise, down to the seed, and all the way around. Remove the peel along with the inner membrane to get to the fruit. Discard (preferably compost) the skin. Then remove the flesh from the seed. Discard the seed. If fresh lychees are unavailable, use a 20-ounce can of lychees, drained of syrup.

go local

Do you live in the North Atlantic region? You're in luck if you're a sea scallop devotee. The sea scallop populations there are healthy. On the other hand, the Mid-Atlantic (North Carolina to New York) area is unfortunately overfished. So think colder for greener sea scallops.

wild salmon rainier

GRILLED WILD ALASKAN SALMON WITH RAINIER CHERRY SAUCE

Makes 4 servings: 1 salmon fillet with 3 tablespoons sauce each

Alaska can boast about many things. One highlight is its wild salmon; it appears to be the greenest of all salmon varieties. But for those of us that don't live in that great state up north, some things are worth the miles they need to travel to get to the table. Sustainable wild Alaskan salmon is worth it. And when coupled with cherries, it's a food experience worth having regularly throughout the summer.

4 (5-ounce) skinless wild Alaskan salmon fillets

½ teaspoon sea salt, or to taste

¼ teaspoon freshly ground black pepper, or to taste

2 teaspoons peanut oil

1 tablespoon unsalted organic butter

1 large shallot, minced

3 tablespoons apple cider vinegar or aged red wine vinegar

1 cup fresh Rainier cherries, pitted and thinly sliced

2 teaspoons mild floral honey

1 teaspoon fresh thyme

little
green
cooking
tip

Consolidate pan use when logical. When you can use one skillet instead of two, it means you'll have one less skillet to clean. It may mean you wipe or rinse out the pan quickly to reuse it but that will save energy during cleanup. And it could even enhance your cooking if the dishes you make have compatible flavors, like Wild Salmon Rainier—no wiping or rinsing required between uses.

1. Pat the salmon fillets dry with an unbleached paper towel. Add the salt and pepper. Heat the oil in a large stick-resistant skillet over medium-high heat. Add the salmon, skinned side up, and cook for 3 minutes. Turn over and sauté until just cooked through, about 2 more minutes. Transfer to a plate and set aside.

2. In the same skillet, melt the butter over medium heat. Add the shallots and sauté until lightly caramelized, about 1 minute. Add the vinegar, cherries, honey, and thyme. Cover and turn off the heat. Let "lid cook" (cook covered while the burner is off) until the cherries are soft, about 3 minutes.

3. Return salmon fillets and any collected juices to the skillet. Cover and "lid cook" for 3 minutes, or just until hot. Taste and adjust seasoning, if necessary. Transfer the salmon and sauce to plates and serve.

PER SERVING: 250 calories, 10g total fat, 3.5g saturated fat, 0g trans fat, 75mg cholesterol, 360mg sodium, 11g total carbohydrate, 1g dietary fiber, 29g protein

a planet-friendly bite

According to the Environmental Defense Fund, salmon caught in Alaska—including pink, sockeye, Chinook/king, chum, and coho—are a green choice. They are low in contaminants, their populations are well managed, and they are caught with gear that has minimal environmental impact.

chicken luau

BREADED ORGANIC CHICKEN PAILLARDS WITH FRESH MANGO RELISH

Makes 4 servings: 1 paillard with 3 tablespoons relish each

Baked chicken breasts can take half an hour or more of roasting time in a conventional oven. Baked in a toaster oven after being pounded into paillards, they'll take just 7 minutes. Not only will you be saving a significant amount of energy, you won't be heating up the kitchen. So get ready for the taste bud luau. This magical mango-lovers' meal is no sweat—literally!

1 cup plain whole-wheat panko breadcrumbs
1 tablespoon mild floral honey
1 large clove garlic, minced
2 (7-ounce) boneless, skinless organic chicken breasts
¼ teaspoon ground cumin
¾ teaspoon sea salt, or to taste
¼ teaspoon freshly ground black pepper, or to taste
¾ cup Mango Tango Topping (page 159)

1. Spread the panko on a plate and set aside.

2. With your fingers, rub the honey and garlic onto the chicken. Sprinkle with the cumin. Add ½ teaspoon of the salt and the pepper.

3. Cut each chicken breast in half to make 4 small breast pieces. Place between sheets of unbleached parchment paper and pound with a kitchen mallet to ½-inch thickness.

4. Dip both sides of each chicken paillard into the panko and place on a toaster oven tray. Lightly spray the chicken paillards with homemade cooking spray.* Sprinkle with the remaining ¼ teaspoon salt.

5. Place the tray in a toaster oven** (do not preheat). Turn the heat to 450°F and bake until well done and golden brown, about 7 minutes. Taste and adjust seasoning, if necessary.

6. Serve with Mango Tango Topping on the chicken breasts. Enjoy warm or cool.

PER SERVING: 210 calories, 3g total fat, 0.5g saturated fat, 0g trans fat, 55mg cholesterol, 650mg sodium, 24g total carbohydrate, 3g dietary fiber, 23g protein

*Fill a Misto or similar spray bottle with oil of choice.
**Toaster oven sizes and cooking times will vary. See page 39.

little **green** cooking tip

Keep the kitchen cool! Use a toaster oven instead of a big ol' conventional oven; you won't heat up your kitchen as it heats up outside. No extra air-conditioning required for cooling down your kitchen.

mango tango topping

FRESH MANGO RELISH

Makes 1 ½ cups

1 medium mango, peeled, pitted, and diced
¼ cup finely diced red onion
1 small jalapeño with some seeds, minced
1 tablespoon finely chopped fresh cilantro
Juice of ½ lime (about 1 tablespoon)
½ teaspoon sea salt, or to taste
⅛ teaspoon ground cumin, or to taste

Stir together the mango, onion, jalapeño, cilantro, and lime in a small bowl. Add salt and cumin to taste. If desired, serve from a mango "peel-up."

use it, don't lose it

When you don't use all of a sauce, salsa, gravy, or dressing that a recipe calls for, consider using it in other dishes at that same meal to better marry all of the separate meal components. Extra salad dressing for a side salad can add intrigue to grilled or steamed veggies. For Chicken Luau, you'll only need half of the Mango Tango Topping recipe for the chicken. So use the remainder to punch up a side of plain grains or as a dip for organic tortilla chips.

a better blt

ORGANIC BACON, LETTUCE, AND TOMATO SANDWICH

Makes 4 servings: 1 sandwich each

You don't need a pound of crisp, salty bacon for a lip-smacking BLT. Half of that amount is actually the just-right amount for this sandwich since it is layered with flavors and textures. In this new-fangled version, the onion provides extra crispness and sharpness, the avocado "mayo" adds saltiness and creaminess, and the basil emphasizes herbaceous freshness. All together, you'll be keener on this greener BLT.

little **green** cooking tip

If you love bacon and don't want to give it up to go green, then go organic and "green-size" it by halving the portion. To make up for some of the bacon's crispness and saltiness, add ingredients that provide those charac-teristics, like crispy onion and a pinch of sea salt. But if you prefer to go meatless, this sandwich will still be scrumptious without bacon—or add a thin slice of natu-rally smoked Gouda cheese to each sandwich.

8 ounces sliced organic turkey or uncured pork bacon
1 Hass avocado, pitted and peeled
Juice of 1 lime (about 2 tablespoons)
3 tablespoons mayonnaise
⅛ teaspoon sea salt, or to taste
⅛ teaspoon freshly ground black pepper, or to taste
2 medium vine-ripened tomatoes, cut into ¼-inch-thick rounds
8 thick slices whole-grain bread
4 romaine lettuce leaves, torn into large pieces
8 large fresh basil leaves
⅓ cup thinly sliced red onion

1. Place the bacon on an unbleached paper towel on a microwave-safe dish and cover with another paper towel. "Micro-roast" (cook in the microwave oven*) on high to desired crispness, about 4 minutes. Set aside to drain on another paper towel.

2. Mash the avocado with a fork in a medium bowl (or using a mor-tar and pestle) until smooth. Add 1 tablespoon of the lime juice and the mayonnaise and stir until well combined. Add salt and pepper. (It's okay if it's a little lumpy.)

3. Sprinkle the tomatoes with the remaining lime juice and strain off excess liquid into a small bowl or cup. (Enjoy the strained tomato-lime liquid as a refreshing drink—or "shot.")

4. Meanwhile, spread half of the avocado mixture on 1 side of 4 of the bread slices. Top each with the bacon, then the lettuce, basil, tomato, and onion. Spread the remaining avocado mixture over the remaining 4 bread slices. Place the bread slices on top of the lettuce. Cut sandwiches in half and serve.

PER SERVING: 370 calories, 22g total fat, 4g saturated fat, 0g trans fat, 25mg cholesterol, 860mg sodium, 30g total carbohydrate, 7g dietary fiber, 15g protein

*Microwave oven cooking times will vary. See page 39.

use it, don't lose it

 Wash, dry, and save the avocado peels. Then use them as single-serve snack bowls or "peel-ups."

groovy grape juice

CALIFORNIA GRAPE GAZPACHO "COCKTAIL"

Makes 8 servings: 1 Champagne flute (½ cup) each

When the weather outside is sweltering, you might want a cool, refreshing drink. But if you need to take the edge off of your hunger, too, then you'll want to reach for this delightful grape "cocktail." It's like gazpacho, a cold soup, yet it's meant to be sipped. No cooking is required. It only takes 1 minute to whirl it up in the blender. And it makes for a very interesting (virgin) drink that also has a little extra texture.

little *green* cooking tip

Instead of using a measuring cup to measure and a bowl to mix ingredients, try to use just the measuring cup for both. Then you'll need to wash just one item, not two.

1½ cups seedless green grapes
1½ cups chopped unpeeled hothouse cucumber
1½ cups chopped iceberg or romaine lettuce
¾ cup sliced celery
3 scallions, white and green parts, sliced
⅓ cup chopped yellow or green bell pepper
1½ cups low-sodium vegetable broth, or to taste
3 tablespoons white wine vinegar or apple cider vinegar
2 tablespoons extra-virgin olive oil
1 large clove garlic, chopped
½ teaspoon sea salt, or to taste
¼ teaspoon cayenne pepper, or to taste

1. Combine the grapes, cucumber, lettuce, celery, scallions, and bell pepper in a large bowl.

2. Whisk together the broth, vinegar, oil, garlic, salt, and pepper in a large liquid measuring cup.

3. Place half of the grape-veggie mixture and half the broth mixture in a blender container. Cover and puree on low for about 30 seconds, then on high until most of the grape skins are just tiny flecks, about 30 seconds. Pour into a 2-quart pitcher and repeat with the remaining grape-veggie mixture and broth mixture. Taste and adjust seasoning.

4. Let chill for at least 1 hour. Serve in Champagne flutes.

PER SERVING: 40 calories, 1.5g total fat, 0g saturated fat, 0 g trans fat, 0mg cholesterol, 170mg sodium, 7g total carbohydrate, 1g dietary fiber, 1g protein

a planet-friendly bite

Sweet bell peppers got their name because they're shaped like bells. Nearly all color varieties start out green. Basically, the green ones are not as ripe as the yellow, orange, and red ones. As they ripen and turn their gorgeous colors, they become sweeter.

superfood smoothie

VERY GREEN MANGO SMOOTHIE

Makes 2 servings: ¾ cup each

This ultra-healthy, thick-n-creamy beverage is inspired by my friend John who lives in Ireland. He loves all things green—and this smoothie definitely is. If you're not so sure about the spinach part, just wean your way up to the full amount, starting with ¼ cup. Try it, you'll like it.

1 large Keitt or other mango, peeled, pitted, and cubed
¾ cup fresh baby spinach
Juice of ½ small lemon (about 1 tablespoon)

1. Add all ingredients to a blender container along with ½ cup cold fresh water or to taste. Cover and puree on low until combined, about 30 seconds, then on high until velvety, about 15 seconds.

(continued)

little
green
cooking
tip

If you don't have one, consider investing in a professional blender. Some less costly ones puree so poorly that you often waste several minutes of excess energy trying to achieve smooth results. And remember, when left plugged in, appliances—even small ones—can still drain "phantom" energy unless they're plugged into a "smart" power strip. So, unplug your blender after every use.

2. If desired, boost sweetness with the addition of 1 teaspoon mild floral honey. Serve in small beverage glasses.

PER SERVING: 70 calories, 0g total fat, 0g saturated fat, 0g trans fat, 0mg cholesterol, 20mg sodium, 19g total carbohydrate, 2g dietary fiber, 1g protein

---

use it, don't lose it

How do you know when a mango is ripe? Position it stem side up. Then take a whiff. It should smell sweet and fresh. The mango itself will give a little with slight pressure, too. If it's not ripe yet, don't use it. Place it in a recycled paper bag and let sit at room temperature for a day or two until softened.

key lime pie-tini

KEY LIME MARTINI WITH GRAHAM CRACKER RIM

Makes 2 servings: 1 martini each

Have your pie and drink it, too! That's only possible to do if your pie is actually a drink—like in this inspired martini. It has all of the flavors of key lime pie, but you don't have to bake it. That's a win for the environment—and potentially a win for your social life.

⅓ cup whole-grain graham cracker crumbs
1 key lime or 1 small lime, halved
½ cup vanilla-flavored vodka, such as Tru vanilla-infused organic vodka
¼ cup organic half-and-half or plain unsweetened soy milk
3 tablespoons fresh Key lime juice
2 tablespoons mild floral honey

1. Pour the graham cracker crumbs onto a shallow dish. Cut one half of the Key lime in half again to make 2 wedges. Rub wedges around the rims of two martini glasses. Dip the rims into the graham cracker crumbs until each rim is completely coated with crumbs.

2. Pour the vodka, half-and-half, Key lime juice, and honey into a cocktail shaker. Squirt the juice from the remaining key lime wedges into the shaker. Add 4 large ice cubes and shake until well mixed. Pour into the prepared martini glasses.

3. Thinly slice the remaining Key lime half. Garnish with the Key lime slices and serve immediately.

PER SERVING: 310 calories, 5g total fat, 2.5g saturated fat, 0g trans fat, 10mg cholesterol, 100mg sodium, 36g total carbohydrate, 2g dietary fiber, 3g protein

a planet-friendly bite

 New York City is not just a concrete jungle. Nature is all around—especially if you head up to the rooftops where the bees can make gloriously sweet honey. What's more, a French beekeepers' association found that city-dwelling bees are more productive and healthier than rural bees. It seems city bees enjoy a wide variety of plants and may be better at filtering pollution.

Oven-baked pies are lovely and should be enjoyed on occasion. But you can enjoy that loveliness in a greener way—and more frequent way—by incorporating the flavor highlights of the pie into a cocktail or a smoothie. No baking required.

summer lassi

FRESH NECTARINE–SOY YOGURT SMOOTHIE

Makes 2 servings: 1 cup each

Sometimes when fruits are in season I get carried away and pick up too many at the market. I often do that with nectarines. So when I have too many ripened nectarines, my favorite way to enjoy them is in a smoothie. This smoothie is actually a nectarine version of a mango lassi. It's fragrant and fruity with a little tang from the yogurt and tiny flecks of nectarine skin . . . so you'll know what you're drinking. Enjoy the sweet taste of summer.

1 cup plain soy or organic yogurt, well-chilled
2 large or 3 medium ripe white or yellow nectarines, well chilled, pitted, and cubed
1 tablespoon mild floral honey or turbinado or Demerara sugar

1. Place all the ingredients in a blender container. Cover and puree on low until just combined, about 15 seconds, then on high until creamy, about 15 seconds more.

2. Serve in skinny glasses.

PER SERVING: 250 calories, 2.5g total fat, 0g saturated fat, 0g trans fat, 0mg cholesterol, 95mg sodium, 51g total carbohydrate, 3g dietary fiber, 6g protein

little *green* cooking tip

Whirling a smoothie is a tasty way to use any fully ripened fruit just before it becomes overripe. And it's green, too—as you won't be tempted to toss out any soon-to-be-rotten fruit. (By the way, nectarines ripen at room temperature. Place them in the fridge only if you need to, such as for Summer Lassi, once they're fully ripened.)

use it, don't lose it

If you only need a lassi for one, go ahead and make this full recipe. The remaining portion can be frozen in Popsicle molds and enjoyed later.

sweet ruby

RHUBARB-STRAWBERRY COMPOTE WITH SOY FROZEN DESSERT TOPPING

Makes 4 servings: ¾ cup compote with ⅓ cup frozen dessert each

The marriage of strawberry and rhubarb is a happy one—and, in this dessert recipe, a saucy one. By using "lid cooking," you'll need very little energy for cooking the rhubarb. And for a finishing touch with eco-flair, a little nondairy frozen dessert is dolloped on top instead of that stuff sprayed from a can.

- 1 cup turbinado or Demerara sugar
- 3 tablespoons local strawberry or other fruit spread or homemade jam or 2 tablespoons mild floral honey
- 1 teaspoon Valencia orange zest
- 2 large stalks rhubarb, sliced into ½-inch pieces
- 2 cups sliced hulled fresh strawberries
- 1⅓ cups vanilla soy or rice frozen dessert

1. Combine the sugar, fruit spread, 3 tablespoons fresh water, and orange zest in a medium saucepan. Place over medium-high heat and bring to a boil. Stir in the rhubarb and cook while stirring for 2 minutes. Cover and turn off the heat. Let "lid cook" (cook covered with the burner off) until the rhubarb is soft but not mushy, about 8 minutes. Uncover and let sit at room temperature until slightly cooled, about 30 minutes. Then chill completely in the refrigerator.

2. Stir the strawberries into the chilled rhubarb. Divide evenly among 4 small dessert dishes. Top each serving with a ⅓-cup scoop of the frozen dessert and serve.

PER SERVING: 330 calories, 2.5g total fat, 0g saturated fat, 0g trans fat, 0mg cholesterol, 40mg sodium, 79g total carbohydrate, 4g dietary fiber, 1g protein

a planet-friendly bite

 Rhubarb is enjoyed as a fruit, though it's botanically a veggie. That's probably no surprise as the tart red stalks looks oddly like celery. Fresh from the field, rhubarb is best enjoyed in late spring and early summer.

little *green* cooking tip

Pick or purchase strawberries when they're fully ripened, since they don't ripen after picking. Wash them only when ready for use. Remove green leafy caps after washing. Then clean and reuse plastic strawberry baskets. They make practical drawer dividers or not-so-practical giant homemade bubble blowing wands.

baked peachy bites

MINI WHITE PEACH-NUT MUFFINS

Makes 24 servings: 1 mini muffin each

If whole-grain muffins are green, then whole-grain mini muffins are greener. When shrinking the size of an oven-baked goody, it'll shrink the baking time. And by using a toaster oven instead of a conventional oven, it'll shrink the energy used. That makes these mini muffins green-green. And that's just peachy!

2 tablespoons canola oil
2 tablespoons unsalted organic butter, at room temperature
½ cup turbinado or Demerara sugar
1 large organic egg
1 large or 2 small white peaches, pitted and very finely chopped
¾ teaspoon pure vanilla extract
¾ cup stone-ground whole-wheat flour
½ teaspoon baking soda
¼ teaspoon sea salt
⅓ cup finely chopped raw walnuts or pecans

1. Line 2 mini muffin trays with unbleached mini muffin liners. Alternatively, use a mini-size silicone cupcake baking pan or cups—without liners.

2. Stir together the oil and butter in a medium mixing bowl until smooth. Add the sugar and stir until well combined. Add the egg and vigorously stir until well mixed. Stir in the peaches and vanilla extract and stir until well combined.

3. Sift the flour, baking soda, and salt directly onto the peach mixture (if you don't have a sifter, shake all ingredients through a mesh strainer), and gently stir until just combined. (Note: Stir in any remaining flour left in the strainer, too.)

4. Spoon 1 tablespoon batter into each muffin cup. Sprinkle and then very lightly press the walnuts onto each mini muffin.

5. Place the trays in the toaster oven* (do not preheat). Turn the heat to 400°F and bake, rotating the trays halfway through baking, until a slight indentation remains after gently pressing the top of a mini muffin, about 9 minutes. Turn off the toaster oven. Let the muffins cook with the residual heat until springy to the touch, about 5 minutes. (Bake in two batches, if necessary.) Let cool in trays on a wire rack.

PER SERVING: 70 calories, 3.5g total fat, 1g saturated fat, 0g trans fat, 10mg cholesterol, 55mg sodium, 8g total carbohydrate, 1g dietary fiber, 1g protein

---

*Toaster oven sizes and cooking times will vary. See page 39.

use it, don't lose it

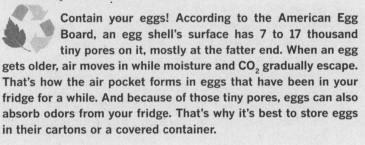

Contain your eggs! According to the American Egg Board, an egg shell's surface has 7 to 17 thousand tiny pores on it, mostly at the fatter end. When an egg gets older, air moves in while moisture and CO_2 gradually escape. That's how the air pocket forms in eggs that have been in your fridge for a while. And because of those tiny pores, eggs can also absorb odors from your fridge. That's why it's best to store eggs in their cartons or a covered container.

rock-n-roll truffles

DARK CHOCOLATE–FRESH RASPBERRY TRUFFLES

Makes 10 servings: about 5 truffles each

Just writing this recipe title makes my mouth water. It sure beats anything found in a box of chocolates that's been overpackaged and filled with who knows what besides chocolate. The only other thing in this rich dark chocolate ganache coating is juicy red raspberries— fresh, flavorful, and eco-licious.

¼ cup organic heavy cream
⅛ teaspoon pure almond extract
⅛ teaspoon pure peppermint extract
7 ounces high-quality semisweet chocolate, finely chopped
6 ounces fresh raspberries
1 tablespoon unsweetened cocoa powder

1. Line a tray with unbleached parchment or wax paper.

2. Bring the cream and both extracts to a simmer (do not boil) in a small saucepan over medium heat. Remove from the heat, then add the chocolate and stir gently until smooth.

3. Pat raspberries dry with an unbleached paper towel, if necessary. Working in batches, add 10 raspberries to the chocolate mixture (ganache) and scoop out one at a time using a slotted spoon. Rock-n-roll each chocolate-covered raspberry in the spoon and tap the spoon against the pan edge to let excess ganache drip back into pan. Transfer to the prepared tray. Repeat with the remaining raspberries.

4. Chill the truffles in the refrigerator on the tray until firm, at least 1 hour. Just before serving, sprinkle with the cocoa powder.

PER SERVING: 130 calories, 8g total fat, 5g saturated fat, 0g trans fat, 15mg cholesterol, 0mg sodium, 15g total carbohydrate, 8g dietary fiber, 2g protein

little *green* cooking tip

Check the label. Make sure that your parchment or wax paper is made from un-bleached paper to ultimately keep chlorine out of our lakes and streams.

berry good micro-bars

BLUEBERRY CRUMBLE BREAD BARS

Makes 12 servings: 1 piece each

I wouldn't have believed that these dessert bars were baked in a microwave oven unless I saw it firsthand. These not only *look* incredibly delicious, they *are*. In fact, this might be my all-time favorite way to enjoy blueberries now.

Bars
¼ cup unsalted organic butter, at room temperature
⅔ cup turbinado or Demerara sugar
1 large organic egg, at room temperature
½ cup plain unsweetened soymilk or whole organic milk
1 teaspoon pure vanilla extract
1⅔ cups stone-ground whole-wheat flour
1½ teaspoon baking powder
½ teaspoon sea salt
1 pint fresh blueberries

Topping
½ cup turbinado or Demerara sugar
¼ cup stone-ground whole-wheat flour
¼ cup unsalted organic butter
½ teaspoon ground cinnamon
⅛ teaspoon sea salt

1. For the bars: Grease a 2-quart microwave-safe dish, such as 8 × 12-inch rectangular or 10-inch round stoneware.

(continued)

Go ahead! It is possible to "bake" divine desserts energy efficiently in a microwave oven. To get that lovely oven-baked brownness, pick naturally brown ingredients, like whole-wheat flour instead of white.

2. Cream the butter and sugar together in a large mixing bowl until smooth. Whisk in the egg, soymilk, and vanilla extract until combined. (The mixture will look oatmeal-like at this point.)

3. Sift the flour, baking powder, and salt directly onto the moist mixture (if you don't have a sifter, shake ingredients through a mesh strainer), and stir until the ingredients are just combined. (Note: Stir in any remaining flour left in the strainer, too.) Gently fold in the berries until just combined. Evenly spread the mixture into the prepared dish.

4. For the topping: Combine the sugar, flour, butter, cinnamon, and salt in a medium mixing bowl. Blend the mixture with a pastry blender or potato masher until the mixture is crumbly. Sprinkle the topping over the mixture in the baking dish.

5. "Micro-bake" (bake in the microwave oven*) on medium until springy to the touch, about 13 minutes, rotating the dish twice during cooking (if necessary). Let cool for at least 20 minutes on a rack. Cut into 12 pieces and serve warm, at room temperature, or cool.

PER SERVING: 250 calories, 9g total fat, 5g saturated fat, 0g trans fat, 40mg cholesterol, 200mg sodium, 40g total carbohydrate, 3g dietary fiber, 4g protein

*Microwave oven cooking times will vary. See page 39.

use it, don't lose it

When a recipe says to "butter" or "grease" a pan or dish, use the remainder of the butter that's left on the wrapper.

oj on ice

FRESH-SQUEEZED VALENCIA ORANGE SOY "ICE CREAM"

Makes 2 servings: 1 cup each

Homemade ice cream is such a treat, even when it's made with soymilk. But the biggest delight may be in how you make it. Though it'd be easy to toss ingredients into an electric ice cream maker, a hand-cranked maker or an ice cream "ball" that you toss around is much greener. (It's fun, too!) Besides, for some reason when you do it yourself, the results taste that much better.

1½ cups plain unsweetened soymilk, chilled
½ cup freshly squeezed Valencia orange juice
⅓ cup turbinado or Demerara sugar
1½ teaspoons pure vanilla extract
½ teaspoon Valencia orange zest

1. Add all ingredients to the container end of an ice cream ball.* Add ice and rock or kosher salt to the other end, per ball instructions. Toss the ball around for 20 minutes, scraping down sides of the ice cream in the container after 10 minutes.

2. Scoop and enjoy. Serve in orange "peel-ups" (halved orange peels) for a green presentation. Sprinkle with additional orange zest, if desired.

PER SERVING: 260 calories, 3.5g total fat, 0g saturated fat, 0g trans fat, 0mg cholesterol, 95mg sodium, 50g total carbohydrate, 1g dietary fiber, 6g protein

*See http://icecreamrevolution.com for information about the ice cream ball.

little
green
cooking
tip

Even if preparing something manually instead of using electricity, don't assume it'll take more time—or that it's hard to do. Whether making homemade ice cream in an electric maker or a manual ice cream ball or hand-cranked version, both only take about 20 minutes.

go local

Though it'd be nice to go to Valencia, Spain, to get these juicy fruits, it's not necessary to do so. Besides, you'd have trouble getting them through customs. Luckily, Valencia oranges are grown in California, Florida, Arizona, and Texas.

AUTUMN

all that's nice nuts

RAW SUGAR-N-SPICE PECANS

Makes 4 servings: ¼ cup each

Pecans are tree nuts that are native to the U.S. Like many other nuts, pecans are actually fruits (or to be botanically correct, they're *drupes*). Like fruits, they have a peak season. Although pecans are available all year, they are most seasonal in fall. So get 'em fresh and try this sweet-n-spicy coating to kick 'em up with fabulousness.

1 cup raw pecan halves
2 tablespoons peanut oil
¼ cup turbinado or Demerara sugar
1½ teaspoons cayenne pepper
1½ teaspoons chili powder

1. Toss the pecans with the oil in a small bowl until fully coated.

2. Sprinkle with the sugar, cayenne, and chili powder and gently toss just until coated.

3. Serve as a snack or on a salad, such as Bartlettuce (page 205).

PER SERVING: 310 calories, 27g total fat, 3g saturated fat, 0g trans fat, 0mg cholesterol, 10mg sodium, 17g total carbohydrate, 3g dietary fiber, 3g protein

little **green** cooking tip

Nuts are often roasted or sautéed in order to coat them with seasonings. But there's no need to roast them as long as the nuts are moist enough for seasonings to "stick." So try this recipe with other nuts, like walnuts, and other favorite coatings, too.

blue boscs

BLUE CHEESE-TOPPED BOSC PEAR "CHIPS"

Makes 8 servings: 1 topped "chip" each

What better way to highlight the sweet-tart Bosc pear than to serve it with tangy blue cheese. The pear "chips" act as the bread, so no bread baking or toasting is required. The pecans provide flavor and textural balance. And no cooking makes this delightful, bruschetta-style appetizer green.

2 (8-ounce) Bosc pears, stems removed

1 lemon, halved

4 ounces organic or locally produced blue cheese, at room temperature

4 ounces organic cream cheese, at room temperature

2 teaspoons mild floral honey

¼ cup raw pecan halves, chopped

8 fresh basil leaves, thinly sliced

1. Cut the pears lengthwise into 7 slices each. Carefully core seeds. Select 8 of the largest pear slices. Rub the cut surfaces of each slice with one of the lemon halves.

2. Dice the remaining pear slices. Place the cubes in a small bowl along with 1 cup fresh water and the juice and rind of the remaining lemon. Let sit in this acidulated water at least 5 minutes.

3. Meanwhile, blend both the cheeses and the honey with a fork in a medium bowl until very smooth. Spread the cut surface of the 8 pear slices with the cheese mixture.

little
green
cooking
tip

It is not always necessary to dirty a measuring cup when you can be flexible with the ingredient amount, like pecan halves for Blue Boscs. Eyeball the portion size. A small handful is about ¼ cup of nuts. Or, if you want to be more precise, simply count out 16 pecan halves.

(continued)

Autumn

4. Thoroughly drain the diced pears. (Enjoy the drained liquid as a little pear-flavored lemonade beverage. Just add a touch of honey.) Mix the diced pears with the pecans and basil. Sprinkle the top of each cheese-topped pear "chip" with the pear-nut mixture. Serve immediately.

PER SERVING: 160 calories, 11g total fat, 6g saturated fat, 0g trans fat, 25mg cholesterol, 240mg sodium, 11g total carbohydrate, 2g dietary fiber, 5g protein

---

go local

Visit area farmers' markets or chat with a local cheese-monger to help you find the best locally produced artisanal blue cheeses in your region. Otherwise, here are a couple of blues that will be divine in this dish: Black River Blue (Wisconsin) and Maytag Blue (Iowa).

caprese skewers

CHERRY TOMATO, BOCCONCINI, AND BASIL PICKS

Makes 6 servings: 2 skewers each

Caprese salad is always a hit, but this skewered version is like a home run—and much more fun. If you grow the tomatoes and basil yourself or if you find your bocconcini locally, then you've got a green grand slam.

3 tablespoons extra-virgin olive oil

2 tablespoons aged balsamic vinegar

½ teaspoon sea salt, or to taste

¼ teaspoon freshly ground black pepper, or to taste

24 unsalted fresh organic or locally produced bocconcini (small balls fresh mozzarella) in water, drained

24 cherry or grape tomatoes (use the size closest in size to the bocconcini)

24 small fresh basil leaves

1. Add the oil, vinegar, salt, and pepper to a small, lidded bowl. Shake to combine. Add the bocconcini. Shake again to combine. Let marinate for 30 minutes to 1 hour at room temperature, shaking gently on occasion.

2. Alternately thread 2 bocconcini, 2 tomatoes, and 2 basil leaves onto each of 12 (6-inch) bamboo or reusable skewers. Serve at room temperature.

PER SERVING: 200 calories, 15g total fat, 8g saturated fat, 0g trans fat, 40mg cholesterol, 360mg sodium, 4g total carbohydrate, 1g dietary fiber, 11g protein

go local

Not surprisingly, most of the olive oil–producing companies in the U.S. are based in California. But domestic producers have established operations in a growing number of states outside of California, too, such as in Texas, Georgia, Idaho, and Arizona.

little *green* cooking tip

Instead of traditional skewers, thread foods onto rosemary twigs from which you've already removed the leaves. If you do this for Caprese Skewers, add about ¼ teaspoon minced rosemary to the marinade, too.

my own private idaho sticks

SPICED SKINNY FRENCH FRIES

Makes 2 servings: 30 to 35 fries each

How do you like your fries? Crispy? Extra-crispy? It's up to you how you favor your fries. But remember, the less you fry them, the smaller your carbon footprint. Focus on enjoying the flavor scrumptiousness rather than extra-crispiness. I'm not talking about wimpy, limpy fries; "just crisp" is just right. That's how these "hyperfried" fries will be enjoyed. Think of it as the Goldilocks of greenness for fries.

2 medium russet potatoes, scrubbed unpeeled, and sliced
    into skinny fries, about ¼-inch thick*
2½ cups peanut oil
¼ teaspoon sea salt, or to taste
⅛ teaspoon garlic powder, or to taste
⅛ teaspoon cayenne pepper, or to taste

(continued)

little *green* cooking tip

The traditional way to fry is to heat the oil then drop in the food. But you can save energy and still have successful French fry results by placing potatoes into the oil, then turning on the heat. Call it "hyperfrying"!

1. Arrange the potatoes in a single layer in a large skillet. Place the skillet on a burner. Pour the oil over the potatoes. Add more oil if needed to completely cover the potatoes. Turn the heat to medium-high. Cover the skillet and cook for 5 minutes.

2. Uncover and fry, stirring occasionally, until the potatoes are golden brown and just crisp, about 8 minutes.

3. Transfer to unbleached paper towels to drain. Add salt, garlic powder, and cayenne. Serve immediately.

PER SERVING: 400 calories, 27g total fat, 4.5g saturated fat, 0g trans fat, 0mg cholesterol, 300mg sodium, 36g total carbohydrate, 3g dietary fiber, 4g protein

*Rinse then dry uncooked fries to reduce stickiness when cooking.

a planet-friendly bite

 How does using your French fry grease as gas sound to you? If intrigued, check out the Veggie Van Voyage at www.veggievan.org. After that, watch the film *Fields of Fuel*. Visit www.fieldsoffuel.com for more. In it, Josh Tickell, who is an expert on alternative fuels, takes you on a real journey toward a decentralized, sustainable energy future. Trickell found that the first diesel engine wasn't designed to run on petroleum; it was designed to run on vegetable oil!

yam bams

SWEET POTATO SKINNY FRIES WITH ROSEMARY

Makes 2 servings: 30 to 35 fries each

Zipping open a can of super-sweet candied sweet potatoes is one way to enjoy this veggie. It's definitely not the greenest or healthiest way, as they're swimming in corn syrup. A greener, healthier, and tastier way to enjoy sweet potatoes is when fresh from the market—prepared nearly any other way you might prepare regular potatoes. "Hyperfrying" them is my pick.

2 medium sweet potatoes, scrubbed unpeeled, and sliced into skinny
   fries, about ¼-inch thick
2½ cups peanut oil
¼ teaspoon sea salt, or to taste
¼ teaspoon minced fresh rosemary, or to taste

1. Arrange the potatoes in a single layer in a large skillet. Place the skillet on a burner. Pour the oil over the potatoes. Add more oil if needed to completely cover the potatoes. Turn the heat to medium-high. Cover the skillet and cook for 5 minutes.

2. Uncover and fry until the potatoes are golden brown (they won't be crispy), about 8 minutes.

3. Transfer to unbleached paper towels to drain. Add salt and rosemary. Serve immediately.

PER SERVING: 390 calories, 27g total fat, 4.5g saturated fat, 0g trans fat, 0mg cholesterol, 400mg sodium, 35g total carbohydrate, 6g dietary fiber, 3g protein

little
green
cooking
tip

Sweet potatoes can be eaten raw—shred like carrots or slice like potato chips to try a taste. But if you want more beta-carotene benefit, it's generally best to cook them. Better yet, sauté or fry them since the dietary fat can enhance beta-carotene absorption. Just enjoy fried food only occasionally to keep your body fat in check.

use it, don't lose it

After frying, there's plenty of oil remaining in the skillet or fryer. If used for preparing plant foods, like sweet potatoes, save the oil for one more use. When cool, simply strain the oil slowly through an unbleached coffee filter–lined strainer or more quickly through cheesecloth. Store in a sealed container in the refrigerator until you're ready again for Yam Bams.

guava glazers

GUAVA-N-LIME-GLAZED FARMED SHRIMP SKEWERS

Makes 4 servings: 2 skewers each

When you think of guava, it might conjure up images of the tropics. But guava grows in the U.S., too. You might not be able to easily find the fresh fruit at your local market, but its nectar is widely available. It adds that tropical—or Floridian, Californian, or Hawaiian—flair to these quick-to-prepare shrimp skewers.

1 cup guava or passion fruit nectar
Juice of 2½ limes (about 5 tablespoons)
2 tablespoons extra-virgin olive oil
1 tablespoon scrubbed unpeeled minced gingerroot
1 large clove garlic, minced
¾ teaspoon crushed red pepper flakes
½ teaspoon sea salt, or to taste
24 medium or large U.S. farmed shrimp, shelled and deveined,
   tails left intact (about 1 pound)
1 large red bell pepper, cut into 24 bite-sized pieces

1. Mix the nectar, ¼ cup of the lime juice, oil, gingerroot, garlic, crushed red pepper, and ¼ teaspoon of the salt in a large bowl. Add the shrimp and bell peppers; toss to coat. Let marinate about 30 minutes.

2. Alternately thread 3 bell peppers and 3 shrimp on each of 8 water-soaked (12-inch) bamboo or reusable skewers.

3. Prepare a grill pan or indoor or outdoor grill (medium-high heat). Grill shrimp until cooked through, about 2½ minutes per side.

4. Sprinkle with the remaining 1 tablespoon lime juice. Add the remaining ¼ teaspoon salt and serve.

PER SERVING: 150 calories, 8g total fat, 1g saturated fat, 0g trans fat, 65mg cholesterol, 370mg sodium, 14g total carbohydrate, 2g dietary fiber, 8g protein

little **green** cooking tip

Grilling kebabs rather than thick steaks or whole fish will keep grilling time to a minimum since food on the skewers is bite-sized and cooks quickly. And it provides an opportunity to incorporate some veggies or fruits. It's more fun to eat food on sticks, too.

little big city sliders

SKILLET-SEARED ORGANIC MINI BURGERS WITH RADICCHIO

Makes 8 servings: 1 burger each

When you hear about green cuisine, you'll likely hear that no-meat cuisine is greenest. So if you enjoy veggie burgers, go for it. (Taste my Homemade Veggie Burgers on page 269.) But if you gotta have a meaty burger on occasion, that's okay. Just choose grass-fed organic beef to start with. Then green-size it by going mini instead of jumbo on portion size. That way when you do eat beef, you're doing so in an earth-friendlier fashion.

⅓ cup grated scrubbed unpeeled sweet potato

3 tablespoons grated white onion

1 tablespoon ketchup

1 large clove garlic, minced

½ teaspoon sea salt, or to taste

¼ teaspoon freshly ground black pepper, or to taste

16 ounces grass-fed organic ground beef (85 percent lean)

6 whole-grain dinner rolls, split

1½ cups shredded radicchio

1. Spread the grated sweet potato in a small microwave-safe dish. "Micro-roast" (cook in the microwave oven*) until cooked through and steaming hot, about 30 seconds. Allow to cool for at least 3 minutes.

(continued)

little
green
cooking
tip

Sneaking veggies into organic burgers, meatloaf, chili, and so on is a green trick, not just a nutrient-boosting treat. It helps to "stretch" your meat so you can use less total beef in each burger.

2. Add the slightly cooled sweet potato, the onion, ketchup, garlic, salt, and pepper to a medium bowl and combine with your hands. Add the beef and combine until just mixed. Form into eight patties (about ¼ rounded cup beef mixture each). Heat a large stick-resistant skillet over medium-high heat. Cook the burgers in two batches until medium doneness, about 45 seconds per side. Taste and adjust seasoning, if necessary.

3. Place each burger on the bottom half of the dinner rolls. Top each beef patty with the radicchio. Place the roll tops on the burgers. Serve with mayonnaise or enjoy with smashed micro-roasted sweet potato as a condiment.

PER SERVING: 170 calories, 7g total fat, 2.5g saturated fat, 0g trans fat, 35mg cholesterol, 300mg sodium, 15g total carbohydrate, 2g dietary fiber, 12g protein

---

*Microwave oven cooking times will vary. See page 39.

a planet-friendly bite

According to the USDA Food Safety and Inspection Service, 1 out of every 4 hamburgers looks done before it has reached a safe internal temperature of 160°F. So use a food thermometer to make sure your food is safe to eat. A thermometer can help prevent overcooking foods, too.

really good dates

RAW ALMOND-STUFFED DATES WRAPPED IN ORGANIC BACON

Makes 8 servings: 3 stuffed dates each

Dates are like candy from trees. Stuff them with crunchy almonds and wrap them in salty organic bacon and you've found the Candy Land of pop-in-your-mouth pleasures. This Spanish tapas–inspired hors d'oeuvres will fill every one of your taste and texture temptations—sweet, yet savory and salty; crunchy, yet chewy and moist. More please!

little **green** cooking tip

24 raw (natural) whole almonds (1 ounce)
24 pitted dates
12 thin slices organic bacon, cut in half crosswise

1. Stuff one almond in the center of each date. Wrap a piece of bacon around each stuffed date.

2. Place stuffed dates onto an unbleached parchment paper–lined toaster oven tray. Place in the toaster oven* (do not preheat). Turn the heat to 425°F and bake until the bacon is nearly crisp, about 15 minutes. Turn off the toaster oven. Let the bacon cook with the residual heat for another 5 minutes.

3. Remove to wire rack to drain. Serve warm.

Measure out nuts into 1-ounce portions to be ready for low-carbon cuisine in an instant. One ounce is about 24 almonds. (Though nutty experts will tell you it's 23!) Repurpose a used (and thoroughly washed) baby food jar, spice bottle, or Altoids mint tin for, curiously, 1 ounce of almonds. Have way too many almonds? Refrigerate the extras in a sealed container to keep them fresh for months.

PER SERVING: 270 calories, 6g total fat, 1.5g saturated fat, 0g trans fat, 10mg cholesterol, 220mg sodium, 55g total carbohydrate, 5g dietary fiber, 6g protein

*Toaster oven sizes and cooking times will vary. See page 39.

a planet-friendly bite

More than five thousand years ago dates helped sustain desert peoples and nomadic wanderers of the Middle East and North Africa. In the eighteenth century, dates were introduced in California by Spanish missionaries. Date palm trees thrive now in Arizona and California.

Autumn

DIPS, SALSAS, & SAUCES

fresh-from-the-bog relish

RAW CRANBERRY RELISH

Makes 10 servings: ¼ cup each

I have to admit . . . I was never a big fan of cranberry sauce at Thanksgiving when I was a child. But as I grew up, I learned to appreciate it. Finally, I've grown very fond of it. You'll understand once you prepare this recipe; it's a marvelous mishmash of sweet, tart, and savory. When cranberries are available at your market (October through December) fresh from the bogs, whirl up this relish regularly. It's a tasty condiment every day, not just on a holiday.

3 cups fresh or thawed frozen cranberries
1 medium red onion, coarsely chopped
½ cup turbinado or Demerara sugar
Juice and zest of ½ navel or Valencia orange (about 3 tablespoons juice)

Place the cranberries, onion, sugar, orange juice, and zest in the bowl of a food processor. Cover and pulse until finely chopped, about 10 seconds total. Chill the relish, covered, for at least 2 hours before serving.

PER SERVING: 60 calories, 0g total fat, 0g saturated fat, 0g trans fat, 0mg cholesterol, 0mg sodium, 16g total carbohydrate, 2g dietary fiber, 0g protein

use it, don't lose it

Get that autumn-fresh, seasonal cranberry taste all year long. Fresh cranberries can be frozen for up to a year.

little **green** cooking tip

Eating seasonally is an eco-conscious concept. Make sure the fresh produce you select is at its peak of ripeness, when possible. For instance, fresh cranberries (which are one of only three fruits native to the U.S. and Canada!) will bounce like baby basketballs when ripe!

papapple sauce

NO-COOK PAPAYA-APPLE SAUCE

Makes 8 servings: ½ cup each

Most people know applesauce as something that comes in a jar from a processing plant. Or if you make it yourself, it typically requires cooking—as much as 45 minutes of stovetop gas or electricity. I've developed a greener way to make applesauce with no cooking at all. The fragrant papaya provides the creaminess of the cooked apple consistency. But it's the sauce's hint of intriguing spice that will really make you go "mmmm . . . !"

1 large papaya, peeled, seeded, and cubed (about 4 cups)

2 large Granny Smith or other sweet-tart apples, quartered

2 tablespoons mild floral honey or brown sugar

¼ teaspoon sea salt, or to taste

¼ teaspoon ground cinnamon, or to taste

⅛ teaspoon ground cardamom, or to taste

Place all ingredients in the bowl of a food processor. Cover and pulse until a fine applesauce-like texture, about 20 seconds. Let chill in the refrigerator at least 1 hour before serving. Taste and adjust seasoning.

PER SERVING: 70 calories, 0g total fat, 0g saturated fat, 0g trans fat, 0mg cholesterol, 75mg sodium, 19g total carbohydrate, 3g dietary fiber, 1g protein

little **green** cooking tip

Go raw! By wise use of a food processor or blender, many fruits and veggies can be whirled into sweet and savory sauces and soups that'll require no cooking at all.

use it, don't lose it

Spices, such as cinnamon and cardamom, add distinctive flavors and unique aromas to both sweet and savory dishes. But if you overdo it, you can ruin the entire dish. That can easily happen when doubling recipes, so remember to increase spices only one and one-half times instead of two.

fruitamole

GUACAMOLE WITH FALL FRUITS

Makes 4 servings: ½ cup each

If I were shipwrecked on a deserted isle, the one food I don't think I could live without is guacamole. So from my own kitchen island, I love to invent new versions of guacamole. In early autumn, when figs or nectarines are still at their peak, this is my version of a life-saver!

1 Hass avocado, pitted, peeled, and cubed (reserve peel)
3 Calimyrna or Mission figs, diced, or 1 large white nectarine, pitted and diced
1 kiwi, scrubbed unpeeled, and finely diced
8 red or black seedless grapes, halved lengthwise and thinly sliced crosswise
Juice of ½ lime, or to taste (about 1 tablespoon)
¼ cup diced white onion
3 tablespoons chopped fresh cilantro
1 small jalapeño with some seeds, minced
½ teaspoon ground cumin, or to taste
¼ teaspoon sea salt, or to taste

1. Gently stir all the ingredients together in a medium bowl until just combined. Taste and adjust seasoning, if necessary.

2. Serve as a condiment for roasted organic pork or chicken or like traditional guacamole with organic red, white, or blue corn tortilla chips. Use avocado "peel-ups" (halved avocado peels) as serving dishes, if desired.

PER SERVING: 110 calories, 6g total fat, 1g saturated fat, 0g trans fat, 0mg cholesterol, 150mg sodium, 16g total carbohydrate, 4g dietary fiber, 1g protein

rootamole

ROOT VEGGIE "GUACAMOLE"

Makes 5 servings: ½ cup each

One day I had some extra potatoes on hand and was experimenting in my kitchen. Since I love the flavors that turn avocado into guacamole but I didn't have any avocados, I took all of the same ingredients and invented a guacamole made with potatoes instead. It's a lovely way to serve root veggies when they're so plentiful.

1 medium sweet potato, scrubbed unpeeled
1 medium Yukon gold potato, scrubbed unpeeled
Juice of 1 lime, or to taste (about 2 tablespoons)
½ cup diced white onion
3 tablespoons finely chopped fresh cilantro
1 small jalapeño with some seeds, minced
½ teaspoon sea salt, or to taste

1. Poke holes with a fork in both potatoes to vent steam. Place potatoes in a microwave-safe dish. Cover well with unbleached parchment paper. "Micro-roast" (cook in the microwave oven*) on high until potatoes are nearly fork tender, yet still slightly firm in the center, about 5 minutes. Let sit covered in the off microwave or set aside to cook by carryover cooking until the potatoes further soften, about 3 minutes. Cool the potatoes and cut into ½-inch cubes.

(continued)

little
green
cooking
tip

Enjoy "earth-style" root veggies. When produce peels and skins are edible, such as potatoes and sweet potatoes, use them whenever possible. But first make sure to scrub them clean using a veggie scrub brush. And go organic whenever possible.

2. Add the cubed potatoes to a medium serving bowl. Gently stir (do not mash) in all the remaining ingredients until just combined. Serve as a side salad, as a scrambled organic egg topping, or just like traditional guacamole with organic tortilla chips.

PER SERVING: 80 calories, 0g total fat, 0g saturated fat, 0g trans fat, 0mg cholesterol, 260mg sodium, 18g total carbohydrate, 3g dietary fiber, 2g protein

*Microwave oven cooking times will vary. See page 39.

go local

One way to access seasonal, local produce is through a community supported agriculture program (CSA). A CSA is a partnership between public supporters and a nearby farm. Basically, when you join one, you're buying direct access to fresh, seasonal food—straight from the farm. Plus, you'll be helping the farm operate successfully because you'll be buying a share of the harvest in advance. The CSA season often runs from late spring or early summer through the fall. As a member (or "shareholder") you'll receive a weekly allotment (or "share") of produce—or whatever else your CSA membership provides, including eggs, flowers, and more. To find a CSA near you, visit Local Harvest at www.localharvest.org/csa.

rock the boat hummus

JALAPEÑO HUMMUS IN CUCUMBER BOATS

Makes 4 servings: ½ cup each

If you were one of those kids that got a kick out of ants-on-a-log, you'll want to fix my made-over adult version of it. I chose to go with hummus instead of peanut butter and cucumber instead of celery. And the "ants" are now parsley. Okay, so it's not really ants-on-a-log anymore, but you'll get a kick out of it anyway.

1 large hothouse cucumber, unpeeled and cut in half lengthwise

1 (15-ounce) can organic chickpeas (with no added salt),
    drained (do not rinse)

1 small jalapeño with some seeds, stem removed

1 large clove garlic, peeled

2 tablespoons tahini (sesame seed paste)

Juice of 1 small or ½ large lemon, or to taste (about 2 tablespoons)

2 tablespoons extra-virgin olive oil, or to taste

¾ teaspoon sea salt, or to taste

3 tablespoons chopped fresh flat-leaf parsley or cilantro

1. With a grapefruit spoon or small paring knife and a melon baller, carefully carve out the cucumber flesh, and reserve, leaving about ⅛ inch of flesh on the skin. Set the cucumber "boats" aside, upside down on a clean kitchen towel or sheet of un- bleached paper towel so juices can drain off.

2. Add the cucumber flesh to a blender container along with the chickpeas, jalapeño, garlic, tahini, lemon juice, oil, and salt. Cover and puree on low until thick and creamy, pulsing if neces- sary. Taste and adjust seasoning, if necessary.

3. Spoon ½ cup of the hummus into each cucumber "boat." (You'll have enough hummus to refill the boats.) Sprinkle with the parsley. Serve as an appetizer with fresh whole-grain pita bread wedges or cherry tomatoes.

PER SERVING: 230 calories, 12g total fat, 1.5g saturated fat, 0g trans fat, 0mg cholesterol, 460mg sodium, 23g total carbohydrate, 6g dietary fiber, 8g protein

little **green** cooking tip

Kick up the kidlike fun. Call it eco-fun. Have your kids help make the cup, bowl, or "boat;" you'll be using every edible part of the foods, which means no waste . . . just great taste. And the kids will enjoy eating what they've created.

use it, don't lose it

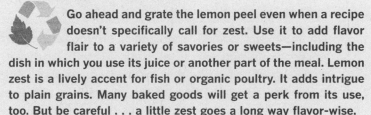

Go ahead and grate the lemon peel even when a recipe doesn't specifically call for zest. Use it to add flavor flair to a variety of savories or sweets—including the dish in which you use its juice or another part of the meal. Lemon zest is a lively accent for fish or organic poultry. It adds intrigue to plain grains. Many baked goods will get a perk from its use, too. But be careful . . . a little zest goes a long way flavor-wise.

baba ghanoush
à la skillet

MIDDLE EASTERN SKILLET-SMOKED EGGPLANT DIP

Makes 6 servings: ⅓ cup each

Eggplant is most enjoyable to me in late summer and early autumn. That's when I find myself diving into this uncommonly divine dip almost daily. I used to roast the whole eggplant in the oven, but it took about 45 minutes. That's so not green. I had to find a way to make this a luscious, lower-carbon part of my recipe repertoire. Luckily, "lid cooking" works. Now we all can have our dipping desires satisfied more sustainably.

1 medium eggplant, unpeeled, cut into ¼-inch cubes
⅓ cup chopped white onion
1 large clove garlic, chopped
¼ cup extra-virgin olive oil
Juice and zest of 1 lemon, or to taste (about 3 tablespoons juice)
2 tablespoons tahini (sesame seed paste)
½ teaspoon sea salt, or to taste
2 tablespoons chopped fresh flat-leaf parsley

1. Add the eggplant, onion, garlic, and oil to a large stick-resistant skillet. Stir to coat eggplant with the oil. Set skillet over medium heat, cover, and cook, stirring twice, until the onion and eggplant are softened, but not completely cooked through, about 10 minutes. Stir, cover, and turn off the heat. Let "lid cook" (cook covered while the burner is off) until the eggplant is completely softened, about 8 minutes. Let cool slightly.

2. Combine the cooled eggplant-onion mixture with the lemon juice, tahini, and salt in a medium bowl. Mash with a potato masher until you reach a desired consistency. (Alternatively, place the eggplant mixture into a blender container with the lemon juice, tahini, and salt. Cover and puree on low until combined, about 30 seconds, then on high until smooth, about 30 seconds more.)

3. Pour the eggplant dip into a serving bowl. Chill in the refrigerator. Taste and adjust seasoning, if necessary. Top with the parsley and some of the lemon zest and serve at room temperature. Enjoy as an appetizer with fresh whole-grain pita bread wedges.

PER SERVING: 140 calories, 12g total fat, 1.5g saturated fat, 0g trans fat, 0mg cholesterol, 200mg sodium, 7g total carbohydrate, 3g dietary fiber, 2g protein

use it, don't lose it

When chopping parsley or other herbs that have non-woody stems, don't worry about being so precise and picking off leaves and leaving all of the stems. You can use both the leaves and the thin, tender stems. Saves time and waste.

little **green** cooking tip

When a recipe requires roasting, put your eco-thinking cap on and consider if it can be prepared in a greener way. Many veggies, like eggplant, can be diced and then basically pan-roasted—with "lid cooking."

utterly addictive artichoke dip

CREAMY SCALLION, SPINACH, AND ARTICHOKE DIP

Makes 8 servings: ½ cup each

One of the most decadent, palate-pleasing appetizers is spinach-artichoke dip. I like my whole-wheat flour–spiked, "micro-steamed" spinach—but still 100% delicious—version better than what I find at a family-style chain restaurant because I know what's in mine. And I know, without a doubt, it's healthier for the planet.

1 pound fresh baby spinach
2 tablespoons extra-virgin olive oil
3 scallions, green and white parts, minced
2 large cloves garlic, minced
¼ cup stone-ground whole-wheat flour
⅔ cup organic half-and-half, at room temperature
Juice of ½ small lemon (about 1 tablespoon)
½ teaspoon vegetarian Worcestershire sauce* or
    hot pepper sauce
1 teaspoon sea salt, or to taste
½ cup freshly grated organic or locally produced
    Parmesan cheese
⅓ cup organic sour cream, at room temperature
1½ cups chopped steamed fresh artichoke hearts or
    1 (9-ounce) package thawed frozen artichoke hearts, chopped
½ cup shredded organic or locally produced Monterey Jack cheese

1. Firmly mound the spinach in a large microwave-safe dish. (Do not add water.) "Micro-steam" (cook in the microwave**) on high until the spinach is fully wilted and steaming hot, about 3 minutes. Set aside. (Do not drain.)

little *green* cooking tip

To help shrink cooking time—and use less cooking energy—take the chill off ingredients from the fridge, like butter, milk, half-n-half, and sour cream. Let premeasured portions of them sit on the counter to warm to room temperature before cooking. But keep them safe—let sit at room temp for no more than 2 hours.

2. Heat the oil in a large skillet over medium heat. Add the scallions and sauté for 1 minute. Add the garlic and sauté for 30 seconds. Add the flour, stirring constantly for 1 minute. Slowly pour in the half-and-half; stir briskly, smashing with the back of the spatula or spoon to prevent lumping, until the mixture is smooth. Stir in the lemon juice, Worcestershire sauce, and salt. Turn off the heat and stir in the Parmesan cheese until melted and smooth. Stir in the sour cream, steamed spinach, artichoke hearts, and Monterey Jack cheese. Taste and adjust seasoning, if necessary.

3. Serve immediately with salsa (or try with Green Green Salsa on page 54) and organic blue corn tortilla chips.

PER SERVING: 160 calories, 9g total fat, 4g saturated fat, 0g trans fat, 15mg cholesterol, 520mg sodium, 14g total carbohydrate, 6g dietary fiber, 7g protein

*Choose a vegetarian Worcestershire sauce which contains no anchovies.
**Microwave cooking times will vary. See page 39.

go local

Lovers of Parmesan cheese will tell you that Parmigiano-Reggiano from Italy is the best Parmesan available. If you live on the East Coast, cheese shipped from Italy logically doesn't leave as large of an environmental footprint as if you live on the West Coast. And there are excellent cheeses made in America that you might want to consider. One of those is eighteen month–aged American Grana that can be used in any recipe that calls for a Parmesan cheese.

tomato velvet

RAW "CREAM" OF TOMATO SOUP

Makes 4 servings: 1 cup each

A gooey grilled cheese sandwich and piping hot tomato soup is one of those dynamic dining duos. But if I'm grilling a sandwich, then I like to pair it with something that doesn't require cooking. That's called finding a sustainable "sweet spot." This righteously creamy (from avocado!) raw soup recipe is my recommended match for a crispy grilled fresh mozzarella cheese sandwich—or just plain toast.

2 medium vine-ripened or 3 large plum tomatoes, quartered
1 Hass avocado, pitted and peeled
1½ cups low-sodium vegetable broth
1 small shallot, coarsely chopped
1 small clove garlic
3 tablespoons extra-virgin olive oil
1 tablespoon aged red wine vinegar, or to taste
1¼ teaspoons sea salt, or to taste
½ teaspoon freshly ground black pepper, or to taste

1. Add the tomatoes to a blender container. Cover and blend on low for 15 seconds.

2. Add all of the remaining ingredients to the blender container. Cover and blend on low until velvety smooth, about 1½ minutes. (Blend in batches, if necessary.)

3. Chill in the refrigerator for at least 1 hour. Taste and adjust seasoning, if necessary. Stir in additional broth for a thinner consistency, if desired.

4. Pour into 4 soup bowls and serve cool or at room temperature.

PER SERVING: 180 calories, 16g total fat, 2g saturated fat, 0g trans fat, 0mg cholesterol, 790mg sodium, 8g total carbohydrate, 3g dietary fiber, 1g protein

little
green
cooking
tip

It's not necessary to add cream to a recipe that you want to be creamy. If it's a hot veggie soup, for instance, cook it with the addition of diced potatoes, then puree all of the soup. Once pureed, the cooked potatoes will provide you with dreamy creaminess. If it's a cold soup, adding avocado, then pureeing, will give you velvety lusciousness.

zoom shroom soup

SAUVIGNON BLANC MUSHROOM-ONION SOUP IN MINUTES

Makes 7 servings: 1 cup each

Growing up in the seventies, canned creamy mushroom soup was always on hand in the pantry. My entire family loved it, except me. I think it was a texture thing. So now that I'm all grown up, I decided to come up with a recipe that was fresher and without all the goop. This is it. Now I can happily join in on the mushroom soup moments. You can, too.

¼ cup extra-virgin olive oil

1 large white onion, finely diced

24 ounces fresh wild mushrooms, such as cremini (baby portobellos) or shiitake, brushed clean, stemmed, thinly sliced

2 teaspoons finely chopped fresh thyme

½ cup Sauvignon Blanc or other white wine

3 tablespoons stone-ground whole-wheat flour

3 cups low-sodium vegetable broth

⅓ cup organic heavy cream (optional)

2½ teaspoons sea salt, or to taste

¼ teaspoon freshly ground black pepper, or to taste

Few drops of hot pepper sauce, or to taste

1. Heat the oil in a large saucepan over medium heat. Add the onion and mushrooms and cover. Cook, stirring once halfway through, until the onions are translucent and mushrooms are just softened, about 10 minutes.

(continued)

little *green* cooking tip

Cook with a wine that you'll actually drink. So when a recipe calls for ½ cup of wine, you won't have to dump the rest or put it back in the fridge or cabinet to use who-knows-when. And remember, go with an organic or bio-dynamic wine when possible. Try one from Frey Vineyards or Cooper Mountain Vineyards.

Autumn

2. Increase heat to medium-high, remove the lid, and cook while stirring for 1 minute.

3. Add the thyme and wine and stir for 1 minute. Add the flour and stir for 30 seconds.

4. Stir in the broth and bring soup to a full boil, uncovered.

5. Turn off the heat. Stir in the cream (if using). Add salt, pepper, and hot pepper sauce and stir. Ladle into mugs or cups and serve.

PER SERVING: 140 calories, 8g total fat, 1g saturated fat, 0g trans fat, 0mg cholesterol, 900mg sodium, 12g total carbohydrate, 2g dietary fiber, 4g protein

go local

If you haven't checked lately, nice wines are being produced all throughout the United States, including Missouri and Texas, not just in the vineyards along our West and East coasts. Aim to cook with those same locally produced wines, too. They'll be less traveled. Some are organic or biodynamic—a definite eco-plus! And many are downright delicious.

smashing sweet potato soup

EARTH-STYLE PUREED SWEET POTATO SOUP

Makes 4 servings: 1 cup each

Sometimes the best approach is "the simpler the better," like for this soup. This velvety cup of pleasure uses the sweet potato peel, too. I refer to that as "earth-style" cuisine. And that helps to make this vibrant orange-colored soup green.

2 medium sweet potatoes, scrubbed unpeeled, and diced*
4 cups low-sodium vegetable or organic chicken broth, or to taste
1¼ teaspoons sea salt, or to taste
Several drops of hot pepper sauce, or to taste

1. Add the sweet potatoes and broth to a large saucepan. Cover and bring to a boil over high heat. Reduce heat to medium-high, and cook until the potatoes are nearly softened, about 8 minutes. Turn off the heat. Let the soup "lid cook" (cook covered while the burner is off) until the potatoes are fully softened and easily mashed, about 12 minutes.

2. Mash soup with a potato masher for a home-style consistency. (For a velvety smooth texture, use an immersion blender until pureed, about 1 minute.)

3. Stir in additional broth for thinner consistency, if desired. Add salt and hot pepper sauce. Serve immediately.

PER SERVING: 120 calories, 0g total-fat, 0g saturated fat, 0g trans fat, 0mg cholesterol, 930mg sodium, 26g total carbohydrate, 4g dietary fiber, 2g protein

---

*Note: Peel off the sweet potato skins before dicing the sweet potatoes if you desire a peel-free soup. Then compost the peels.

little *green* cooking tip

Unless you're working with eco-friendly recipes, like those in this book, lengthy ingredient lists may mean many of the ingredients only get partially used—which can create waste. For those recipes, plan ahead and find uses for all of the ingredients. Otherwise, go for short ingredient lists. Cooking simply can be a green thing!

go local

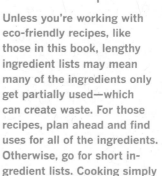

Need to "beef" up your dicing and slicing skills? Look for a knife skills class at a cooking school near you. If in New York, or planning a trip to the city, take a recreational class at the Institute of Culinary Education: www.iceculinary.com.

fennel and beans

ITALIAN FENNEL SALAD WITH BEANS

Makes 4 servings: 1 cup each

The form of fennel with the big bulb that we eat as a veggie is cultivated in the U.S., not just the Mediterranean, even though it's called Florence (or Italian) fennel. And it's 100 percent edible—the base, the stems, and the feathery leaves, or fronds, which look like dillweed. Since you can use every part of the fennel leaving virtually no waste, it's a particularly green vegetable. And since it can be eaten raw, it's extra-green.

2 tablespoons extra-virgin olive oil

1 tablespoon aged red wine vinegar

1 (15-ounce) can organic white cannellini or
    Great Northern beans, drained (do not rinse)

¼ cup finely diced red onion

1 large vine-ripened tomato, seeded and diced

1 small fennel bulb, trimmed, cored, cut
    into short matchstick-size strips or finely diced
    (reserve fronds)

¼ cup finely chopped fresh basil leaves, or mixture of
    basil and flat-leaf parsley

½ teaspoon sea salt, or to taste

¼ teaspoon freshly ground black pepper, or to taste

1. Whisk together the oil and vinegar in a medium serving bowl.

2. Stir in the remaining ingredients and let the salad stand at least 20 minutes.

3. Stir, taste, and adjust seasoning, if necessary. Serve at room temperature. If desired, sprinkle with some of the reserved fennel fronds.

PER SERVING: 180 calories, 8g total fat, 1g saturated fat, 0g trans fat, 0mg cholesterol, 350mg sodium, 21g total carbohydrate, 6g dietary fiber, 6g protein

little
green
cooking
tip

Go ahead. Chop up and add the fennel stems to this salad if you're a fennel fan. Otherwise save them for another meal and toss them onto a leafy salad or into a stir-fry.

use it, don't lose it

autumn black bean salad

CHERRY TOMATO, CHARD, AND BLACK BEAN SALAD WITH SPICY LIME VINAIGRETTE

Makes 4 servings: ¾ cup each

Swiss chard is one of those veggies I nearly always ate cooked. But I now enjoy it raw—leaves and stalks and all. If you're looking for a use for chard when it's plentiful, give this salad a shot. I think you might become happily hooked. Then if you're anything like me, you'll double the portion and have it as a vegetarian no-cook entrée.

Juice of 1 lime (about 2 tablespoons)
2 tablespoons extra-virgin olive oil
1 small jalapeño with some seeds, minced
1 large clove garlic, minced
¾ teaspoon sea salt, or to taste
1½ cups finely chopped fresh green or red chard leaves and tender stalks
1 (15-ounce) can organic black beans, drained (do not rinse)
10 cherry tomatoes, sliced
⅓ cup finely diced red onion

1. Whisk together the lime juice, oil, jalapeño, garlic, and salt in a medium serving bowl.

(continued)

little
green
cooking
tip

Just because you always cook a veggie, doesn't mean it needs to be cooked. Though not all veggies can be enjoyed raw, most can. Chard, green asparagus, and beets are examples of veggies you can go raw with. Enter the green zone and try it.

2. Add the chard, beans, tomato, and red onion and gently toss.

3. Serve at room temperature.

PER SERVING: 160 calories, 7g total fat, 1g saturated fat, 0g trans fat, 0mg cholesterol, 580mg sodium, 20g total carbohydrate, 5g dietary fiber, 6g protein

use it, don't lose it

If you don't use all of the chard stalks in this salad, try them quickly cooked in a stir-fry or with pasta—similar to the way you might use asparagus.

speckled carrot salad

CARROT SALAD WITH BLACK SEEDLESS RAISINS

Makes 5 servings: ½ cup each

Like probably anyone who's ever been to a Whole Foods Market or other specialty food shop, once you go, you can't stop going. It's a healthy type of addiction—although it can be expensive. I love to stop at their fresh food bars on occasion and pick up a few new items. I recently tried a prepared carrot salad. It was so wholly satisfying and refreshing that I had to create my own recipe for it.

4 large carrots, scrubbed unpeeled, and coarsely grated

⅔ cup black seedless raisins or dried tart cherries

¼ cup mayonnaise

2 tablespoons local apricot or other fruit spread or homemade jam or 1 tablespoon mild floral honey

Juice of ½ lemon (about 1½ tablespoons)

1½ teaspoons white wine vinegar

1½ teaspoons sesame oil

1 teaspoon stone-ground mustard

1 teaspoon grated scrubbed unpeeled gingerroot

¼ teaspoon sea salt, or to taste

¼ teaspoon freshly ground black pepper, or to taste

Gently stir together all the ingredients in a medium serving bowl. Taste and adjust seasoning, if necessary. Serve cool or at room temperature.

PER SERVING: 190 calories, 10g total fat, 1.5g saturated fat, 0g trans fat, 5mg cholesterol, 230mg sodium, 25g total carbohydrate, 2g dietary fiber, 1g protein

use it, don't lose it

 When a recipe requires only half of a fruit, slice the remaining fruit and add to your accompanying beverage, such as freshly brewed iced tea, water, or a cocktail. And if a recipe hands you leftover lemons, make fresh lemonade. It's delicious any time of the year.

little **green** cooking tip

If you don't feel like cooking, go to an eco-conscious market near you for something to eat in the short term but also for inspiration to create your own green recipes.

the champagne of salads

CHAMPAGNE ARUGULA SALAD WITH RED DELICIOUS APPLES AND WALNUTS

Makes 4 servings: 1½ cups each

When it's autumn time, it's prime time for apples. Meticulously biting your way around a caramel apple is probably one of the most scrumptious ways to enjoy them. But if your dentist is doing the judging, this salad will take home the tooth-friendly prize—as it won't destroy all of that fancy dental work! If you're looking for a planet-pleasing (and dentist-pleasing) salad for a sophisticated supper or soiree, this salad will make anyone smile. Just be sure to keep total fat in check the rest of the day to assure a healthy smile.

⅓ cup walnut oil
2 tablespoons Champagne vinegar or white wine vinegar
2 teaspoons aged balsamic vinegar
1 tablespoon mild floral honey or turbinado or Demerara sugar
¼ teaspoon sea salt, or to taste
¼ teaspoon freshly ground black pepper, or to taste
1 large Red Delicious apple, thinly sliced
5 cups arugula leaves
½ small red onion, very thinly sliced
4 ounces organic or locally produced Parmesan cheese, shaved (optional)
½ cup raw walnut halves

1. Whisk together the oil, both vinegars, and honey in a large serving bowl. Add salt and pepper.

2. Add the apple slices, arugula, and onion to the Champagne-walnut vinaigrette. Toss to combine. Sprinkle with the cheese (if using) and walnuts and serve.

PER SERVING: 300 calories, 26g total fat, 2.5g saturated fat, 0g trans fat, 0mg cholesterol, 160mg sodium, 17g total carbohydrate, 3g dietary fiber, 3g protein

little **green** cooking tip

If preparing and serving this in a nice serving bowl that you don't want to scratch, use a silicone-coated whisk for preparing the dressing. That way you won't need to dirty two bowls—one for mixing and one for serving.

a planet-friendly bite

About three out of every four of the world's flowering plant species rely on pollinators—such as insects and birds—to carry pollen from the male to the female parts of flowers to reproduce. And roughly one out of every three bites of food we eat requires bees for pollination. According to the National Academy of Sciences, there's direct evidence of the North American decline of some pollinator species. Unfortunately, honeybees have been disappearing in the U.S.—which may be connected to something called Colony Collapse Disorder. But you can help; plant wildflower seeds! Grow them in your garden to give bees a healthy home if you desire. And be sure to purchase foods from local organic farmers to keep pesticides out of the environment—and make it bee-friendlier. You can also support companies who are helping to fund research into this environmental threat. Visit Pollinator Partnership for more: www.pollinator.org.

little **green** cooking tip

When sprinkling organic or locally produced cheese on a salad, use a sharp, full-flavored one, like Roquefort or other blue cheese. A little bit of high-flavored, full-fat cheese will be more satisfying than a lot of flavor-lacking, low-fat cheese.

bartlettuce

BARTLETT PEAR AND MESCLUN SALAD WITH SUGAR-N-SPICE PECANS

Makes 4 servings: 2 cups each

Iceberg lettuce swimming in a pool of bottled ranch dressing was what I considered the only salad worth eating when I was sweet sixteen. Boy, times have changed. I'm a little older now—and thankfully a little wiser, and greener, around the edges. A perfect salad for me today is this one. For salad perfection with a sprinkling of pecan divinity and fresh pear vinaigrette, look no further. This'll please any salad aficionado at any age.

    3 tablespoons extra-virgin olive oil
    3 tablespoons apple cider vinegar
    2 medium Bartlett or Asian pears, thinly sliced
    ½ small red onion, thinly sliced
    ½ teaspoon sea salt, or to taste
    5 cups mesclun mix or mixed baby greens
    ⅓ cup crumbled organic or locally produced Roquefort cheese (optional)
    ⅓ cup All That's Nice Nuts (page 176) or raw pecan halves

(continued)

Autumn

205

1. Place the oil, vinegar, ¼ of the pear slices, ½ of the sliced onion, and salt in a blender container. Cover and puree on low speed, about 15 seconds. Taste and adjust seasoning, if necessary.

2. Arrange the mesclun, the remaining sliced pears, and the remaining onion on a large serving platter or individual salad plates. Sprinkle with the cheese (if using) and pecans. Serve with the dressing on the side.

PER SERVING: 220 calories, 18g total fat, 2g saturated fat, 0g trans fat, 0mg cholesterol, 310mg sodium, 19g total carbohydrate, 4g dietary fiber, 2g protein

go local

Planning to add cheese to your salad? Visit your local cheesemonger and ask for a locally produced blue cheese that's piquant and pairs perfectly with pears and pecans. Hey East Coasters! Try Great Hill Blue in this recipe.

tabbouleh of the sea

TANGY TUNA TABBOULEH

Makes 4 servings: 1½ cups each

My mother is Lebanese, so I grew up eating tabbouleh. Little did I know it's an eco-friendly food. You don't need to cook the bulgur wheat since it is sold already steamed and then dried. Though many people will rehydrate it with boiling water, it's unnecessary. Just plain ol' cool fresh water will do the job, as I've done here. This isn't my mom's tried-n-true tabbouleh; it has a modern twist with tuna and basil. I don't know if my mother will approve of this nontraditional version, so let's keep it our secret!

little *green* cooking tip

Are you a vegetarian, flexitarian, or ecotarian? Many recipes, especially salads, that normally feature meat, poultry, or fish, can be prepared without. Simply skip the tuna from the Tabbouleh of the Sea recipe for a vegetarian tabbouleh—or tabbouleh of the land.

1 cup bulgur wheat

2 (6-ounce) cans minimal mercury albacore tuna, drained and flaked with a fork

½ of a large hothouse cucumber, unpeeled and finely diced

1 medium vine-ripened tomato, diced

¼ cup chopped fresh flat-leaf parsley

¼ cup chopped fresh basil (optional)

2 scallions, green and white parts, minced

1 large clove garlic, minced

⅓ cup extra-virgin olive oil

Juice of 1 lemon (about 3 tablespoons)

1 teaspoon sea salt, or to taste

½ teaspoon freshly ground black pepper, or to taste

1. Place the bulgur wheat in a medium bowl and completely cover with cool fresh water, about 1 cup. Let stand for 1 hour. Drain any remaining liquid.

2. Place the soaked bulgur wheat in a large serving bowl along with the tuna, cucumber, tomato, parsley, basil (if using), scallions, and garlic. Stir to combine.

3. Stir in the oil and lemon juice. Add salt and pepper.

4. If desired, stir in some lemon zest for added zing. Serve at room temperature.

PER SERVING: 410 calories, 20g total fat, 3g saturated fat, 0g trans fat, 25mg cholesterol, 880mg sodium, 32g total carbohydrate, 7g dietary fiber, 27g protein

a planet-friendly bite

To be an eco-conscious albacore tuna connoisseur, make sure to choose a variety with minimal mercury. When going the canned route, there's one environmentally conscientious brand that stands out: Wild Planet. Check them out: 1wildplanet.com.

Whenever there's a simple way to use less energy, just do it. And spread the word. Here's a simple green tip for cooking the turkey for this salad recipe: thin is in. Choose thin-sliced turkey cutlets or pound them with a kitchen mallet (½ inch or thinner). Place cutlets in a large stick-resistant skillet over medium-high heat. Cover and cook for 5 minutes. Flip cutlets and cook covered for 2 more minutes, or until cooked through.

cool curry turkey cups

CURRIED ORGANIC TURKEY SALAD WITH GRAPES IN LETTUCE BOWLS

Makes 4 servings: 1 stuffed lettuce bowl each

Not only is it cool to serve salad in an edible bowl made of lettuce, it's ultimately better for the environment—no bowl washing required. Though all you might really care about when you're actually eating this salad is how delicious it is.

2 cups cubed cooked boneless, skinless organic turkey breast, chilled
⅓ cup plain soy or organic yogurt
3 tablespoons mayonnaise
3 tablespoons mango chutney
2 teaspoons curry powder
1 teaspoon sea salt, or to taste
4 red radishes, diced
½ cup red or white seedless grapes, thinly sliced
1 tablespoon finely chopped fresh cilantro
4 leaves Bibb or Boston lettuce

1. Stir together the turkey, yogurt, mayonnaise, chutney, curry powder, and salt in a medium bowl. Add the radishes, grapes, and cilantro and stir.

2. Stuff each lettuce "bowl" with ¾ cup turkey salad. Enjoy with a fork or roll up and eat as a wrap.

PER SERVING: 250 calories, 9g total fat, 1.5g saturated fat, 0g trans fat, 75mg cholesterol, 700mg sodium, 14g total carbohydrate, 1g dietary fiber, 27g protein

use it, don't lose it

There's no need to buy an entire pound of turkey if you don't need to use an entire pound in the recipe. When you have the opportunity, befriend your butcher (if you haven't already) so you can then make specific requests, like for this recipe. If you're preparing turkey just for this dish, you'll need 14 ounces raw boneless turkey breast to yield 2 cups cubed cooked turkey.

VEGETARIAN DISHES

new age navel entrée

ORANGE-BULGUR STACK WITH TOMATOES, HERBS, AND ALMONDS

Makes 5 servings: 1 cup each

This recipe is like tabbouleh salad, but it's fruitier and nuttier. The fresh juices in this give it a refreshing flair. The nuts will make it extra-satisfying. And the shapely presentation will turn it into a savory spectacle. Serve this as an entrée, rather than a salad. You can plate fish or organic poultry on the side, if you like.

Juice of 4 medium navel oranges (about 1⅓ cups)
Juice of 1 lemon (about 3 tablespoons)
1 cup bulgur wheat
1 cup finely chopped fresh herbs, such as basil, mint, and flat-leaf parsley
4 medium or 3 large vine-ripened tomatoes, diced
2 scallions, green and white parts, minced
¼ cup extra-virgin olive oil
1 large clove garlic, minced
¾ teaspoon sea salt, or to taste
¼ teaspoon freshly ground black pepper, or to taste
½ cup slivered raw (natural) almonds or pine nuts

1. Pour the orange and lemon juices over bulgur wheat in a large bowl. Chill in the refrigerator at least 3 hours, or overnight.

2. Stir the herbs, tomatoes, scallions, oil, and garlic into the soaked bulgur wheat. Add salt and pepper. Chill in the refrigerator to let flavors blend, about 1 hour.

(continued)

little **green** cooking tip

Grain-based salads, such as quinoa or bulgur wheat that are mixed with seasonal produce, are planet-friendly. So turn those little green salads usually served like sides into big green entrées.

3. When ready to serve, stir well then drain of excess liquid into a little bowl or cup. (Use the excess liquid as a cold soup or as a healthy shot! You'll likely have about ¾ cup.)

4. Stir the almonds into the bulgur mixture. Firmly pack the mixture 1 cup at a time into a 1-cup dry measure and invert onto a plate. Alternatively, use a round biscuit cutter as a mold. Garnish the top of each stack with additional fresh herbs, if desired, and serve.

PER SERVING: 310 calories, 17g total fat, 2g saturated fat, 0g trans fat, 0mg cholesterol, 360mg sodium, 36g total carbohydrate, 8g dietary fiber, 7g protein

use it, don't lose it

Before you recycle a can, such as from vegetable broth or tomato puree, consider if it can be reused. Using a smooth-edged manual can opener, open both ends of the can, wash it, and dry it. Then, instead of using a measuring cup or buying a professional mold, use the can to perfectly form a molded or stacked salad, side, or entrée, like New Age Navel Entrée.

hot beans

SZECHUAN GREEN BEAN STIR-FRY

Makes 2 servings: 2 cups each

Even though I love to cook, sometimes I just want Chinese takeout. I probably order Szechuan green beans the most—it's tasty, filling, and healthy. I enjoy it as an entrée—so I've developed this recipe for you to do the same. Whenever you can make seasonal veggies the center of attention, it's going to be the greenest plate. I'm sure I'll still get takeout Chinese on occasion, but now that I've developed this stir-fry recipe, I'm sure I'll make it most often myself. So before you pick up the phone to place an order, try this out yourself. It's takeout worthy—only tastier.

2 tablespoons naturally brewed soy sauce

2 tablespoons sesame oil

2 tablespoons turbinado or Demerara sugar

1 tablespoon rice vinegar (preferably brown rice)

1 large clove garlic, minced

½ teaspoon grated scrubbed unpeeled gingerroot

¼ teaspoon crushed red pepper flakes

1½ pounds green beans, trimmed

2 tablespoons raw sesame seeds

1. Combine the soy sauce, oil, sugar, vinegar, garlic, gingerroot, and crushed red pepper in a small bowl. Set aside.

2. Add the green beans and ¼ cup fresh water to a large stick-resistant skillet or wok and set over high heat. Cover and cook, stirring once, until the green beans are crisp-tender, about 4 minutes.

3. Add the soy sauce mixture to the green beans and stir-fry until the sauce reduces slightly and lightly coats the beans, about 2 minutes. Turn off the heat. Add the sesame seeds and toss to coat.

4. Serve beans on a platter or in a medium serving bowl. Drizzle with the remaining sauce from the skillet and serve immediately.

PER SERVING: 350 calories, 19g total fat, 3g saturated fat, 0g trans fat, 0mg cholesterol, 930mg sodium, 41g total carbohydrate, 12g dietary fiber, 11g protein

little **green** cooking tip

For the eco-friendliest plate, make the veggies the center of the plate—the entrée. If you choose to enjoy organic meat, serve it on the side, rather than the other way around.

use it, don't lose it

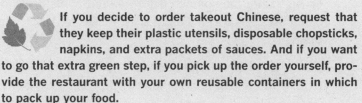

If you decide to order takeout Chinese, request that they keep their plastic utensils, disposable chopsticks, napkins, and extra packets of sauces. And if you want to go that extra green step, if you pick up the order yourself, provide the restaurant with your own reusable containers in which to pack up your food.

loaded veggie curry

EGGPLANT, SPINACH, ONION, AND CHICKPEA CURRY

Makes 8 servings: 1¼ cups each

While my idea of a food I could never live without is guacamole, my friend John's idea is a good curry. So my dear John, this recipe is for you (and all the other curry lovers out there). Though I have to admit, I might not want to live without this recipe, too. It definitely takes time to chop up all of the spinach, but look at it as a calming activity; there's no need to do it in a hurry. Besides, this makes such a large amount of curry, you'll be enjoying it for days.

2 pounds fresh baby spinach, finely chopped
¼ cup canola or peanut oil
1 large eggplant, unpeeled, cut into ½-inch cubes
1 extra-large or 2 medium red onions, finely chopped
1 (15-ounce) can organic chickpeas, drained (do not rinse)
1 serrano pepper with some seeds, halved lengthwise and
   thinly sliced
2 large cloves garlic, minced
1 tablespoon curry powder, or to taste
1 (14-ounce) can diced organic tomatoes
1½ tablespoons mango chutney
2 teaspoons sea salt, or to taste

1. Firmly mound the spinach in a large microwave-safe dish. (Do not add water.) "Micro-steam" (steam in the microwave oven*) on high until the spinach is fully wilted and steaming hot, about 3 minutes. (Work in batches, if necessary.) Set aside. Do not drain.

2. Heat the oil in a large stick-resistant skillet over medium-high heat. Add the eggplant, onion, chickpeas, serrano pepper, garlic, and curry powder and stir to coat with the oil. Cover and cook, stirring once, until the onion is soft, about 8 minutes.

3. Stir in the tomatoes, chutney, and salt. Cover and turn off the heat. Let "lid cook" (cook covered while the burner is off) until the eggplant is soft, about 3 minutes.

little *green* cooking tip

When you use your stovetop to cook one meal, but it makes enough leftover for two, three, or more meals, you're saving energy since you're only cooking once. That means not only are you shrinking your carbon footprint, you're saving valuable time.

4. Combine the spinach and the eggplant mixture in a large serving bowl. Cover with a lid or recycled aluminum foil and allow to steam until the flavors are blended and the eggplant is fully cooked, about 5 minutes. Taste and adjust seasoning, if necessary. Serve immediately or store in a covered container in the refrigerator for up to two days.

PER SERVING: 210 calories, 8g total fat, 0.5g saturated fat, 0g trans fat, 0mg cholesterol, 890mg sodium, 33g total carbohydrate, 11g dietary fiber, 7g protein

*Microwave oven cooking times will vary. See page 39.

a planet-friendly bite

When a recipe calls for lots of chopping, such as finely chopping 2 pounds of fresh baby spinach, you might be tempted to do it in a food processor. But try your best to give your chef's knife and a bamboo or Paperstone cutting board a workout. It'll take time for you to do all the chopping, but you'll feel good that you expended your own energy instead!

tlc panini

GRILLED HEIRLOOM TOMATO AND CHEESE SOURDOUGH SANDWICH

Makes 2 servings: 1 sandwich each

When heirloom tomatoes can be fresh-plucked from nearby (or backyard!) vines in early autumn, incorporate them as often as you can. Since they're at their succulent best, they add mouthwatering magic anywhere you add them. It's hard to imagine a grilled cheese sandwich needing any help, but abracadabra! It works—even for a food that's already amazing.

2 tablespoons extra-virgin olive oil

1 large clove garlic, minced

4 thick slices whole-grain sourdough bread

1½ ounces fresh organic or locally produced mozzarella cheese,
   thinly sliced

1 ounce organic or locally produced feta cheese,
   crumbled (optional)

1 medium or ½ large ripe heirloom or vine-ripened tomato,
   thinly sliced

⅛ teaspoon sea salt, or to taste

⅛ teaspoon crushed red pepper flakes, or to taste

¼ cup finely chopped arugula or other leafy green

1½ ounces organic or locally produced Asiago cheese,
   thinly sliced

1. Whisk together the oil and garlic in a small bowl. Rub with your fingers or brush 1 side of each bread slice with the garlic oil, using about 2 teaspoons total.

2. On 2 of the bread slices, arrange the mozzarella cheese, feta cheese (if using), and tomato. Add the salt and crushed red pepper. Top with the arugula and Asiago cheese and then top with the remaining bread slices, oil side down. Rub or brush tops of sandwiches with about 2 teaspoons of the remaining garlic oil.

little *green* cooking tip

When heirloom produce is available (and you can afford it!), choose it instead of its conventional counterpart. They're produced from many varieties of open-pollinated seeds—so generations to come can enjoy the tomatoes, potatoes, beans, and more from the natural seeds.

3. Heat a panini grill to medium-high heat. Place each sandwich oil side down in the grill. (Cook in batches, if necessary.) Rub or brush bread tops with the remaining 2 teaspoons oil, then cook until the sandwiches are golden brown and the cheese is melted, about 3 minutes. Serve while warm. (Alternatively, pan-toast each sandwich in a preheated skillet or grill pan over medium-high heat until lightly toasted on the bottom, about 1½ minutes; then flip, turn off the heat, and cook while the burner is off until lightly toasted and cheese is melted, about 1½ minutes more.)

PER SERVING: 490 calories, 29g total fat, 10g saturated fat, 0g trans fat, 40mg cholesterol, 810mg sodium, 38g total carbohydrate, 7g dietary fiber, 21g protein

go local

Looking for farmers' markets in your area? Or doing some travel in the U.S. and want to know where the markets are at your destination? Visit the USDA Farmers' Market Locator at http://apps.ams.usda.gov/FarmersMarkets. Search by a market's name or location for a full listing.

little
green
cooking
tip

When you want a hearty, protein-rich entrée, but don't want to fix something big and beefy, think eggs. Since they're quick cooking, organic eggs fit nicely into the low-carbon cuisine category—any time of the day.

don't cry for me omelet

ARGENTINE-ACCENTED POTATO AND ONION OMELET

Makes 3 servings: ⅓ of 12-inch omelet each

Any crying over chopped onions is worth it for this omelet. Those tears will turn into tears of joy because you're using green cooking methods—"micro-roasting" and "lid cooking"—and because you can't believe you've made the best-tasting egg dish ever. In fact, it's an omelet worthy of serving for a candlelit dinner. (By the way, that lit candle may help prevent crying when dicing onions—or stick the onion in the freezer for 10 minutes before dicing.)

1 medium russet potato with skin, scrubbed unpeeled,
    and cut into ½-inch cubes
2 tablespoons canola or peanut oil
1 large white onion, finely diced
2 teaspoons minced fresh oregano
1 teaspoon minced fresh thyme or ½ teaspoon minced fresh rosemary
¾ teaspoon sea salt, or to taste
¼ teaspoon cayenne pepper, or to taste (optional)
6 large organic eggs
¾ cup shredded organic or locally produced sharp white
    Cheddar cheese or Swiss cheese (optional)
¼ teaspoon freshly ground black pepper, or to taste

1. Arrange the potatoes in a single layer on a microwave-safe plate. Cover well with unbleached parchment paper. "Micro-roast" (cook in the microwave oven*) on high until the potato is nearly tender, about 3 minutes. Let sit covered in the off microwave to cook by carryover cooking and further soften, about 2 minutes.

2. Heat 1 tablespoon of the oil in a large stick-resistant skillet or saucepan over medium-high heat. Add the onion and sauté until the onion is just beginning to caramelize, about 5 minutes. Stir in the cooked potato, the oregano, thyme, ½ teaspoon of the salt, and cayenne (if using). Turn off the heat and cover to keep warm.

Big Green Cookbook

3. Meanwhile, whisk together the eggs, 1 tablespoon cold fresh water, the remaining ¼ teaspoon salt, and the black pepper in a medium bowl. (Alternatively, quickly whisk all of these ingredients directly into the heated, oil-coated skillet in step 4.)

4. Heat the remaining 1 tablespoon oil in a large stick-resistant skillet over medium-high heat and add the egg mixture. Tilt the pan slightly and use a silicone spatula to lift the edges of the omelet, allowing uncooked egg to flow under cooked portion. Cook until the omelet is nearly set, about 3 minutes. Cover with a lid and turn off the heat. Let "lid cook" (cook covered while the burner is off) until the omelet is fully cooked and set, yet still moist, about 3 minutes.

5. Sprinkle with the cheese, if using. Sprinkle half of the omelet with the potato-onion filling. Slide the omelet out of the pan onto a platter, while using the edge of the pan to help fold the unfilled side over the potato-onion filling. Taste and adjust seasoning, if necessary. Serve immediately.

PER SERVING: 340 calories, 20g total fat, 4g saturated fat, 0g trans fat, 425mg cholesterol, 710mg sodium, 25g total carbohydrate, 3g dietary fiber, 16g protein

*Microwave oven cooking times will vary. See page 39.

use it, don't lose it

 Have extra eggs? Start a new holiday tradition. Hard-cook them (see page 251) and color them for a Halloween basket. Foods that stain, like fresh or frozen blueberries, can work as dyes. Make devilish deviled eggs from them, too, using slices of olives, carrots, and fresh herb leaves or stems to create spooky faces.

sesame celery root batons

MINI CELERY ROOT STICKS WITH SESAME DRESSING

Makes 4 servings: ½ cup each

Stir things up a bit. Add late-autumn pizzazz to the plate with a veggie that's no ordinary veggie. It's the extraordinary celery root. Extraordinary because of its looks! It's definitely the ugly ducking of root vegetables—knobbiness and all. Its taste, however, is a refreshing change of pace. Go ahead, give it a try. You might fall for it.

1 tablespoon canola or peanut oil
1 pound celery root (celeriac), peeled,
    cut into matchstick-size strips
1 scallion, green and white parts, minced
1 tablespoon raw black sesame seeds
    (or mixture of black and white sesame seeds)
1½ teaspoons sesame oil
1½ teaspoons rice vinegar (preferably brown rice)
½ teaspoon sea salt, or to taste

1. Heat the canola oil in a large skillet over medium-high heat. Add the celery root and stir to coat with the oil. Reduce heat to medium, cover, and cook, stirring halfway through, until the celery root is nearly done, yet still crunchy, about 5 minutes.

2. Stir in the scallion, sesame seeds, sesame oil, vinegar, and salt. Cover and turn off the heat. Let "lid cook" (cook covered while the burner is off) until the celery root is fully cooked, yet al dente, about 5 more minutes. Serve immediately.

PER SERVING: 110 calories, 7g total fat, 0.5g saturated fat, 0g trans fat, 0mg cholesterol, 410mg sodium, 11g total carbohydrate, 2g dietary fiber, 2g protein

little *green* cooking tip

See lots of a veggie at a market? It often means it's at its seasonal peak—the best time to buy it. The same applies to produce that's not über-popular, like celery root. Enjoy it while in season—cooked or raw. In fact, choose the seasonal produce, then choose the recipe, not vice versa.

brussels and balsamic

CARAMELIZED BALSAMIC BRUSSELS SPROUTS WITH SHALLOTS

Makes 2 servings: 1 cup each

When Brussels sprouts are overcooked, I can't bear those funny-smelling mini cabbage heads. When they're fresh, seasonal, and properly cooked, please pass those immediately. When they're cooked in an earth-friendly fashion—or "lid cooked"—please pass me seconds. But before you do, take a bite of these aged balsamic-splashed sprouts. They're noteworthy—and nose-worthy.

1½ tablespoons canola or peanut oil

12 ounces Brussels sprouts, trimmed, thinly sliced lengthwise

1 large shallot, sliced

1 teaspoon aged balsamic vinegar

½ teaspoon sea salt, or to taste

⅛ teaspoon freshly ground black pepper, or to taste

2 teaspoons extra-virgin olive oil

1. Heat the canola oil in a large skillet over medium-high heat. Add the Brussels sprouts and shallot. Cook while stirring until the sprouts and shallots are just beginning to caramelize, about 5 minutes. Cover and turn off the heat. Let "lid cook" (cook covered while the burner is off) until the sprouts are just tender, about 5 minutes.

little
green
cooking
tip

Skinny-size your veggies before preparing them, even if you don't usually slice or dice them. It'll speed up cooking, which will use less cooking energy—and less of your time. Try it with Brussels sprouts, baby potatoes, and baby carrots.

(continued)

2. Stir in the aged balsamic vinegar. Add the salt and pepper. Drizzle with the olive oil and serve.

PER SERVING: 210 calories, 16g total fat, 1.5g saturated fat, 0g trans fat, 0mg cholesterol, 620mg sodium, 16g total carbohydrate, 5g dietary fiber, 5g protein

a planet-friendly bite

What can you do if you're cooking a lot, but don't want "green guilt" that comes with using a lot of energy? If you haven't already done so, switch your energy source to wind power—or other green power. You don't need to install your own windmill or solar panels, unless, of course, you have the resources to do so. Instead, just visit www.eere.energy.gov/greenpower/buying/buying_power.shtml to find out how you can make the switch.

ali baba beans

PRESSURE-COOKED LEBANESE GREEN BEANS WITH TOMATOES

Makes 4 servings: 1½ cups each

Loubya bi Zayt is one dish my mother made regularly when I was growing up. It's slow-stewed green beans, although she usually stewed cubes of beef along with hers to make it more of a meal. Sorry, Mom . . . this is a green cookbook. So here's an ecotarian version of my own. And to make it extra-green, I've converted it into a pressure cooker recipe—so it'll stew in a few minutes instead of an hour. While my mother may not approve of my messing with culinary tradition, I hope you'll approve of how it tastes.

3 tablespoons extra-virgin olive oil

1 large yellow onion, minced

1 large clove garlic, minced

1½ pounds green beans, trimmed

3 medium vine-ripened tomatoes, chopped

2 teaspoons turbinado or Demerara sugar

1 teaspoon sea salt, or to taste

½ teaspoon ground allspice or cinnamon, or to taste

1. Heat the oil in a pressure cooker over medium heat. Add the onion and sauté until fragrant and nearly soft, about 3 minutes. Add the garlic and sauté until garlic is fragrant, about 1 minute.

2. Stir in the beans, tomatoes, sugar, salt, allspice, and ¼ cup fresh water.

3. Close the pressure cooker lid and turn to the high pressure setting. Increase the burner heat to high. Once the pressure cooker hisses, adjust the heat as necessary to maintain high pressure with gentle hissing and cook for 3 minutes.

4. Turn off the pressure cooker or remove from the heat. Carefully release the pressure and remove the lid. Taste and adjust seasoning, if necessary, and serve as a side dish or as a stew with whole-wheat couscous or orzo.

PER SERVING: 190 calories, 11g total fat, 1.5g saturated fat, 0g trans fat, 0mg cholesterol, 590mg sodium, 23g total carbohydrate, 7g dietary fiber, 4g protein

---

a planet-friendly bite

 Recycle your glass bottles, such as olive oil bottles. Recycling just one glass bottle may save enough energy to watch three hours of your favorite eco-friendly television shows, like *Emeril Green* on Discovery's Planet Green channel.

little ***green*** cooking tip

A pressure cooker is a beloved item in a low-carbon kitchen because you're cooking with pressure instead of with extra electricity or gas. The result is stewlike lusciousness in a few minutes, not an hour.

sweet-n-sour savoy

GOLDEN DELICIOUS SWEET-N-SOUR SAVOY CABBAGE

Makes 4 servings: 1 cup each

Two standout ingredients of autumn are apples and cabbage. Unite them in a harmony of sweet-n-sour sublimity, and you'll remember why you're meant to enjoy produce when it's at its peak. Pair this recipe with organic turkey sausage, and you'll have found culinary ecstasy on a plate.

3 tablespoons unsalted organic butter or canola oil
1 medium white onion, very thinly sliced
1 large head savoy cabbage, very thinly sliced
1 large Golden Delicious apple, very thinly sliced
¼ cup turbinado or Demerara sugar
⅓ cup apple cider vinegar
¾ teaspoon sea salt, or to taste
¼ teaspoon freshly ground black pepper, or to taste

1. Add the butter, onion, and cabbage to a large saucepan and set over medium-high heat. Sauté until the cabbage is slightly wilted and has reduced in volume by about half, about 8 minutes.

2. Stir in the apple, sugar, and vinegar. Cover and cook, stirring once, until the cabbage is soft and apples are nearly tender, about 4 minutes.

3. Turn off the heat. Let "lid cook" (cook covered while the burner is off) until the apples are soft, about 4 minutes. Add salt and pepper and serve.

PER SERVING: 210 calories, 9g total fat, 6g saturated fat, 0g trans fat, 25mg cholesterol, 490mg sodium, 33g total carbohydrate, 7g dietary fiber, 4g protein

---

little **green** cooking tip

The less processed a food, the greener it'll be. It usually has more flavor characteristics—so the tastier it'll be, too. So pass on the white granulated sugar. Try turbinado or Demerara sugar whenever a recipe just calls for sugar. Pick an organic brand when you can.

a planet-friendly bite

To reduce your exposure to pesticide residue on produce, wash produce thoroughly in cold water and go organic when possible. Eat a variety of foods, too. If you need to prioritize purchasing of organic foods due to cost, check out the list of produce from the Environmental Working Group at http://foodnews.org/index.php. You'll find produce listed in order of the level of potentially harmful chemicals they contain. Try to at least go organic for the first dozen fruits and veggies listed, which includes apples. Onions are the best; they contain the lowest level of pesticides of all fruits and veggies listed!

tropicalaf

NUT-STUDDED STEWED MANGO QUINOA PILAF

Makes 4 servings: 1 cup each

This is not your light and fluffy pilaf. It's actually meant to be a bit mushy like oatmeal or polenta, but oh so much yummier. And since it uses quinoa, it cooks in minutes. That makes it an environmentally friendly winner. It's a taste winner, too, as you might just be tempted to eat this comfort food straight from the pan!

1 cup quinoa, rinsed and drained

2 cups plain unsweetened soymilk*

1 large mango, peeled, pitted, and diced

1 teaspoon sea salt, or to taste

¼ teaspoon ground cumin

½ teaspoon pure coconut extract (optional)

2 tablespoons finely chopped fresh cilantro

2 tablespoons finely chopped fresh mint

¼ cup slivered raw (natural) almonds or coarsely chopped macadamia nuts

little *green* cooking tip

Coconut milk is usually shipped from more tropical locations. To get full coconut flavor without the can (and without the fat), choose a little bottle of coconut extract that you'll be able to use for months and months. Just a tiny drop provides that distinctive coconut essence whenever you desire.

(continued)

Autumn

1. Combine the quinoa, soymilk, mango, salt, cumin, and coconut extract (if using) in a medium saucepan. Place over high heat. Bring to a boil. Cover and turn off the heat. Let "lid cook" (cook covered while the burner is off) until the quinoa is tender, fully cooked, and liquid is absorbed, about 30 minutes. Taste and adjust seasoning, if necessary.

2. Stir in the fresh herbs and almonds and serve immediately.

PER SERVING: 310 calories, 8g total fat, 1g saturated fat, 0g trans fat, 0mg cholesterol, 650mg sodium, 49g total carbohydrate, 6g dietary fiber, 12g protein

*For a less sticky version, use 1½ cups soymilk and "lid cook" for about 25 minutes.

a planet-friendly bite

If trying to eat less meat for environmental, health, or other reasons, getting enough protein becomes more of a nutritional priority. That's where quinoa comes in. It has more protein than any other whole grain. Plus, it cooks super-fast, unlike many other whole grains that can take a full hour!

pink and green pilaf

MINTED PILAF WITH POMEGRANATE SEEDS

Makes 4 servings: ¾ cup each

Since couscous is a quick-cooking pasta, it means nearly no cooking time is required on your end. That leaves you extra time to remove the precious juicy seeds from the pomegranate. You'll wanna eat 'em up when they're plentiful in autumn—especially October and November. Pomegranates are not available locally most of the winter or spring. Pair them with fresh mint, like in this pilaf, and the flavor memory will last until they're back on the market again.

2 tablespoons extra-virgin olive oil

1 large shallot, minced

1 cup whole-wheat couscous

⅓ cup fresh pomegranate seeds or dried tart cherries

Juice and zest of ½ lemon (about 1½ tablespoons juice)

¼ cup finely chopped fresh mint

1 teaspoon sea salt, or as needed

1. Heat the oil in a large saucepan over medium heat. Add the shallots and sauté for 1 minute. Stir in the couscous until coated with oil.

2. Add 1½ cups fresh water, about ¾ of the pomegranate seeds, and lemon juice and bring to boil over high heat. Cover and turn off the heat. Let "lid cook" (cook covered while the burner is off) until the water is absorbed, about 5 minutes.

3. Remove from the burner and stir in the mint and lemon zest. Add salt. Sprinkle with the remaining pomegranate seeds to garnish and serve.

PER SERVING: 200 calories, 8g total fat, 1g saturated fat, 0g trans fat, 0mg cholesterol, 580mg sodium, 29g total carbohydrate, 4g dietary fiber, 5g protein

go local

 There's no need for bottled water when you can get fresh local tap water anytime you want. How do you know how fresh your water is? According to the U.S. Environmental Protection Agency, you should be mailed a short report from your water supplier by July first every year that tells you what's in your water and where it comes from. If not (or anytime), see if your drinking water quality report is available online at www.epa.gov/safewater/dwinfo/index.html.

FISH, POULTRY, & MEAT DISHES

papaya gone wild fishin'

PAN-SEARED ALASKAN WILD SALMON WITH PAPAYA SAUCE

Makes 4 servings: 1 salmon steak with ⅓ cup sauce each

Today, there are ecological issues with some salmon, such as Atlantic or farmed salmon. But luckily there is one sustainable salmon choice that's considered "eco-best" by the Environmental Defense Fund; it's Alaskan wild salmon. It's caught from well-managed, healthy populations. And when fresh, it makes this light and refreshing dish absolutely delish.

1 medium or ½ large papaya, peeled, seeded, and
cubed (about 2 cups)
1 small jalapeño without seeds, minced
1 tablespoon chopped fresh mint
Juice of ½ lime, or to taste (about 1 tablespoon)
1 teaspoon grated scrubbed unpeeled gingerroot
¾ teaspoon sea salt, or to taste
4 (5-ounce) Alaskan wild salmon steaks or fillets,
about ½-inch thick*
1 tablespoon canola or peanut oil
¼ teaspoon freshly ground black pepper, or to taste
2 scallions, white and green parts, minced

1. Mash the papaya with a potato masher in a medium bowl until it has an applesauce-like consistency. Stir in the jalapeño, mint, lime juice, gingerroot, and ½ teaspoon of the salt until combined.

2. Rub the salmon with the oil. Heat a panini grill to high heat. Place the salmon in the grill. Cook until desired doneness, about 2 minutes. Add the remaining ¼ teaspoon salt and the pepper.

3. Spoon the papaya sauce onto a serving platter, and place the salmon on top. Sprinkle with the scallions and serve.

PER SERVING: 230 calories, 9g total fat, 1.5g saturated fat, 0g trans fat, 65mg cholesterol, 510mg sodium, 8g total carbohydrate, 2g dietary fiber, 29g protein

---

*Or buy two 1-inch-thick 10-ounce steaks; halve into four ½-inch-thick steaks.

use it, don't lose it

When a recipe uses a pepper, such as jalapeño or serrano, but the seeds aren't used in the recipe, save the seeds anyway. If you can handle the heat, sprinkle them (sort of like crushed red pepper flakes) on other parts of the meal to add a little kick. Or freeze seeds for later use if you choose.

chili con turkey under pressure

PRESSURE-COOKED SPICY BEAN AND TURKEY CHILI

Makes 8 servings: 2 cups each

Fall is my favorite season because I love when the leaves change colors. I love the crispness in the air. I love football. (That's because I went to Ohio State—and it's a requirement there!) If you're like me, a football-watching party is always on the schedule, and there's no better party food than chili. This winning recipe can be made during halftime—in a pressure cooker. And you won't miss the beef as this eco-friendlier turkey version is heavy on the beans and the spice. It's a touchdown for the taste buds!

½ cup canola or peanut oil
1 pound ground organic turkey*
2 large red onions, finely chopped
1 large jalapeño with some seeds, minced
4 large cloves garlic, minced
2 (15-ounce) cans organic kidney beans, drained (do not rinse)
4 medium vine-ripened tomatoes, chopped
2 bay leaves
3 tablespoons chili powder, or to taste
2 tablespoons organic tomato paste
2½ teaspoons sea salt, or to taste
1 teaspoon ground cumin, or to taste
½ teaspoon ground cinnamon, or to taste
½ teaspoon freshly ground black pepper, or to taste

1. Heat the oil in a large stick-resistant skillet over medium-high heat. Add the turkey, onions, jalapeño, and garlic and sauté until the turkey is just cooked through, about 5 minutes. Cover, turn off the heat, and "lid cook" (cook covered while the burner is off) until the turkey mixture is fully cooked and onions are soft, about 5 minutes.

2. Meanwhile, add the beans, tomatoes, bay leaves, chili powder, tomato paste, salt, cumin, cinnamon, and pepper to the pressure cooker. Stir in the turkey mixture along with any liquids in the skillet. Close the pressure cooker lid and turn to the high pressure setting. Increase the burner heat to high. Once the pressure cooker hisses, adjust the heat as necessary to maintain high pressure with gentle hissing and cook for 8 minutes, or until stew-like.

3. Turn off the pressure cooker or remove from the heat. Carefully release the pressure and remove the lid. Remove and discard the bay leaves. Taste and adjust seasoning, if necessary.

4. Serve while hot. If desired, serve in whole-wheat sourdough bread bowls (middle of bread loaf is torn out to create a "bowl")—and enjoy the chili along with the torn-out bread pieces.

If you don't have a pressure cooker, get one! It's so cool because it cooks food so fast. In fact, it can cook food about three times as fast! Plus, you'll potentially be retaining more nutrients while saving as much as 70% of the usual required energy.

PER SERVING: 330 calories, 18g total fat, 2g saturated fat, 0g trans fat, 30mg cholesterol, 820mg sodium, 26g total carbohydrate, 11g dietary fiber, 20g protein

*Choose ground turkey with at least 7 percent fat for best culinary results.

a planet-friendly bite

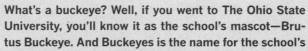

What's a buckeye? Well, if you went to The Ohio State University, you'll know it as the school's mascot—Brutus Buckeye. And Buckeyes is the name for the school's football team, too. But it you're thinking in earthier terms, a buckeye is a shiny, small dark brown nut that has a light tan patch; it comes from Ohio's official state tree, the buckeye tree. The trees are relatively common in Ohio, growing along streams and rivers and in floodplains. The fallen nuts aren't edible, but can be replanted . . . to grow more buckeyes. And according to folklore, carrying a buckeye brings good luck.

curry chicken ciabatta

CURRIED ORGANIC CHICKEN MANGO SALAD ON CIABATTA BREAD

Makes 3 servings: 1 sandwich each

If forty is the new thirty, and green is the new black, then chicken thigh is the new breast. The richer-tasting thigh is actually a better match for the distinctive flavors of ginger, curry, and cilantro. For planet-friendliness, rather than poaching or roasting a whole chicken or chicken parts as is often done when making chicken salad, you'll be dicing the thigh meat before cooking. That will save valuable resources since it'll cook in a jiffy. This tantalizing savory treat will likely be gone in a jiffy, too.

1 (7-ounce) boneless, skinless organic chicken thigh,
    cut into ⅓-inch cubes
½ teaspoon sea salt, or as needed
3 tablespoons plain soy or organic yogurt
2 tablespoons mayonnaise
1 teaspoon grated scrubbed unpeeled gingerroot
1 teaspoon curry powder, or to taste
¼ cup thinly sliced celery
½ cup finely diced mango
1 tablespoon finely chopped fresh cilantro
1 (8-ounce) whole-grain ciabatta or whole-wheat
    Italian bread loaf, cut into 3 pieces and split

1. Add the chicken, ¼ teaspoon of the salt, and ¼ cup fresh water to a small skillet set over high heat. Cook while stirring until the chicken is fully cooked, about 3 minutes. Cover and turn off the heat. Let "lid cook" (cook covered while the burner is off) until the chicken is slightly tender, about 5 minutes.

2. Let the chicken and any accumulated liquids cool slightly in a small bowl, then place in the refrigerator to fully chill. Once the chicken is chilled, drain off extra liquid.

little *green* cooking tip

When choosing meat or poultry, try a "head to tail" approach and use parts that you might not normally consider. Remember, a chicken has many parts, not just breasts! So even if a recipe calls for breast meat, consider chicken thigh, leg, or wing meat—or some of the lesser-used parts.

3. Stir together the cold chicken, yogurt, mayonnaise, ginger-root, curry powder, and remaining ¼ teaspoon salt. Then stir in the celery, mango, and cilantro. Taste and adjust seasoning, if necessary.

4. Spoon ½ scant cup of the chicken salad onto each piece of bread and serve as a sandwich.

PER SERVING: 400 calories, 16g total fat, 3g saturated fat, 0g trans fat, 45mg cholesterol, 810mg sodium, 41g total carbohydrate, 6g dietary fiber, 23g protein

use it, don't lose it

Curry powder is a variable mixture of finely ground spices, herbs, and seeds, such as cumin, turmeric, fenugreek, coriander, red pepper, and cloves. If it's not already on your spice shelf and you prefer not to buy curry powder for one recipe, create your own spice mixture from what you have, even if that's only a couple of the ingredients, like ground cumin and red pepper.

star chicken stir-fry

STAR FRUIT ORGANIC CHICKEN STIR-FRY WITH PINE NUTS

Makes 4 servings: 1 cup each

One reason stir-fries can be considered green is because they often include plenty of veggies. This recipe is no exception. Plus, it includes seasonal star fruit as a bonus. Also called Chinese star fruit or carambola, star fruit has been grown in the U.S. for over a century. Florida can boast that star fruit is the VIP (or is that VIF . . . Very Important Fruit) of its state's tropical fruit.

¾ cup low-sodium vegetable or organic chicken broth
1 tablespoon naturally brewed soy sauce
1 tablespoon cornstarch
1 tablespoon turbinado or Demerara sugar
3 tablespoons canola or peanut oil
1 pound boneless, skinless organic chicken thighs,
    cut into ⅓-inch cubes
½ teaspoon sea salt, or to taste
1 large red or orange bell pepper, diced
4 scallions, green and white parts, thinly sliced
3 large cloves garlic, very thinly sliced
1 tablespoon grated unpeeled scrubbed gingerroot
¼ teaspoon crushed red pepper flakes
2 star fruits, very thinly sliced
⅓ cup raw pine nuts

1. Whisk together the broth, soy sauce, cornstarch, and sugar in a liquid measuring cup or small bowl. Set aside.

2. Heat the oil in a wok or large stick-resistant skillet over medium-high heat. Add the chicken and stir-fry until cooked through, about 4 minutes. Transfer the chicken with a slotted spoon to a bowl and add salt. Set aside.

3. Add the bell pepper and white portion of the scallions to the wok; stir-fry until the scallions are slightly caramelized, about 2 minutes. Add the garlic, gingerroot, and crushed red pepper and stir-fry until the bell peppers are crisp-tender and the garlic is fragrant, about 30 seconds.

little **green** cooking tip

When you have an array of veggies and you're not quite sure what to do with them, stir-fry them. It's a low-carbon cooking method because it's so quick and provides an easy way to boost your veggie intake.

4. Give the broth mixture a quick stir and pour into the wok. Reduce the heat to medium-low, and simmer, stirring until thickened, about 1 minute. Turn off the heat.

5. Stir in the star fruit, pine nuts, green portion of scallions, and cooked chicken along with any accumulated juices until heated through, about 1 minute. Serve with steamed whole grains, such as quinoa, and enjoy with bamboo or other reusable chopsticks.

PER SERVING: 390 calories, 27g total fat, 3.5g saturated fat, 0g trans fat, 75mg cholesterol, 620mg sodium, 15g total carbohydrate, 3g dietary fiber, 24g protein

use it, don't lose it

When a recipe calls for a portion of a can or carton, such as ¾ cup broth, plan ahead and use the remainder in another part of the meal. For instance, leftover broth can be used to make a quick soup or as a simmering liquid for quinoa. Don't want to use it right away? Freeze the remainder for future Star Chicken Stiry-Fry preparation in ¾-cup portions in small lidded storage bowls that are oven-, microwave-, freezer-, and dishwasher-safe.

september submarine

SUBMARINE WRAP WITH ARUGULA AND VINE-RIPENED TOMATO SALSA

Makes 4 servings: 1 wrap each

For a back-to-school sandwich like no other, take a bite out of this wrap—even if your schooldays are long behind you. It's like an Italian party sub, but it's easier to eat, filled with more local ingredients, and bursting with flavor. And if you'd like to make this more Italian, make it with love—that's *amore!*

4 (8-inch) stone-ground whole-wheat tortillas
4 ounces sliced smoked deli organic turkey breast
4 ounces sliced baked deli organic ham or genoa salami
5 ounces organic or locally produced provolone cheese
    or other cheese of choice, thinly sliced
2 tablespoons freshly grated organic or locally produced
    Parmesan cheese
2 cups baby arugula or chopped arugula
1 recipe Spicy Ciao Salsa (page 235)
½ teaspoon freshly ground black pepper, or to taste

1. Top each tortilla with the turkey, ham, provolone and Parmesan cheeses, and arugula.

2. Then top each with ¼ cup Spicy Ciao Salsa, straining excess liquids before adding to the tortilla. Add pepper.

3. Roll up tightly and secure with toothpicks. Serve immediately.

PER SERVING: 290 calories, 12g total fat, 7g saturated fat, 0g trans fat, 55mg cholesterol, 950mg sodium, 26g total carbohydrate, 3g dietary fiber, 24g protein

---

little
green
cooking
tip

If you choose to eat deli meat, go organic. Organic varieties are more available than ever before. It means the animals were fed organic feed and given no antibiotics. It's an investment in your health and the environment's.

spicy ciao salsa

"HOT" ITALIAN VINE-RIPENED TOMATO SALSA

Makes 1 cup

1 medium vine-ripened tomato, diced
¼ cup finely diced white onion
¼ cup well-drained hot pickled peppers, finely chopped
2 tablespoons aged balsamic vinegar
½ teaspoon finely chopped fresh oregano

Combine all ingredients in a small bowl and serve.

use it, don't lose it

When salsa, such as Spicy Ciao Salsa, is added to a sandwich or wrap, it can make it soggy. Straining salsa before use can help prevent that sogginess. But save what you strain; that salsa liquid can make a tasty salad dressing if you choose to serve some leafy greens on the side. Or drizzle it onto cooked grains or veggies to perk them up.

saucy shell steak

CRANBERRY-PORT SAUCED ORGANIC SHELL STEAK

Makes 4 servings: 1 steak with ⅓ cup sauce each

Talk about orgasmic (I mean, *organic*) steak with fresh cranberries . . . it's like sex on a plate. It's hot and steamy with a wildly sweet-savory balance that'll leave you breathless, especially if it only takes a couple minutes to enjoy it. Your taste buds will be so excited that they'll be ready to go at it again—and again.

3 tablespoons canola or peanut oil
2 large cloves garlic, sliced
1 large shallot, sliced
1 cup ruby port
¾ cup low-sodium vegetable broth
½ cup fresh or thawed frozen cranberries
2 tablespoons turbinado or Demerara sugar
½ teaspoon minced fresh rosemary
4 (3½-ounce) well-trimmed grass-fed organic shell steaks
  or filets mignons
½ teaspoon sea salt, or to taste
½ teaspoon freshly ground black pepper, or to taste

1. Heat 2 tablespoons of the oil in a saucepan over medium-high heat. Add the garlic and shallot, and cook until the garlic is fragrant, about 1 minute. Add the port, broth, cranberries, sugar, and rosemary. Bring to a boil and simmer until the liquid is reduced by half, about 8 minutes. Turn off the heat and set aside.

2. Heat the remaining 1 tablespoon oil in a large skillet over medium-high heat. Season steaks with salt and pepper. Add the steaks to the skillet; cook to desired doneness, about 2½ minutes per side for medium-rare. Transfer steaks to a serving platter.

little
green
cooking
tip

Aim for medium-rare for organic steaks—this is long enough to assure meat is cooked safely, yet energy is saved since they're not overcooked. It'll lessen the amount of CO_2 entering the atmosphere.

3. Add the reserved sauce to the skillet. Bring to a boil over medium-high heat and simmer, while scraping up any browned bits, until desired consistency, about 2 minutes. Taste and adjust seasoning, if necessary.

4. Spoon the sauce over the steaks and serve.

PER SERVING: 350 calories, 14g total fat, 2.5g saturated fat, 0g trans fat, 35mg cholesterol, 360mg sodium, 18g total carbohydrate, 1g dietary fiber, 20g protein

a planet-friendly bite

By not overcooking meats, it may help lessen the amount of potentially cancer-causing chemicals, such as heterocyclic amines, that can form when meat is cooked for a long time at a high temperature.

SIPS & SWEETS

favorite fall fruit smoothie

TRIPLE FRUIT SMOOTHIE

There's really no need to follow a smoothie recipe. But if you like, here's one that's full of fall fruit goodness that's sure to satisfy a sweet tooth. It's one of the easiest ways to meet your daily fruit servings, too.

1½ cups sliced hulled fresh strawberries or other seasonal berries
1 cup pure apple juice, not from concentrate
Juice from 7 passion fruits (⅓ cup juice)

1. Freeze the sliced strawberries on a baking sheet for at least 1 hour.

2. Place the frozen strawberries, apple juice, and passion fruit juice in a blender container. Cover and blend on low until the fruit is chopped, about 15 seconds, then on high until smooth, about 15 seconds more.

3. Serve immediately sprinkled with some passion fruit seeds, if desired.

PER SERVING: 120 calories, 0.5g total fat, 0g saturated fat, 0g trans fat, 0mg cholesterol, 5mg sodium, 30g total carbohydrate, 3g dietary fiber, 1g protein

little *green* cooking tip

If unable to find a fresh fruit that's meant to be juiced, such as passion fruit, there's no need to hunt for the bottled version that may be shipped from a faraway land. Rather, head to your local farmers' market and use any juicable fruit that's available instead. While you're there, check if freshly pressed apple juice is available.

use it, don't lose it

Look for passion fruit that's partially deflated, a sign of ripeness. Halve the passion fruit. Scrape out the pulp (flesh and seeds) with a spoon. Press pulp through a fine strainer to remove the tiny seeds. Save seeds for garnishing.

mango tea

MANGO-INFUSED ICED BLACK TEA

Makes 4 servings: 1¼ cup each

A lovely way to sweeten tea is to actually use no sugar at all. Sweeten it with real fruit instead, like the juicy and fragrant mango. Its natural sugars will provide all of the sweetness you need—plus exotic fruity flavor.

4 Earl Grey, English Breakfast, or other black tea bags
1 medium mango, peeled, pitted, and sliced

1. Place tea bags into a medium bowl or teapot. Add 2 cups boiling fresh water, making sure the tea bags are completely immersed in the water. Let steep for 5 minutes, then remove the tea bags.

2. Meanwhile, place the mango slices and ½ cup fresh water in a blender container. Cover and puree, about 15 seconds. Pour pureed mango into a 2-quart pitcher along with 2 cups of cold fresh water.

3. Pour the tea into the pitcher and chill in the refrigerator until ready to serve.

4. Sweeten with honey or turbinado or Demerara sugar, if desired. Add ice cubes to serve.

PER SERVING: 35 calories, 0g total fat, 0g saturated fat, 0g trans fat, 0mg cholesterol, 0mg sodium, 9g total carbohydrate, 1g dietary fiber, 0g protein

little **green** cooking tip

When boiling water for tea, use a whistling tea kettle . . . so you know when the water is ready. When boiling water for other recipes, consider using a kettle for that, too. A tea kettle isn't just for making tea when you're cooking green.

a planet-friendly bite

If you need to shop far and wide to find organic tea that's Fair Trade Certified, you might consider purchasing it online instead. It has been estimated that every one minute you spend driving a car to the store may use as much as 10 times the energy of doing that same shopping online from home.

mangotini

FRESH MANGO MARTINI

Makes 2 servings: 1 martini each

The matchup of mango and martini in this creamy, dreamy Mangotini is on-the-level delicious, but this is also a deceptively addictive drink that comes with a warning: you might not be able to stop at one!

⅔ cup diced mango
2 ounces vodka
1 ounce Triple Sec
Juice of ½ lime (about 1 tablespoon)

1. Add all the ingredients and 4 large ice cubes to a blender container. Cover and puree on low speed, about 30 seconds.

2. Pour into two martini glasses and serve.

PER SERVING: 140 calories, 0g total fat, 0g saturated fat, 0g trans fat, 0mg cholesterol, 0mg sodium, 10g total carbohydrate, 1g dietary fiber, 0g protein

use it, don't lose it

 If it's a party, one way to keep from imbibing in too much alcohol is by drinking something nonalcoholic between drinks. Slice the other half of lime left over from the Mangotini and toss a couple slices into seltzer water for a between-drink refresher.

fig newgents

THIN-N-CRISPY OATMEAL FIG COOKIE SANDWICHES

Makes 8 servings: 1 large (3⅓-inch) cookie sandwich each

It's rather indulgent to name a cookie after yourself like I did here. But these "hyperbaked" cookies are themselves indulgent. Swap out my last name for yours and join in on the indulgence, if you prefer. But if the name of these fig-filled delights is of no interest to you, then all that's left to do is enjoy one. Just one . . . they're cookie sandwiches, after all.

1 cup old-fashioned oats
¼ cup stone-ground whole-wheat flour
1½ teaspoons baking powder
¾ teaspoon sea salt
⅛ teaspoon ground cinnamon
½ cup unsalted organic butter, at room temperature
¾ cup turbinado or Demerara sugar
¼ cup brown sugar
1 large organic egg
1 teaspoon pure vanilla extract
5 medium Calimyrna or Mission figs, stems removed

1. Combine the oats, flour, baking powder, salt, and cinnamon in a medium bowl. Mix with a spoon to combine. Set aside.

2. Stir the butter and sugars in a medium bowl until well combined. Vigorously stir in the egg and vanilla extract. Add the oat mixture to the butter-egg mixture and stir until well combined.

3. Line 2 baking sheets with unbleached parchment paper. Drop the dough by rounded tablespoon onto the sheets, at least 2 inches apart (8 cookies per sheet). These spread out a lot!

4. Place the baking sheets in the oven, then turn the heat to 400°F (do not preheat). Bake until the cookies just spread out to cookie shape but are not browned, about 12 minutes. As quickly as possible (so you don't let out too much heat), open the oven and swap the trays—move the tray on the top rack to the bottom and bottom rack to the top.

(continued)

little
green
cooking
tip

We're trained to preheat the oven. In many cases, it's unnecessary, such as for baking cookies. You'll need to adjust other recipes. But in *Big Green Cookbook*, it's done for you. By not preheating, you'll use less energy by taking advantage of all the heat. It's called "hyperbaking"!

5. Close the oven, then turn the oven off and let the cookies continue baking in the off oven with the residual heat until desired brownness, 6 to 8 minutes. Remove from the oven. (If necessary, gently separate cookies, if any of them slightly run together, with the edge of a spatula.) Let cool completely on baking sheets on wire racks. The cookies will be thin and crispy when cooled.

6. Meanwhile, mince the figs. Then "cream" them with a chef's knife or mash them using a mortar and pestle. Chill the creamed fig in the refrigerator.

7. When the cookies are cool and crisp, gently and thinly spread the chilled creamed fig onto the bottom side of 8 cookies. Top each with another cookie, bottom to bottom, so it forms a sandwich, and serve.

PER SERVING: 280 calories, 13g total fat, 8g saturated fat, 0g trans fat, 55mg cholesterol, 330mg sodium, 41g total carbohydrate, 2g dietary fiber, 4g protein

a planet-friendly bite

According to the California Fig Advisory Board, the fig is not technically a fruit! It's a flower that's inverted into itself. The seeds are the real fruit—otherwise known as drupes. Figs are the only fruit to fully ripen and semi-dry while still on the tree.

apple of my eye

HOT FUJI APPLE SUNDAE

Makes 2 servings: 1 sundae each

It's apple season. That means apple *pie* season, too. So when you have a craving for a pie, it's now easy to please that passion. This Fuji apple dessert conjures up those flavor memories in every mouthful. It only takes minutes to make since it's "micro-roasted." And you even get to enjoy it à la mode.

1 large Fuji apple, cored, halved lengthwise
2 tablespoons turbinado or Demerara sugar
⅛ teaspoon ground cinnamon, or to taste
⅛ teaspoon sea salt
½ cup vanilla soy or rice frozen dessert
1 tablespoon chopped raw pecans or walnuts

1. Place the apple halves, cut side up, on a microwave-safe dish.

2. Stir together the sugar, cinnamon, and salt in a small bowl. Sprinkle the mixture over the cut surface of the apple halves.

3. "Micro-roast" (cook in the microwave oven*) on high until the apple is tender and the sugar mixture melts, about 3½ minutes.

4. Serve each apple half in a dessert dish. Top with a scoop of the frozen dessert. Drizzle with any remaining syrup. Sprinkle with extra cinnamon, if desired, and the pecans. Serve immediately.

PER SERVING: 190 calories, 4.5g total fat, 0g saturated fat, 0g trans fat, 0mg cholesterol, 170mg sodium, 40g total carbohydrate, 5g dietary fiber, 1g protein

*Microwave oven cooking times will vary. See page 39.

little
green
cooking
tip

You don't need to bake a pie to get all of the mouthwatering flavors of a fresh-baked one. Fruit can be "micro-baked" in minutes and topped with nondairy frozen dessert. A sprinkling of nuts on top will give you a crust-like crunch.

go local

Most Americans live an average of about sixty miles from an apple orchard. Unfortunately, the apples usually purchased from a typical grocery store travel over 1,700 miles from orchard to your table. That's about the distance from New York City to Colorado Springs!

winter

bites & snacks

wild winter mushroom pâté . . . 246
cumin-accented wild mushroom spread

grape poppers . . . 248
pistachio–goat cheese stuffed red globe grapes

southwestern sweet potato "sushi" . . . 249
spicy sweet potato–cream cheese tortilla roll-up bites

sunny-side up starter . . . 251
shallot-spiked egg salad bruschetta

dips, salsas, & sauces

pulpy papaya . . . 252
tropical papaya sauce

guacamole rápido . . . 253
speedy guacamole

not your ordinary pesto . . . 254
fresh parsley–triple nut pesto

soups & salads

nine veggie stew . . . 255
winter vegetable stew with Middle Eastern spices

lotsa veggie clam chowder . . . 257
leek and Yukon gold clam chowder

wintercress salad . . . 258
watercress salad with winter fruits

fall into winter salad . . . 259
mixed green salad with pears, walnuts, cranberries, and maple dressing

yin-yang orange . . . 261
leafy Asian mandarin orange salad

tabbouleh twist . . . 262
tabbouleh salad with Meyer lemon

broccoli trifle . . . 263
layered broccoli salad

salad of citrus cheer . . . 265
pink grapefruit and endive salad with Champagne vinaigrette

salad melody . . . 266
blood orange, arugula, and Maytag blue cheese salad with blood orange vinaigrette

pinky potato salad . . . 267
winter fingerling potato salad

vegetarian dishes

homemade veggie burgers . . . 269
vegetarian soy burgers

peanutty citrus stir-fry . . . 271
thai peanut pink–grapefruit tofu stir-fry

granny cakes . . . 273
Granny Smith apple pancakes with cinnamon butter

"that's not broccoli" capellini . . . 275
lemon-zested rapini capellini

wild winter mushroom pâté

CUMIN-ACCENTED WILD MUSHROOM SPREAD

Makes 10 servings: ⅓ cup each

Pâté de foie gras, which translated from French means "fatty liver," is an epicurean delicacy. But there's concern over its production, which involves force-feeding ducks and geese. So keep those birds happy and choose a vegetarian version in its place. This savory pâté has an array of flavor nuances that's sure to please the gourmand palate.

1 large white onion, chopped
2 tablespoons extra-virgin olive oil
4 cups sliced wild mushrooms of choice or cremini mushrooms
1 cup unsalted natural almond butter
¼ cup packed fresh flat-leaf parsley
Leaves from 2 sprigs fresh thyme (optional)
¾ teaspoon sea salt, or to taste
½ teaspoon ground cumin, or to taste
½ teaspoon freshly ground black pepper, or to taste

1. Stir together the onions and oil in a large microwave-safe dish until onions are well coated. "Micro-roast" (cook in the microwave oven*) on high until the onions are soft, about 4 minutes, stirring once.

2. Rinse and drain the mushrooms and stir into the onions. "Micro-roast" on high until the mushrooms are soft, about 2 minutes, stirring once.

3. Transfer the cooked onion and mushrooms to the bowl of a food processor along with any accumulated juices. Add the almond butter, parsley, and thyme (if using). Cover and pulse briefly until nearly smooth or desired texture. Add salt, cumin, and pepper.

4. Spoon the pâté into 10 small dishes or ramekins. Chill thoroughly in the refrigerator for at least 1 hour. Garnish with additional parsley, if desired. Serve with thin slices of toast, pita crisps, or celery or cucumber slices, or use it as a sandwich condiment.

PER SERVING: 200 calories, 18g total fat, 2g saturated fat, 0g trans fat, 0mg cholesterol, 180mg sodium, 8g total carbohydrate, 2g dietary fiber, 5g protein

*Microwave oven cooking times will vary. See page 39.

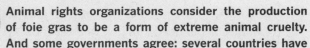

a planet-friendly bite

Animal rights organizations consider the production of foie gras to be a form of extreme animal cruelty. And some governments agree: several countries have barred its production. The sale of foie gras was prohibited in Chicago for a couple years, though Chicagoans now can enjoy it freely again. A state ban in California is next—in 2012. Your city or state may be next. The Humane Society of the United States (HSUS) is a resource for more details. Download "An HSUS Report: The Welfare of Animals in the Foie Gras Industry" at www.hsus.org/web-files/PDF/farm/HSUS-Report-on-Foie-Gras-Bird-Welfare.pdf.

little
green
cooking
tip

Mushrooms are earthy. They provide "meatiness," as well as flavor and texture. Use them in place of meats on occasion, like Wild Winter Mushroom Pâté or serve mushrooms like you would a steak.

grape poppers

PISTACHIO-GOAT CHEESE STUFFED RED GLOBE GRAPES

Makes 16 servings: 5 stuffed grape halves each

Globe grapes are the gorgeously plump ones with seeds—which are actually edible. But for this recipe, go ahead and scoop out the seeds to make a bed for the little balls of equally gorgeous goat cheese. You'll find this to be one of the most popular hors d'oeuvres at any party you toss—mostly because these are so easy to toss into your mouth.

1 pound red globe grapes
6 ounces organic or locally produced soft goat cheese
¼ teaspoon freshly ground black pepper, or to taste
½ cup finely chopped salted pistachios

1. Cut each grape in half lengthwise and scoop out a pea-size amount of the flesh along with the seeds. (Try this using a small parisienne scoop; it's like a mini melon-baller.)

2. Form the goat cheese into small balls, about ¼ teaspoon each, and place in the cavity of the grapes. Add pepper.

3. Dip each grape half, cheese side down, into the pistachios. Serve at room temperature, pistachio side up.

PER SERVING: 70 calories, 4g total fat, 2g saturated fat, 0g trans fat, 5mg cholesterol, 55mg sodium, 6g total carbohydrate, 1g dietary fiber, 3g protein

little *green* cooking tip

Look for ways to incorporate more fresh seasonal produce into your eating plan—or your party plan. Fruits are ideal cracker replacements, such as Grape Poppers, right, or Blue Boscs (page 177), pear slices spread with blue cheese.

a planet-friendly bite

California's Paramount Farms is the largest grower of pistachios in the world. They pride themselves on using environmentally friendly farming techniques, including water conservation. Plus, they have invested millions of dollars building North America's largest privately owned solar farm.

southwestern sweet potato "sushi"

SPICY SWEET POTATO–CREAM CHEESE TORTILLA ROLL-UP BITES

Makes 6 servings: 5 roll-ups each

Need to take some finger foods to a party? These "sushi" morsels will get a thumbs-up. There's nothing fishy here, just fresh ingredients designed for fun. And the earth-style, micro-roasted sweet potato surprise inside is sure to add green intrigue.

⅓ cup grated scrubbed unpeeled sweet potato
8 ounces organic cream cheese or soy-based cream cheese spread,
   at room temperature
3 tablespoons salsa or Green Green Salsa (page 54)
1 small jalapeño with seeds, minced
2 scallions, green and white parts, minced
2 tablespoons finely chopped plus 30 whole leaves fresh cilantro
5 (8-inch) stone-ground whole-wheat or sprouted-grain tortillas

1. Spread the grated sweet potato in a small microwave-safe dish. "Micro-roast" (cook in the microwave oven*) until cooked through and steaming hot, about 30 seconds. Allow to cool for at least 3 minutes.

2. Thoroughly combine the sweet potato, cream cheese, salsa (drained of excess liquids), jalapeño, scallions, and chopped cilantro in a medium bowl. (Makes about 1½ cups filling.)

3. Spread about ¼ rounded cup filling on the entire area of one side of each tortilla and tightly roll up.

4. Slice about ½-inch off each end of the rolled tortillas. (These "rejects" are for nibbling!) Then slice each rolled tortilla into 6 equal-sized pieces.

(continued)

When throwing a party, make sure to have an array of vegetarian appetizers so there's something for everyone. If you make mini burgers, also serve mini veggie burgers. If there's sushi, also prepare vegetarian sushi—or at least Southwestern Sweet Potato "Sushi."

5. Stand each piece of "sushi" on a cut edge and garnish the top with one cilantro leaf. Chill in the refrigerator until ready to serve.

PER SERVING: 210 calories, 14g total fat, 8g saturated fat, 0g trans fat, 40mg cholesterol, 310mg sodium, 22g total carbohydrate, 2g dietary fiber, 6g protein

*Microwave oven cooking times will vary. See page 39.

use it, don't lose it

Some fresh herbs have tender, very edible stems, like parsley and cilantro. Some have woody, rather inedible stems, like rosemary and thyme. When a recipe calls for a chopped or minced fresh herb that has tender stems, don't waste your time pulling off just the leaves. Instead, tear off a portion of the leaves and stems and chop away.

sunny-side up starter

SHALLOT-SPIKED EGG SALAD BRUSCHETTA

Makes 6 servings: 2 medium or 4 small bruschetta each

A bruschetta-style appetizer nearly always means a topping on toasted bread. But there are eco-savvier ways to prepare it. One way is to not toast the bread. If the bread is thick and hearty to start, it'll stand up to nearly any topper. If that topping is a delicate salad of organic eggs, you might prefer an uncrisp bread bottom anyway.

⅓ cup mayonnaise

2 teaspoons stone-ground mustard

1 large shallot, minced

1 scallion, green and white parts, very thinly sliced

2 teaspoons finely chopped fresh dill, 1 teaspoon finely chopped fresh tarragon, or ¾ teaspoon dried dill

7 large hard-cooked organic eggs, peeled and diced

¼ teaspoon sea salt, or to taste

⅛ teaspoon cayenne pepper, or to taste

12 medium or 24 small slices firm pumpernickel or rye bread

1. Stir together the mayonnaise and mustard in a medium bowl to combine. Stir in the shallot, scallion, and dill. Gently stir in the eggs and add salt and cayenne. (Makes about 2¼ cups egg salad.)

2. Top each medium bread slice with 3 tablespoons egg salad (or each small slice with 1½ tablespoons egg salad). Garnish each with additional dill sprigs, if desired, and serve.

PER SERVING: 310 calories, 17g total fat, 3.5g saturated fat, 0g trans fat, 250mg cholesterol, 610mg sodium, 27g total carbohydrate, 4g dietary fiber, 12g protein

---

little **green** cooking tip

Make hard-cooked green eggs! Place eggs in a single layer in a large saucepan. Cover with fresh water, ½ inch above the eggs. Place over high heat. Bring just to a boil. Cover and turn off the heat. Let "lid cook" (cook covered while the burner is off) for 9 minutes. Pour off the water, cool to room temperature, then chill in the refrigerator.

a planet-friendly bite

The microwave oven can come in handy when scrambling or frying eggs. But don't try to microwave an egg when it's in its shell. The steam will build up so quickly that the egg can explode. That's called green eggs and a mess!

DIPS, SALSAS, & SAUCES

pulpy papaya
TROPICAL PAPAYA SAUCE

Makes 5 servings: ⅓ cup each

Looking for a transporting experience to take you away from the wintertime blues? Dollop this exotically fruity sauce onto your dishes and rid yourself of those doldrums. Swirl it over vanilla soy frozen dessert. Stir it into mixed winter fruit to create a tropical fruit salad. Or slather it as a pan-grilling sauce onto wild salmon.

1 medium or ½ large papaya, peeled, seeded, and cubed (about 2 cups)
¼ cup turbinado or Demerara sugar
Juice and zest of 1 lime (about 2 tablespoons juice)
1 tablespoon finely chopped fresh mint (optional)
¼ teaspoon sea salt, or to taste

1. Add the papaya, sugar, lime juice, and mint (if using) into a medium bowl. Mash with a potato masher until smooth (some lumps will remain).

2. Add salt as needed. Cover and refrigerate until ready to use.

3. Sprinkle with a little lime zest, if desired, and serve.

PER SERVING: 60 calories, 0g total fat, 0g saturated fat, 0g trans fat, 0mg cholesterol, 120mg sodium, 16g total carbohydrate, 1g dietary fiber, 0g protein

a planet-friendly bite

 Papaya contains a natural enzyme called papain. It can be used as a natural tenderizer for meat and poultry.

---

little *green* cooking tip

There's no need to go "plain Jane" when eating green. Smash up fresh seasonal fruit into a sauce to add pizzazz to nearly anything that's plain. By the way, sauces are a terrific use of fruit that's just about to become overripe.

guacamole rápido

SPEEDY GUACAMOLE

Makes 6 servings: ⅓ cup each

When I crave guacamole, sometimes I have a hard time waiting long enough to make it from scratch. But after a bad experience buying a commercial brand, I absolutely need to have it freshly made. (My store-bought guacamole was green from artificial food coloring, not avocados. It was fake!) So enjoy this freshly made 100 percent real guacamole—rápido.

2 Hass avocados, pitted, peeled, and cubed
¼ cup chopped red onion
2 tablespoons chopped fresh cilantro
Juice of ½ lime (about 1 tablespoon)
½ teaspoon sea salt, or to taste
¼ teaspoon hot pepper sauce, or to taste

1. Gently stir all the ingredients together in a medium serving bowl until just combined. Alternatively, combine ingredients in a *molcajete* (large Mexican-style mortar). Taste and adjust seasoning.

2. Serve from the bowl or the *molcajete* with organic blue, white, or yellow corn tortilla chips.

PER SERVING: 80 calories, 7g total fat, 1g saturated fat, 0g trans fat, 0mg cholesterol, 200mg sodium, 5g total carbohydrate, 3g dietary fiber, 1g protein

little *green* cooking tip

Fast food doesn't need to include a drive-through window. It can incorporate fresh seasonal ingredients right from your own kitchen. If you have a favorite (mine is guacamole), look for shortcuts. Just keep them as natural as possible.

a planet-friendly bite

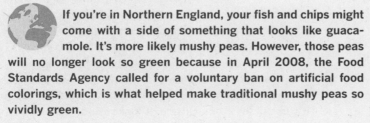

If you're in Northern England, your fish and chips might come with a side of something that looks like guacamole. It's more likely mushy peas. However, those peas will no longer look so green because in April 2008, the Food Standards Agency called for a voluntary ban on artificial food colorings, which is what helped make traditional mushy peas so vividly green.

not your ordinary pesto

FRESH PARSLEY-TRIPLE NUT PESTO

Makes 4 servings: ¼ cup each

When life hands you too much parsley, make parsley pesto. You can use it just like you might typical basil pesto. But you might find this delicious in more places as the flavors amplify, not overpower. Plus, pesto is so much better when prepared this seemingly old-fashioned way . . . by hand.

2 cups packed fresh flat-leaf parsley
3 tablespoons unsalted chopped raw mixed nuts, such as
    pine nuts, natural almond slivers, or chopped walnuts
Juice of ½ lemon (about 1½ tablespoons)
1 large clove garlic
⅓ cup extra-virgin olive oil
¼ cup freshly grated organic or locally produced Parmesan cheese
    (optional)
¼ teaspoon sea salt, or to taste

Add the parsley, nuts, lemon juice, and garlic to a *molcajete* or large mortar. With a pestle, pound into a paste, slowly adding the olive oil while pounding. Stir in the cheese (if using). Add salt and serve with pasta or use as a sandwich spread.

PER SERVING: 220 calories, 23g total fat, 3g saturated fat, 0g trans fat, 0mg cholesterol, 160mg sodium, 3g total carbohydrate, 1g dietary fiber, 2g protein

little *green* cooking tip

Move over food processor. There's a better, greener processor in town. It's you. Some foods, like pesto, have better textures when made by hand—in a *molcajete* or mortar with a pestle. That means it's electricity-free.

a planet-friendly bite

A *molcajete* is a Mexican version of a mortar. (Its pestle is called a *tejolote*.) It's quite the earthy piece as it's made from real volcanic rock. But if you're in the market for one, beware of the inexpensive, softer-stoned versions—which will keep producing sand when you grind in it. Do choose an authentic, high-quality, basalt lava, hand-carved *molcajete*. It's useful for green cuisine. It looks good, too.

nine veggie stew

WINTER VEGETABLE STEW WITH MIDDLE EASTERN SPICES

Makes 4 servings: 1½ cups each

A rustic stew can take hours of simmering time. This aromatic veggie-packed stew takes only minutes to simmer—as it's "micro-stewed." Don't be worried about the time it'll take to prep all of the ingredients, either. Most are earth-style, which means they don't need to be peeled. That'll save time, and add planet-friendly panache.

1½ cups low-sodium vegetable broth

2 large carrots, scrubbed unpeeled, and thinly sliced

1 parsnip, scrubbed unpeeled, and thinly sliced

2 stalks celery, thinly sliced

1 large vine-ripened tomato, diced

1 small yellow onion, sliced

1 (15-ounce) can organic chickpeas, drained (do not rinse)

1 medium sweet potato, scrubbed unpeeled, and cut into ½-inch cubes

1 medium Yukon gold or red potato, scrubbed unpeeled,
    and cut into ½-inch cubes

3 tablespoons chopped fresh mint or 1 tablespoon dried crushed mint

1 tablespoon ground cumin

¼ teaspoon ground cinnamon or allspice

1¼ teaspoons sea salt, or to taste

½ teaspoon freshly ground black pepper, or to taste

1. Add the broth, carrots, parsnip, celery, tomato, and onion to a large 2-quart microwave-safe dish. Cover with unbleached parchment paper and "micro-stew" (stew in the microwave oven*) on high for 5 minutes.

(continued)

little
green
cooking
tip

Low-carbon cooking usually involves plenty of veggies. Serve them "earth style" so it'll take little time to prep—and it'll leave less waste. That means don't peel foods like carrots or parsnips. Just scrub them and then they're ready for cooking.

2. Add the chickpeas, sweet potato, Yukon gold potato, mint, cumin, and cinnamon to the vegetables and stir well. Cover with unbleached parchment paper and "micro-stew" on high until the vegetables are nearly tender, about 10 minutes, stirring twice.

3. Let sit covered until all the vegetables are tender, about 8 minutes. Add salt and pepper. Serve hot as is or over whole-wheat couscous.

PER SERVING: 260 calories, 1.5g total fat, 0g saturated fat, 0g trans fat, 0mg cholesterol, 880mg sodium, 53g total carbohydrate, 11g dietary fiber, 9g protein

*Microwave oven cooking times will vary. See page 39.

a planet-friendly bite

Since 1994, the U.S. Department of Agriculture has been publishing the National Directory of Farmers' Markets every two years. It lists all farmers' markets operating in the U.S. According to Directory listings, there were 1,755 farmers' markets in 1994. In 2006, there were 4,385. Now that's a good green trend.

lotsa veggie
clam chowder

LEEK AND YUKON GOLD CLAM CHOWDER

Makes 4 servings: 2 cups each

If the weather outside is frightful, this bowl of chowder is so delightful. It's green comfort food in a bowl prepared with produce of the season using "lid cooking" to save energy. So let this chowder flow, let it flow, let it flow.

little
green
cooking
tip

2 tablespoons extra-virgin olive oil

4 medium leeks, white and light green parts only, very thinly sliced

2 large Yukon gold potatoes, scrubbed unpeeled, and diced

2½ pounds farm-raised littleneck clams, well scrubbed

2 cups low-sodium vegetable or organic chicken broth

½ teaspoon ground sage

1 cup organic half-and-half or plain unsweetened soymilk

¼ cup chopped fresh flat-leaf parsley

1¼ teaspoons sea salt, or to taste

¼ teaspoon freshly ground black or white pepper, or to taste

1 scallion, green and white parts, minced

Gone vegetarian? You can often make nonvegetarian soups or chowders vegetarian simply by leaving out the meat, fish, or poultry and using vegetable stock or broth as the base. For Lotsa Veggie Clam Chowder, simply don't add the clams, use vegetable broth, and proceed with rest of the recipe.

1. Heat the oil in a large saucepan over medium heat. Add the leeks and sauté until soft, about 5 minutes.

2. Increase the heat to high. Add the potatoes, clams, broth, and sage and bring to a boil. Cover, reduce the heat to medium, and cook 10 minutes or until the potatoes are nearly tender. (Discard any unopened clams after 10 minutes.)

3. Add the half-and-half. Cook for 3 minutes. Cover and turn off the heat. Let "lid cook" (cook covered while the burner is off) until the potatoes are fully cooked, about 5 minutes.

(continued)

4. Remove the lid and stir in the parsley. Add salt and pepper. Sprinkle with the scallion to serve.

PER SERVING: 410 calories, 15g total fat, 5g saturated fat, 0g trans fat, 50mg cholesterol, 900mg sodium, 51g total carbohydrate, 5g dietary fiber, 18g protein

use it, don't lose it

 After enjoying your chowder, repurpose the leftover clam shells—if you're crafty. Perhaps turn them into holiday decorations, a wreath, or a wind chime.

 little **green** cooking tip

If you don't have a vegetable brush, get one. It'll come in handy as you'll be using plenty of unpeeled fruits and veggies for eco-conscious cooking. When scrubbing, do so in a bowlful of water rather than continuously running the tap.

wintercress salad

WATERCRESS SALAD WITH WINTER FRUITS

Makes 4 servings: 1¾ cup each

Having a tough time getting all of your fruit and veggie servings in the winter? Solution: Wintercress Salad. It helps you meet those servings scrumptiously. It's filling, too, as the added texture of the pear and kiwi skins provides chewy eco-satisfaction.

2 tablespoons apple cider vinegar
2 teaspoons stone-ground mustard
¼ cup extra-virgin olive oil
1 Bosc pear, finely diced
2 kiwis, scrubbed unpeeled, and finely diced
⅓ cup finely diced red onion
¾ teaspoon sea salt, or to taste
½ teaspoon freshly ground black pepper, or to taste
2 bunches watercress, thick stems trimmed
1 head Boston lettuce, leaves torn into bite-sized pieces

1. Whisk together the vinegar and mustard in a large serving bowl. Whisk in the oil. Stir in the pear, kiwi, and onion. Add salt and pepper.

2. Add the watercress and lettuce and toss to combine and serve.

PER SERVING: 190 calories, 14g total fat, 2g saturated fat, 0g trans fat, 0mg cholesterol, 490mg sodium, 15g total carbohydrate, 3g dietary fiber, 2g protein

go local

Not all produce will be locally available since not all produce can be grown in all regions of the country—especially during the winter. But visit localharvest.org for places to buy sweet potatoes, jalapeños, or other local produce in your area.

fall into winter salad

MIXED GREEN SALAD WITH PEARS, WALNUTS, CRANBERRIES, AND MAPLE DRESSING

Makes 4 servings: 1½ cups each

Having family or friends over for a holiday dinner? This salad will knock their stockings off! The maple syrup in the dressing coupled with the mixture of seasonal fruits and nuts create a concoction worthy of an elegant affair or casual merrymaking.

2 teaspoons Champagne or white wine vinegar
2 teaspoons pure maple syrup
1 teaspoon Dijon mustard
¼ cup extra-virgin olive oil
1 small shallot, finely diced
½ teaspoon sea salt, or to taste
¼ teaspoon freshly ground black pepper, or to taste
5 cups mixed salad greens, such as chopped endive, frisée, and radicchio
1 Seckel or Comice pear, sliced
½ cup raw walnut halves
¼ cup dried cranberries or dried tart cherries

little
green
cooking
tip

Experiment with ingredients that you already have on hand to help prevent food waste. For instance, the pears in this salad can be replaced with apples or grapes. The walnuts and dried cranberries can be replaced with trail mix or fruit and nut granola. Be creative!

Winter

(continued)

1. Whisk together the vinegar, maple syrup, and mustard in a large serving bowl. Whisk in the oil. Stir in the shallot and add salt and pepper.

2. Add the greens and pear and toss with the maple dressing. Top with walnuts and cranberries and serve.

PER SERVING: 280 calories, 22g total fat, 3g saturated fat, 0g trans fat, 0mg cholesterol, 320mg sodium, 19g total carbohydrate, 3g dietary fiber, 3g protein

a planet-friendly bite

Pure maple syrup is truly a gift from nature. It's basically sap from maple trees that has been cooked down until it's a thick syrup. But watch out for maple-flavored syrup; it's basically corn syrup with just a touch of maple syrup. And pancake syrups can be almost entirely corn syrup with artificial maple flavoring.

yin-yang orange

LEAFY ASIAN MANDARIN ORANGE SALAD

Makes 4 servings: 1½ cups each

Yin and yang is about the uniting of opposites. This salad is about the harmonious unity of vinegar and oil, honey and soy sauce, fruit and nuts. It's a union that's like a storybook romance—a beautiful Asian one—though it's likely a taste tale enjoyed by those who are enchanted by novels rather than nursery rhymes.

little **green** cooking tip

If you usually toast or roast nuts to boost their flavors, you can skip that step to save energy. To up the nutty flavor instead, mix two types of nuts together for flavor synergy. And if tossing nuts onto a salad, use a flavorful nut or seed oil, like sesame, in the dressing to carry the flavors throughout.

1 tablespoon rice wine vinegar (preferably brown rice) or apple cider vinegar
1 tablespoon mild floral honey
2 teaspoons naturally brewed soy sauce
2 tablespoons peanut oil
2 teaspoons sesame oil
¼ teaspoon sea salt, or to taste
¼ teaspoon freshly ground black pepper, or to taste
6 cups mixed salad greens
2 mandarin oranges, tangerines, or Clementines, peeled, sliced
2 scallions, green and white parts, thinly sliced
¼ cup sliced raw (natural) almonds or chopped peanuts, or mixture of almonds and peanuts

1. Whisk together the vinegar, honey, and soy sauce in a large serving or mixing bowl. Whisk in the oils. Add salt and pepper.

2. Add the salad greens, oranges, and scallions and toss with the soy dressing. Sprinkle with the almonds and serve.

PER SERVING: 160 calories, 12g total fat, 1.5g saturated fat, 0g trans fat, 0mg cholesterol, 310mg sodium, 13g total carbohydrate, 3g dietary fiber, 3g protein

a planet-friendly bite

There are many different varieties of soy sauces, but avoid any that are chemically manufactured. To do that, look for one that is naturally brewed. It'll generally be made with just three ingredients: soybeans, wheat, and salt.

tabbouleh twist

TABBOULEH SALAD WITH MEYER LEMON

Makes 4 servings: 1 cup each

Meyer lemons look and smell like they should be summer fruits. But when it's winter, it's the best time to treat yourself to their juicy goodness. A cross between and a tangerine and a lemon, they're a little sweeter than their regular counterpart. Meyer lemon juice is enjoyable in most places that you normally use lemon juice; it adds a hint of sweetness, like in this no-cook bulgur salad.

1 cup bulgur wheat
¼ cup extra-virgin olive oil
3 tablespoons fresh Meyer or regular lemon juice
2 large cloves garlic, minced
1 cup grape tomatoes, halved lengthwise
⅓ cup finely chopped fresh flat-leaf parsley
2 scallions, green and white parts, thinly sliced
¼ cup finely diced unpeeled hothouse cucumber
2 tablespoons finely chopped fresh mint or
    2 teaspoons dried crushed mint
1 teaspoon sea salt, or to taste
¼ teaspoon freshly ground black pepper, or to taste
1 teaspoon Meyer lemon zest, or to taste (optional)

1. Place the bulgur in a medium bowl and completely cover with cool fresh water, about 1 cup. Allow to stand for 1 hour. Drain well of any remaining liquid.

2. Meanwhile, whisk together the oil, lemon juice, and garlic in a medium bowl. Stir in the tomatoes, parsley, scallions, cucumber, and mint.

3. Add the vegetable mixture to the drained bulgur and gently stir. Add salt and pepper.

4. Serve at room temperature. Sprinkle with Meyer lemon zest, if desired.

PER SERVING: 260 calories, 15g total fat, 2g saturated fat, 0g trans fat, 0mg cholesterol, 590mg sodium, 31g total carbohydrate, 7g dietary fiber, 5g protein

little **green** cooking tip

If preparing a planet-pleasing dish and a specific fresh herb isn't available, make it anyway. Use any available fresh herb, such as flat-leaf parsley. Or use 1 teaspoon of the dried herb for 1 table-spoon of the fresh chopped version. Dried organic herbs and spices are now widely available!

broccoli trifle

LAYERED BROCCOLI SALAD

Makes 4 servings: 2 cups each

I remember a version of this salad back from the oddly fashionable seventies when I was a schoolgirl with very picky taste. Other than potato chips and French fries, it was tough to get me to eat veggies. (Well, at least I counted those both as veggies!) But serve me a layered broccoli salad, and I would eat it like I never had a persnickety past. Part of what I discovered back then is that I preferred my broccoli raw. Then topped with a sweet-n-tangy yogurt dressing and sprinkled with salty nuts, you had me at hello. Hello, broccoli—raw food is green and it's back in fashion!

7 cups bite-sized broccoli florets with some of the tender stems

1 small red onion, very thinly sliced

⅔ cup shredded organic or locally produced extra-sharp or sharp Cheddar cheese (optional)

⅓ cup dried tart cherries or cranberries

½ cup plain soy or organic yogurt

2 tablespoons mayonnaise

2 tablespoons apple cider vinegar

2 tablespoons mild floral honey or 3 tablespoons local fruit spread or homemade jam

¼ cup chopped raw cashews or peanuts

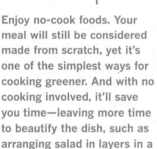

little *green* cooking tip

Enjoy no-cook foods. Your meal will still be considered made from scratch, yet it's one of the simplest ways for cooking greener. And with no cooking involved, it'll save you time—leaving more time to beautify the dish, such as arranging salad in layers in a trifle bowl.

(continued)

Winter

1. Layer the broccoli, onion, cheese (if using), and cherries in a large glass trifle or serving bowl.

2. Whisk together the yogurt, mayonnaise, vinegar, and honey in a small bowl or liquid measuring cup. Pour the dressing evenly over the salad.

3. Sprinkle with the cashews and serve.

PER SERVING: 240 calories, 10g total fat, 1.5g saturated fat, 0g trans fat, 5mg cholesterol, 100mg sodium, 35g total carbohydrate, 7g dietary fiber, 7g protein

---

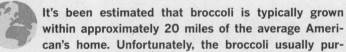

a planet-friendly bite

It's been estimated that broccoli is typically grown within approximately 20 miles of the average American's home. Unfortunately, the broccoli usually purchased from a typical supermarket travels more than 1,800 miles from ground to grocery store. That's like driving from Los Angeles to St. Louis!

salad of citrus cheer

PINK GRAPEFRUIT AND ENDIVE SALAD WITH CHAMPAGNE VINAIGRETTE

Makes 4 servings: 1½ cups each

This recipe takes the grapefruit out of the image of the dreaded diet plate, and onto the lively pages of this stylin' cookbook. This precious pink fruit is what makes this salad so elegant. The sweetness in the vinaigrette mellows its sharpness and pine nuts bring balance. Savor it slowly to appreciate its fine intonations.

2 tablespoons Champagne vinegar

2 teaspoons mild floral honey or 1 tablespoon local fruit spread or homemade jam

¼ cup extra-virgin olive oil

¼ teaspoon sea salt

¼ teaspoon freshly ground black pepper

2 Belgian endives, cored, halved lengthwise, and cut into strips

1 head frisée, torn into bite-sized pieces

1 cup fresh baby arugula or baby spinach

1 large pink grapefruit, peeled, halved, and very thinly sliced

1 ounce organic or locally produced Parmesan cheese, shaved (optional)

3 tablespoons raw pine nuts

1. Whisk together the vinegar and honey in large serving bowl. Whisk in the olive oil. Add salt and pepper. Add the endive, frisée, and arugula and toss to coat. Taste and adjust seasoning.

2. Arrange the grapefruit on top of the salad. Top with the cheese (if using) and pine nuts and serve.

PER SERVING: 220 calories, 19g total fat, 2.5g saturated fat, 0g trans fat, 0mg cholesterol, 160mg sodium, 13g total carbohydrate, 3g dietary fiber, 2g protein

use it, don't lose it

Consider selecting exact recipe ingredients from a salad bar to help prevent waste. A University of Arizona study suggested that U.S. households waste about 14 percent of the food they buy! That means hundreds of dollars a year—plus a harmful environmental impact to go with it.

Winter

salad melody

BLOOD ORANGE, ARUGULA, AND MAYTAG BLUE CHEESE SALAD WITH BLOOD ORANGE VINAIGRETTE

Makes 4 servings: 1½ cups each

This salad will put your back up against the dining chair and make you pay attention. The ruby-red orange is worth appreciating when blood oranges are available. For me, its sweet-tartness in concert with the tangy-saltiness of the blue cheese creates a melody for the palate.

1 blood orange
Juice of ½ lemon (about 1½ tablespoons)
2 teaspoons mild floral honey or 1 tablespoon local fruit spread or
   homemade jam
3 tablespoons extra-virgin olive oil
¼ teaspoon sea salt, or to taste
¼ teaspoon freshly ground black pepper, or to taste
6 cups arugula leaves
¼ cup very thinly sliced red onion
¼ cup crumbled organic or locally produced Maytag or
   other blue cheese

1. Grate the orange zest and set aside. Remove or cut away the remaining peel and slice the orange. Set aside

2. Whisk together the lemon juice, honey, and 1 teaspoon of the orange zest in a large serving bowl. Whisk in the oil. Add salt and pepper.

3. Add the arugula and onion and toss to coat. Add the sliced orange and gently toss. Taste and adjust seasoning.

4. Sprinkle with the cheese and reserved zest, if desired, and serve.

PER SERVING: 170 calories, 13g total fat, 3g saturated fat, 0g trans fat, 5mg cholesterol, 270mg sodium, 10g total carbohydrate, 1g dietary fiber, 3g protein

little **green** cooking tip

Blood orange zest punches up flavor. But, if you prefer, store the scrubbed peel in olive oil for a week or two to make citrusy oil. Or add the peel to a package of hardened brown sugar to soften overnight.

pinky potato salad

WINTER FINGERLING POTATO SALAD

Makes 4 servings: 1½ cups each

This potato salad represents low-carbon cuisine lusciousness at its finest. The potatoes are sliced before cooking so they take little time on the stovetop. Everything is mixed in the bowl you plan to serve it in so there's less to wash. But equally important is that it's filling (in a good way) and tastes great. It'll give you a reason to have a picnic in the winter wonderland—even if indoors.

2 pounds small banana fingerling potatoes, scrubbed unpeeled, and cut into ¼-inch rounds

1 teaspoon sea salt, or to taste

¼ cup mayonnaise

3 tablespoons stone-ground mustard

2 tablespoons organic sour cream or soy-based sour cream alternative

3 scallions, green and white parts, thinly sliced

1 tablespoon chopped fresh dill or 1 teaspoon dried dill

1 large stalk celery, thinly sliced

¼ teaspoon cayenne pepper, or to taste

1. Add the sliced potatoes to a large saucepan or stockpot and cover with cold water. Add ¾ teaspoon of the salt. Bring to a boil over high heat. Cover and reduce the heat to medium. Cook for 2 minutes. Turn off the heat. Let "lid cook" (cook covered while the burner is off) until the potatoes are just tender, about 8 minutes.

(continued)

little
green
cooking
tip

When root veggies, like potatoes, are to be boiled, start them in cold water, let them boil for just a couple minutes, and then "lid cook" the rest of the way. You'll use less energy. Plus, the end result may be a preferable texture since they will be more delicately cooked.

2. Meanwhile, stir together the mayonnaise, mustard, sour cream, scallions, and dill in a large serving bowl.

3. Drain the potatoes. Add the warm potatoes along with the celery to the mayonnaise mixture and stir gently to combine. Add the remaining ¼ teaspoon salt and cayenne.

4. Serve while warm or chill in the refrigerator until ready to serve and enjoy cool. Garnish with additional dill, if desired.

PER SERVING: 290 calories, 13g total fat, 2.5g saturated fat, 0g trans fat, 10mg cholesterol, 620mg sodium, 40g total carbohydrate, 5g dietary fiber, 5g protein

use it, don't lose it

 When boiling potatoes, you'll be left with extra cooking liquid. Use it like a vegetable broth for a base of a soup. Freeze it if you don't need it right away.

VEGETARIAN DISHES

homemade veggie burgers

VEGETARIAN SOY BURGERS

Makes 6 servings: 1 burger each

Burgers . . . not-so-green. Veggie burgers . . . green. Homemade Veggie Burgers . . . very green. You can actually see the veggies so you know the burgers are 100 percent real. They're real good for you and real good tasting, too. So good, in fact, you won't need to glam them up with gobs of condiments; they're actually tasty enough as is.

3 tablespoons peanut oil, or to taste
1 cup finely chopped broccoli florets and tender stems
1 cup finely chopped portobello or cremini mushrooms
1 large shallot, minced
1 large clove garlic, minced
2 large organic eggs*
2 tablespoons unsalted natural almond, cashew, or peanut butter
1 tablespoon turbinado or Demerara sugar
2 teaspoons naturally brewed soy sauce
1 teaspoon sea salt, or to taste
½ teaspoon freshly ground black pepper, or to taste
1 (14-ounce) package firm tofu, well drained and patted dry
1 cup whole-wheat breadcrumbs
1 medium carrot, scrubbed unpeeled, and finely grated

(continued)

little **green** cooking tip

Vegetarian foods are not just for vegetarians anymore, especially vegetarian burgers. Instead of buying a packaged variety of veggie burgers, try them homemade—at least from time to time.

1. Heat 1 tablespoon of the oil in a large stick-resistant skillet over medium heat. Add the broccoli and stir to coat with the oil. Cover and cook until just tender, about 3 minutes. Stir in the mushrooms, shallot, and garlic. Cover with the lid, and cook for 1 minute, then turn off the heat. Let "lid cook" (cook covered while the burner is off) until all vegetables are tender, about 3 minutes.

2. Meanwhile, lightly beat the eggs with a fork in a large mixing bowl. Stir in the almond butter, sugar, soy sauce, salt, and pepper until combined. Stir in the tofu, breadcrumbs, and carrot until combined. Stir in the broccoli mixture, then thoroughly combine with your hands. Firmly form the mixture into 6 patties, about ½ cup mixture each.

3. Heat 1 tablespoon of the oil in the skillet over medium-high heat. Sauté 3 of the patties until well-browned and cooked through, about 3 minutes per side. Repeat with the remaining oil and patties. Taste and adjust seasoning.

4. Serve on whole-grain (egg- and dairy-free, if desired) rolls or buns with lettuce, tomato, onion, and condiments of choice.

PER SERVING: 250 calories, 15g total fat, 2.5g saturated fat, 0g trans fat, 70mg cholesterol, 540mg sodium, 19g total carbohydrate, 4g dietary fiber, 12g protein

*This recipe can be made without eggs. If making without eggs, form this more delicate mixture into 12 mini burgers.

go local

Fresh is best. Instead of buying a jar of nut butter that's made halfway across the country, head to a local market or health food store where you may find them freshly grinding peanut, almond, or other nut butters. Some markets even have do-it-yourself stations set up so you can grind just the amount you need, even if just 2 tablespoons.

peanutty citrus stir-fry

THAI PEANUT–PINK GRAPEFRUIT TOFU STIR-FRY

Makes 4 servings: 1 cup each

I'm a tofu liker, not lover—unless you serve it to me in a full-flavored stir-fry recipe. I'm in love with this ecotartian one. The tofu picks up amazing flavor from the marinade. The grapefruit adds instantaneous flavor intrigue. And the peanuts make it marriage material for the mouth.

1 medium pink grapefruit, peeled, chopped (remove any seeds)
2 teaspoons turbinado or Demerara sugar
3 tablespoons naturally brewed soy sauce
1 tablespoon rice vinegar (preferably brown rice)
2 tablespoons local fruit spread or homemade jam or
   1 tablespoon mild floral honey
2 teaspoons Asian garlic-chili sauce
1 teaspoon sesame oil
1 (12-ounce) package extra-firm tofu, well drained,
   cut into ½-inch cubes
1 teaspoon cornstarch or arrowroot powder
2 tablespoons peanut oil
8 ounces baby bok choy, thinly sliced
3 large cloves garlic, minced
1 tablespoon grated scrubbed unpeeled gingerroot
4 scallions, green and white parts, thinly sliced on diagonal
3 tablespoons finely chopped fresh cilantro
¼ cup raw peanuts, coarsely chopped

1. Toss the grapefruit with the sugar in a small bowl and set aside.

2. Whisk together the soy sauce, vinegar, fruit spread, garlic-chili sauce, and sesame oil in a medium bowl. Add the tofu and stir to coat; let marinate 20 minutes. Drain, reserving the marinade in a small bowl. Whisk ¼ cup fresh water and the cornstarch into the marinade until smooth.

(continued)

little **green** cooking tip

Stir-frying is a quick-cooking technique, which helps to make it an eco-conscious cooking technique, too. Be sure to serve stir-fries with eco-conscious sides as well, such as steamed quinoa, whole-wheat couscous, or soba noodles. For Peanutty Citrus Stir-Fry, serve the side of choice in a grapefruit "peel-up."

Winter

3. Heat 1 tablespoon of the peanut oil in a large stick-resistant skillet or a wok over medium-high heat. Add the tofu and stir-fry until golden, about 3 minutes. Transfer the tofu to a serving plate or bowl and set aside.

4. Add the remaining 1 tablespoon oil to the skillet. Add the bok choy and reserved grapefruit (along with any liquid from the bowl) and stir-fry until the bok choy is tender, about 3 minutes. Add the garlic and gingerroot and stir-fry for 30 seconds.

5. Return the tofu to the skillet along with the scallions and the reserved marinade mixture. Stir-fry until the marinade thickens slightly, about 30 seconds.

6. Sprinkle with the cilantro and peanuts. Enjoy over steamed quinoa. Serve with additional soy sauce on the side, if desired.

PER SERVING: 280 calories, 18g total fat, 2.5g saturated fat, 0g trans fat, 0mg cholesterol, 720mg sodium, 20g total carbohydrate, 3g dietary fiber, 14g protein

use it, don't lose it

 A single stir-fry order from a Chinese fast-food restaurant in the U.S. is notoriously much larger than one serving. So when making your own stir-fry, be conscientious of portion size. Take just what you can eat, regardless of what a recipe says it serves. It's a good green habit to be a "clean your plate" club member—as long as you've placed the just-right amount of food on it to start.

granny cakes

GRANNY SMITH APPLE PANCAKES WITH CINNAMON BUTTER

Makes 4 servings: 4 (2½-inch) pancakes each

These pancakes will make you feel like the morning sun. You'll be glowing with Granny Smith apple goodness. And though you'll be tempted to eat the entire batch, stick to just four or you might start glowing (and growing) all over. It's that cinnamon butter that's like a ray of lusciousness. But it's oh-so worth it!

¼ cup unsalted organic butter, at room temperature

3 tablespoons mild floral honey or ¼ cup local fruit spread
    or homemade jam

½ teaspoon ground cinnamon

½ teaspoon lemon or orange zest

¾ cup stone-ground whole-wheat flour

2 tablespoons turbinado or Demerara sugar

1½ teaspoons baking powder

¼ teaspoon sea salt

⅓ cup whole organic milk or plain unsweetened soymilk

1 large organic egg

3 tablespoons peanut oil

1 medium Granny Smith apple, cored, halved

1. Stir the butter, honey, cinnamon, and zest in a small bowl until smooth. Set aside.

2. Whisk the flour, sugar, baking powder, and salt in a large bowl. Make a well in the center of the dry ingredients. Whisk in the milk, egg, and 2 tablespoons of the oil until smooth. Coarsely grate the apple into the mixture. Cover and let the batter stand at room temperature about 20 minutes.

3. Heat a large stick-resistant skillet or griddle over medium-high heat for 1 minute. Brush the skillet with half of the remaining oil. Spoon the batter, about 1 tablespoon per pancake onto the skillet, to make 8 pancakes. Cook until golden and cooked through, about 2 minutes per side.

(continued)

4. Transfer the cooked pancakes to a plate and cover with a lid or recycled aluminum foil to keep warm. Repeat with the remaining batter to make another 8 pancakes, brushing the skillet with oil before the second batch.

5. Arrange the pancakes on plates. Top with the reserved cinnamon butter mixture.

PER SERVING: 390 calories, 24g total fat, 9g saturated fat, 0g trans fat, 85mg cholesterol, 380mg sodium, 42g total carbohydrate, 4g dietary fiber, 6g protein

use it, don't lose it

Eat the apple peel! One reason is that the peel is nutritionally powerful—containing more antioxidants than apple flesh. Research finds that apples with the peels are better able to inhibit cancer cell growth and inhibit LDL oxidation (that's the bad cholesterol in the blood) when compared to peeled apples. But remember, choose organic apples whenever possible.

"that's not broccoli" capellini

LEMON ZESTED RAPINI CAPELLINI

Makes 6 servings: 1⅓ cups each

Super-skinny is in—well, only if you're talking about pasta. Super-skinny capellini, otherwise called angel hair, cooks so quickly because of its size. That can help keep your carbon footprint on earth a small one. But don't douse the angelic noodles with sauce full of devilish ingredients. Toss them with fresh ingredients, like rapini and olive oil. The result . . . well, heavenly.

1 bunch rapini (broccoli rabe), trimmed and chopped

3 large cloves garlic, minced

2 teaspoons sea salt, or to taste

12 ounces whole-wheat capellini or angel hair pasta

Juice and zest of 1 lemon (about 3 tablespoons juice)

⅓ cup extra-virgin olive oil

½ cup freshly grated organic or locally produced Parmesan cheese (optional)

¼ teaspoon crushed red pepper flakes, or to taste

1. Add the rapini, garlic, and 1 teaspoon of the salt to a large saucepan. Cover with 9 cups of cool fresh water. Bring to a boil over high heat.

2. Stir in the pasta and bring back to a boil. Cover and turn off the heat. Let "lid cook" (cook covered while the burner is off) until the pasta is al dente, about 4 minutes. Drain the pasta and rapini, reserving the cooking liquid.

(continued)

little **green** cooking tip

Save cooking liquids in which you prepare pasta or veggies. Use the water from cooked pasta to add moistness or nicely thin a sauce that's otherwise too thick. Use extra water from cooked veggies in which to prepare grains. Freeze it and use as stock or cooking broth for later use, too.

3. Place the drained pasta and rapini back into the dry pot. Add the lemon juice and zest and toss to coat. Drizzle with the oil and toss to coat. Add desired amount, about ¼ cup, of the reserved cooking liquid. (Use the remaining cooking liquid for another purpose, such as a broth in which to cook whole grains.) Sprinkle with the cheese (if using) and toss to coat. Add the remaining teaspoon salt and crushed red pepper.

PER SERVING: 330 calories, 13g total fat, 2g saturated fat, 0g trans fat, 0mg cholesterol, 610mg sodium, 45g total carbohydrate, 4g dietary fiber, 11g protein

use it, don't lose it

 If you don't want to cook with extra pasta water, you can even use the nutrient-rich liquid (once it cools completely) for watering your plants.

jolly green eggs

BIG BROCCOLI OMELET

Makes 3 servings: ⅓ of 12-inch omelet each

Get that chef's knife out and get ready for action. That's one secret weapon to this recipes greenness. By finely chopping the broccoli, it'll need less cooking time. The end result is an omelet with plenty of green goodness—and plenty of delectableness.

2 tablespoons canola or peanut oil

10 ounces broccoli florets and tender stems, finely chopped

3 ounces shitake or cremini mushrooms, very thinly sliced

2 scallions, green and white parts, very thinly sliced

¾ teaspoon sea salt, or to taste

⅛ teaspoon freshly grated or ground nutmeg, or to taste

6 large organic eggs

¼ teaspoon freshly ground black pepper, or to taste

3 ounces organic or locally produced Swiss cheese, shredded (optional)

1. Heat 1½ tablespoons of the oil in a large stick-resistant skillet over medium-high heat. Stir in the broccoli, mushrooms, the white and most of the green part of the scallions, ¼ teaspoon of the salt, and the nutmeg. Cover and cook until the broccoli is cooked but still firm, about 4 minutes. Pour the broccoli mixture onto a large plate, and cover to keep warm.

2. Meanwhile, whisk together the eggs, 1 tablespoon cold fresh water, the remaining ½ teaspoon salt, and pepper in a medium bowl.

3. Heat the remaining ½ tablespoon oil in the skillet over medium-high heat and add the eggs. (It's okay if there are still some small pieces of the broccoli mixture in the pan.) While slightly tilting the pan and using a silicone spatula, lift the edges of the omelet, allowing uncooked portion of eggs to flow under cooked portion. Cook until the omelet is nearly set, about 3 minutes. Cover with the lid and turn off the heat. Let "lid cook" (cook covered while the burner is off) until the omelet is fully cooked and set, yet still moist, about 3 minutes.

4. Sprinkle with the cheese (if using). Spread half of the omelet with the broccoli filling. Slide the omelet out of the pan onto the large plate, while using the edge of the pan to help fold the unfilled side over the broccoli filling.

5. Taste and adjust seasoning, if necessary. Sprinkle with the remaining scallions. Cut in three portions and serve.

PER SERVING: 270 calories, 20g total fat, 4g saturated fat, 0g trans fat, 425mg cholesterol, 730mg sodium, 8g total carbohydrate, 3g dietary fiber, 16g protein

little *green* cooking tip

Every time you cook, try to find ways to save a little energy. One way is to cut off the energy flow just before the end of the cooking time. Aim to save two or more minutes when giving a green makeover (a "greenover") to a not-so-green recipe.

a planet-friendly bite

Are brown-shelled eggs better? No. Go with brown or white. Eggshell color has nothing to do with egg nutrition, quality, or flavor. The color actually comes from pigments in the shell's outer layer. The hen's breed is what determines the shell color. Breeds with red ear lobes and feathers lay brown eggs. That means breeds with white ear lobes and feathers lay white eggs.

side of supergrains

LEMON-PISTACHIO QUINOA PILAF

Makes 4 servings: ¾ cup each

I haven't found a nut I don't like. But I do play favorites . . . I have three of them. The pistachio is one. I especially love that it's green, literally. It adds distinctive color, crunch, and flavor to this otherwise "plain Jane" quinoa dish. What's more, unlike a brown rice pilaf, this whole-grain pilaf represents the supergrain of low carbon cuisine. It requires only about 5 minutes of cooking energy, not 50.

1 cup quinoa, rinsed and drained
1 small shallot, minced
Juice and zest of 1 small lemon (about 2 tablespoons juice)
¾ teaspoon sea salt, or to taste
2 tablespoons extra-virgin olive oil, or to taste
½ cup unsalted raw shelled pistachios, chopped

1. Combine the quinoa, 1⅔ cup fresh water, shallot, lemon juice and zest, and salt in a small saucepan. Place over high heat and bring to a boil. Cover and turn off the heat. Let "lid cook" (cook covered while the burner is off) until the quinoa is tender, fully cooked, and the liquid is absorbed, about 20 minutes.

2. Stir in the oil. Taste and adjust seasoning, if necessary. Stir in the pistachios and serve immediately.

PER SERVING: 310 calories, 17g total fat, 2g saturated fat, 0g trans fat, 0mg cholesterol, 440mg sodium, 33g total carbohydrate, 5g dietary fiber, 9g protein

use it, don't lose it

Sometimes grain dishes are even better chilled the next day. So if you have leftover pilaf, serve the spare as a savory salad. Squirt it with a lemon wedge for fresh flair.

savory celeriac smash

MASHED CELERY ROOT

Makes 2 servings: ¾ cup each

In the mood for something like mashed potatoes? This knobby root veggie might just be the fix. You'll get a little bit of creaminess with an intriguing celery- and parsley-like taste. By cutting the celery root into tiny cubes, they'll cook quickly. Pair them with organic poultry dishes or leafy greens. Or serve them anytime you might mashed potatoes. They're smashing.

1 medium celery root (celeriac), peeled, cut into ⅓-inch cubes
1 cup low-sodium vegetable broth
¼ cup plain unsweetened soymilk, at room temperature
1 tablespoon unsalted organic butter, at room temperature,
   or extra-virgin olive oil
¼ teaspoon sea salt, or to taste

1. Add the celery root and broth to a large saucepan. Cover and place over medium-high heat. Cook until the celery root is nearly tender, about 5 minutes. Turn off the heat and keep covered. Let "lid cook" (cook covered while the burner is off) until the celery root is tender, about 5 minutes.

2. Add the soymilk and butter. Mash with a potato masher until a chunky applesauce-like consistency. Add salt and serve.

PER SERVING: 150 calories, 7g total fat, 4g saturated fat, 0g trans fat, 15mg cholesterol, 550mg sodium, 19g total carbohydrate, 3g dietary fiber, 4g protein

little *green* cooking tip

A ruler doesn't just belong in a school box or a desk drawer. It's a helpful tool for a low-carbon kitchen. It'll help you slice and dice foods to even-sized—and green-sized—pieces.

use it, don't lose it

Extra celery root? Since it's a root of a unique celery, not potato-like, go raw. Enjoy it uncooked and shredded in a salad. Just toss it in a little acidulated water (lemon juice squirted into water) first to help keep it from turning brownish.

squash-studded orzo

BUTTERNUT SQUASH ORZO WITH FRESH SAGE

Makes 6 servings: 1½ cups each

Perhaps the most unforgettable wintertime flavor duet is butternut squash and sage. When those flavors join synergistically with the rest of the orchestra of ingredients, you have a savory symphony. The petite cubes of squash and rice-sized orzo both allow this dish to cook quickly. That's music to the eco-savvy ear.

2 tablespoons extra-virgin olive oil
2 tablespoons unsalted organic butter
1 medium white or yellow onion, finely chopped
1 large clove garlic, minced
1 medium butternut squash, peeled, seeded, and cut into ¼-inch cubes
4 cups low-sodium vegetable broth
1 cup whole-wheat orzo
½ cup freshly grated organic or locally produced Asiago cheese (optional)
2 tablespoons finely chopped fresh sage
¼ teaspoon cayenne pepper
⅛ teaspoon freshly ground or grated nutmeg
1¼ teaspoons sea salt, or to taste
¼ teaspoon freshly ground black pepper, or to taste

1. Heat the oil and butter in a large stick-resistant skillet over medium heat until the butter melts. Add the onion and sauté until soft, about 5 minutes. Add the garlic and sauté until fragrant, about 1 minute. Add the butternut squash and stir to coat. Add ¾ cup of the broth and cover. Simmer until the squash is only slightly firm, about 6 minutes. Turn off the heat and let "lid cook" (cook covered while the burner is off) until the squash is just tender and liquid is nearly absorbed, about 5 minutes. Immediately transfer the squash mixture along with any remaining liquid to a large serving bowl.

little *green* cooking tip

Orzo is shaped like rice, but it's a pasta. Instead of utilizing nearly an hour of cooking energy to prepare traditional brown rice, consider enjoying whole-wheat orzo in its place. It requires only a few minutes of energy. Though, quicker-cooking rice is available, if you prefer.

2. Meanwhile, add the orzo and the remaining broth in a large saucepan. Bring to a boil over high heat. Cover and turn off the heat. Allow to "lid cook" (cook while covered with the burner off) until the orzo is al dente, about 7 minutes. Drain well, reserving the cooking broth for other purpose.

3. Transfer the orzo to the serving bowl with the squash mixture. Stir in the cheese (if using), sage, cayenne, and nutmeg. Add the salt and black pepper. Serve while warm.

PER SERVING: 240 calories, 9g total fat, 3g saturated fat, 0g trans fat, 10mg cholesterol, 590mg sodium, 37g total carbohydrate, 6g dietary fiber, 5g protein

use it, don't lose it

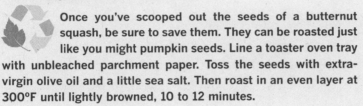 Once you've scooped out the seeds of a butternut squash, be sure to save them. They can be roasted just like you might pumpkin seeds. Line a toaster oven tray with unbleached parchment paper. Toss the seeds with extra-virgin olive oil and a little sea salt. Then roast in an even layer at 300°F until lightly browned, 10 to 12 minutes.

FISH, POULTRY, & MEAT DISHES

tangy tarragon tuna

HONEY-N-GRAPEFRUIT PAN-SEARED TUNA STEAKS WITH TARRAGON

Makes 4 servings: 1 steak each

Yellowfin tuna is a planet-pleaser when it comes to sustainability. Its winning taste is a palate-pleaser. Since it's a fish that's actually better tasting when cooked a little, not a lot, it allows you to enjoy it greenly. When topped with grapefruit, it allows you to enjoy it tartly and sweetly, too.

1 medium pink or white grapefruit
¼ cup peanut oil
1 small shallot, minced
1 small jalapeño with some seeds, minced
2 teaspoons finely chopped fresh tarragon or ½ teaspoon dried tarragon
¾ teaspoon sea salt, or to taste
½ teaspoon freshly ground black pepper, or to taste
2 (10-ounce) Atlantic yellowfin tuna steaks, cut in half to make
   4 (5-ounce) thin-cut tuna steaks, ½-inch thick
1 tablespoon orange blossom or other mild floral honey

1. Grate 1 teaspoon of the grapefruit zest and set aside. Cut off the peel and pith from the grapefruit and cut flesh into 4 thin slices. (Eat any extra grapefruit!)

2. Whisk the oil, shallot, jalapeño, reserved zest, 1 teaspoon of the tarragon, salt, and pepper in a 9 × 13-inch glass baking dish to blend. Add the tuna and completely coat with the marinade. Let marinate for 20 minutes.

3. Heat a large stick-resistant skillet over high heat. Add the tuna along with the marinade and cook until the bottom is just browned, about 1 minute. Turn over the steaks. Top each steak with a grapefruit slice and drizzle with the honey. Cover and turn off the heat. Let "lid cook" (cook covered while the burner is off) until the tuna is cooked to desired doneness, about 1 minute for medium rare.

4. Taste and adjust seasoning, if necessary. Sprinkle with the remaining teaspoon tarragon.

PER SERVING: 310 calories, 15g total fat, 2.5g saturated fat, 0g trans fat, 65mg cholesterol, 490mg sodium, 11g total carbohydrate, 1g dietary fiber, 34g protein

a planet-friendly bite

 There's no need for fancy pans. A well-seasoned cast-iron skillet is the original stick-resistant surface and meant to be used for a lifetime! It's great for low-carbon cooking as it distributes and retains heat very well. The key to getting regular cast iron to be at its stick-resistant best is to use it often.

little **green** cooking tip

Even if you choose foods that are eco-friendly to start with, you can be greener by preparing them in an eco-friendly way, too. For instance, cut a thick sustainable tuna steak into two thinner steaks so it'll cook more quickly. Then pair it with fresh local fruit for green bonus points.

golden gravy— and turkey, too

ROSEMARY-ROASTED ORGANIC TURKEY BREAST WITH GOLDEN DELICIOUS APPLE GRAVY

Makes 4 servings: 3½ ounces turkey with 3 tablespoons apple gravy each

Here you'll find turkey and apples together in perfect harmony on your dinner plate. The rosemary adds an unexpected yet joyful bang. It'll taste like Thanksgiving dinner—ready in minutes, not hours.

3 tablespoons extra-virgin olive oil
1 teaspoon minced fresh rosemary or ¼ teaspoon dried crushed rosemary
1 teaspoon sea salt, or to taste
½ teaspoon freshly ground black pepper, or to taste
1 (1-pound) boneless, skinless organic turkey breast, cut into 4 (2-inch-thick) mini-roasts
1 large Golden Delicious apple, finely diced
2 teaspoons apple cider vinegar

1. Stir the oil, rosemary, salt, and pepper on a toaster oven tray until combined. Add the turkey mini-roasts and apple and toss to fully coat.

2. Place the tray into the toaster oven* (do not preheat). Turn the heat to 400°F and roast the turkey and apples until a thermometer inserted into the thickest part of the turkey registers 170°F and the juices run clear when pierced with a fork, about 16 minutes. Let stand for 5 minutes to allow to finish cooking.

3. Meanwhile, transfer the apples and any pan juices into a bowl. Add the vinegar and mash with a potato masher until a thick applesauce-like consistency.

4. Taste and adjust seasoning. Serve turkey topped with the apple gravy. If desired, garnish with additional fresh rosemary.

PER SERVING: 250 calories, 11g total fat, 1.5g saturated fat, 0g trans fat, 75mg cholesterol, 630mg sodium, 8g total carbohydrate, 1g dietary fiber, 27g protein

*Toaster oven sizes and cooking times will vary. See page 39.

little **green** cooking tip

By downsizing (or greensizing) a traditional entrée, such as roasted turkey, pairing it with fruit, such as apples, and preparing it in greener way, such as in a toaster oven, you'll create an eco-conscious meal to be enjoyed often. Plus, when you cook green, you can save green—since you're preparing healthy portions, not costlier hefty portions.

One of the reasons to use extra-virgin olive oil is because of its robust olive taste. When you want that taste, steer clear of labels that say "light." It's basically an American marketing term that means that the olive oil is heavily filtered, making it light on flavor, not on calories. However, if you want to cook at high temperatures or bake with olive oil, then "light" is fine because of its higher smoke point and plain flavor.

flash dancin' chickenwich

POACHED ORGANIC CHICKEN SALAD SANDWICH WITH BLACK GRAPES

Makes 4 servings: 1 sandwich with ¾ cup chicken salad each

Whether a tea lover or simply an occasional sipper, consider becoming a tea eater! Here, chicken is steeped in tea to punch up the flavor, color, and antioxidants. But you really don't taste tea; you'll taste richer chicken—along with all of the other glorious ingredients that'll have your taste buds dancing like they've never danced before.

1 pound boneless, skinless organic chicken breast, cut into ½-inch cubes
1½ teaspoons sea salt, or to taste
2 tea bags black or green tea
2 stalks celery, thinly sliced on the diagonal
1 large shallot, minced
⅓ cup mayonnaise
2 teaspoons apple cider vinegar
1 tablespoon apricot or favorite local fruit spread or homemade jam or 2 teaspoons mild floral honey
1 cup black seedless grapes, halved lengthwise
¼ teaspoon freshly ground black pepper, or to taste
⅓ cup raw pecan halves
2 teaspoons poppy seeds (optional)
8 thick slices whole-grain bread

(continued)

When choosing to cook with chicken, choose organic when you can. Your next best bet is to choose natural. But don't hunt for "hormone-free" labeling. Hormones are not used in poultry production in the U.S.; it's illegal.

1. Add the chicken to a large saucepan. Add cool fresh water until the chicken is just covered (about 2 cups) and 1 teaspoon of the salt. Place over medium-high heat. Bring to a boil, reduce heat to medium, and cook until the chicken is nearly cooked through, about 5 minutes. Add the tea bags, cover, and turn off the heat. Let "lid cook" (cook covered while the burner is off) until the chicken is fully cooked, about 5 minutes. Drain the chicken and remove the tea bags. (Reserve the chicken cooking liquid for other purpose, if desired.)

2. Gently combine the tea-poached chicken cubes, celery, shallot, mayonnaise, vinegar, and fruit spread in a large bowl. Gently stir in the grapes. Add the remaining ½ teaspoon salt and pepper. Chill in the refrigerator until ready to serve.

3. Just before serving, stir in the pecans and poppy seeds (if using). Serve ¾ cup chicken salad per sandwich.

PER SERVING: 500 calories, 26g total fat, 4g saturated fat, 0g trans fat, 70mg cholesterol, 970mg sodium, 35g total carbohydrate, 5g dietary fiber, 31g protein

use it, don't lose it

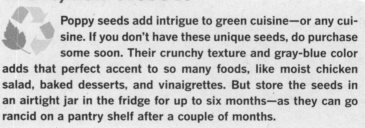

Poppy seeds add intrigue to green cuisine—or any cuisine. If you don't have these unique seeds, do purchase some soon. Their crunchy texture and gray-blue color adds that perfect accent to so many foods, like moist chicken salad, baked desserts, and vinaigrettes. But store the seeds in an airtight jar in the fridge for up to six months—as they can go rancid on a pantry shelf after a couple of months.

bring home the bacon

KUMQUAT ORGANIC CANADIAN BACON

Makes 3 servings: 2 slices each

This dish sounds like breakfast, but it can be anything you want it to be. Ready to enjoy in a pinch, it's delicious for dinner along with steamed whole-wheat couscous or polenta and steamed greens. The pretty slivers of kumquats add allure. And the combination of sweet, tart, salty, and smoky flavors will have you coming back for more.

little **green** cooking tip

1 tablespoon unsalted organic butter

4 kumquats, very thinly sliced

1 scallion, green and white parts, minced

6 slices Canadian-style organic bacon

1 teaspoon mild floral honey or 2 teaspoons local fruit spread or homemade jam

⅛ teaspoon freshly ground black pepper, or to taste

Canadian-style bacon is not any regular bacon. It's actually more like ham—it's fully cooked and smoked. It's from the eye of the loin, so it's lean. And, like poultry, it's hormone-free. But do choose organic when you can to assure it's nitrite-free, too

1. Melt the butter in a large stick-resistant skillet over medium heat. Add the kumquats and scallion and sauté for 1 minute; remove to a plate. Add the bacon and sauté for 1 minute.

2. Turn over, top each slice with the honey, cover, and turn off the heat. Let "lid cook" (cook covered while the burner is off) until fully cooked through, about 3 minutes.

3. Add pepper. Serve the bacon topped with the kumquats.

PER SERVING: 110 calories, 6g total fat, 3g saturated fat, 0g trans fat, 25mg cholesterol, 420mg sodium, 7g total carbohydrate, 2g dietary fiber, 7g protein

a planet-friendly bite

A basic guideline for eco-friendly eating is to choose food with as little packaging as possible. Then, make sure to use as much of that food as you can. Selecting kumquats is a win-win. You can eat the whole fruit. It's the only citrus fruit whose skin is fully edible. In fact, the sweetest part is the skin. Watch this fun video to see how to eat a kumquat: http://dadecity.tbo.com/video.shtml.

Winter

papaya pork

HAWAIIAN ORGANIC PORK LOIN WITH TROPICAL PAPAYA SAUCE

Makes 4 servings: 1 mini-roast each

Using small kitchen appliances is back in fashion as they require less energy than major ones. And you'll find out they can help create tasty dishes, too. This absolutely yummy organic pork entrée is delightfully easy to prepare . . . using a panini grill. Since the grill cooks two sides at once, cooking time is halved.

1 medium papaya, peeled, seeded, and chopped (about 1½ cups)
2 tablespoons naturally brewed soy sauce
1 tablespoon peanut oil
2 teaspoons grated scrubbed unpeeled gingerroot
3 scallions, green and white parts, thinly sliced
1 pound organic pork tenderloin, cut into 4 mini-roasts

1. Mash the papaya, soy sauce, oil, and gingerroot with a potato masher in a medium bowl until a salsalike texture. Stir in half of the scallions. Remove half of the papaya mixture to a small bowl and set aside.

2. Add the pork to the papaya mixture (about ¾ cup) in the medium bowl. Allow to marinate at least 30 minutes. (Cover and marinate in the refrigerator if more than 1 hour.)

3. Remove the pork from the marinade and discard the marinade. Cook the pork in a panini grill on high heat for 4 minutes. (Alternatively, grill the pork or broil it in a toaster oven.) The pork should be very slightly pink in the middle.

4. Top with the reserved papaya mixture and remaining scallions. Serve each pork mini-roast whole or sliced.

PER SERVING: 230 calories, 10g total fat, 3g saturated fat, 0g trans fat, 80mg cholesterol, 520mg sodium, 6g total carbohydrate, 1g dietary fiber, 26g protein

a planet-friendly bite

 Though native to Central America, one of the largest commercial producers of papayas today is the U.S.

little **green** cooking tip

A potato masher isn't just for mashing potatoes. Use it for mashing fruits into salsa-textured sauces. Sauces don't always need to be perfectly pureed using electric kitchen appliances. A little extra texture can add extra interest . . . and that special "homemade" touch.

SIPS & SWEETS

pink bubbles

PINK GRAPEFRUIT COCKTAIL IN GRAPEFRUIT CUP

Makes 4 servings: about 1 cup each

No glass or cup is required to sip this fruity, spirited beverage. It's served right in its own grapefruit peel. Who knew going green could be so much fun?

2 large pink grapefruits, halved
¾ cup lemon-flavored light rum
1½ cups seltzer water
¼ cup turbinado or Demerara sugar
¼ teaspoon finely chopped fresh mint (optional)

1. Using a reamer or hand juicer, juice the grapefruit halves directly into a pitcher through a strainer (to catch seeds).

2. Add the remaining ingredients into the pitcher. Stir or whisk until the sugar dissolves.

3. Slice a very thin piece of peel from the bottom of the grapefruit halves in order for them to stand like a cup. Pour ½ cup of the beverage into each grapefruit half "peel-up." Drink, then refill.

PER SERVING: 190 calories, 0g total fat, 0g saturated fat, 0g trans fat, 0mg cholesterol, 0mg sodium, 25g total carbohydrate, 2g dietary fiber, 1g protein

little **green** cooking tip

Keep a reamer at the ready in the winter. It'll come in handy with the seasonal citrus fruits that are so prevalent. No reamer? No problem. A dinner fork can work as a juicer, too.

go local

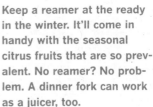

Rather than buying bottled seltzer water, make it yourself using your fresh "local" tap water. You'll need a home seltzer/soda maker (see www.sodaclubusa.com). If you drink fizzy water often, the homemade version will save you money and shrink your carbon footprint. After all, beverages have a high ratio of packaging to liquid and are one of the heaviest food items to ship.

mojit-oj

NAVEL ORANGE MOJITO

Makes 2 servings: 1 cup each

I'm going through a mojito phase. When I'm out with friends, it's my drink of choice. To add a seasonal spin, here I've created one using fresh-squeezed navel orange juice. I know it's not traditional . . . but most things in this cookbook aren't traditional anyway! So shake it up, raise your glass, and make a toast to the planet.

2 large navel oranges, halved
1 lime, halved
½ cup lemon-flavored light rum
2 tablespoons turbinado or Demerara sugar
2 tablespoons finely chopped fresh mint

1. Using a reamer or hand juicer, juice the orange halves (1 cup juice) and lime halves (2 tablespoons juice) directly into a cocktail shaker through a small strainer (to catch any orange seeds).

2. Add the rum, sugar, mint, and 6 large ice cubes.

3. Cover with the shaker lid and shake until the drink is mixed and well-chilled, at least 30 seconds. Strain into two glasses, add extra ice, and serve.

PER SERVING: 270 calories, 0g total fat, 0g saturated fat, 0g trans fat, 0mg cholesterol, 0mg sodium, 37g total carbohydrate, 5g dietary fiber, 2g protein

little **green** cooking tip

Need oranges or grapefruits for a recipe? When buying large produce from a market, put them straight into your basket or cart instead of using a tear-off type plastic produce bag. It'll mean less waste in landfills. Just scrub produce well before preparation—even if not using the peels.

use it, don't lose it

Anytime you're left with orange, lime, or other citrus peels, take full culinary advantage of them. You can just slice orange and lime peels and use them for garnishing. But if you wanna up the fun quotient, serve beverages in orange half "peel-ups." To kick that fun quotient up another notch, use lime "peel-ups" as cool shot glasses. (Of course, remember to consume alcoholic beverages in moderation!)

kool kiwi cheesecake parfait

LAYERED KIWI AND VANILLA CHEESECAKE "MOUSSE"

Makes 3 servings: 1 parfait (1 kiwi and ⅓ cup mousse) each

Cheesecake can take so long to bake. This cheesecake-inspired dessert requires none. That's lucky for you, because you won't want to wait to dive into its decadence. The earth-style kiwi fruit adds freshness, sweetness, and intriguing textural contrast to the creaminess. The graham cracker to finish is like a crispy no-bake crust. Voilà . . . a luscious, low-carbon cheesecake in a wine glass.

1 (8–ounce) package soy-based cream cheese spread or organic or locally produced Neufchâtel cheese, at room temperature

¼ cup plain unsweetened soymilk or whole organic milk

1 tablespoon mild floral honey

Juice of ½ small lemon (about 1 tablespoon)

¼ teaspoon pure vanilla extract

⅛ teaspoon pure almond extract (optional)

⅛ teaspoon sea salt

3 large kiwis, scrubbed unpeeled, and finely diced

3 whole-grain graham cracker squares or quarters

1. Whisk together the soy-based spread, soymilk, honey, lemon juice, vanilla extract, almond extract (if using), and salt in a medium bowl until smooth, about 1 minute.

2. In three sturdy wine glasses, small parfait glasses, or dessert dishes, arrange the cheesecake "mousse" and kiwis in layers. Chill in the refrigerator until ready to serve.

(continued)

3. Serve each with a graham cracker on top. Enjoy with additional graham crackers, if desired.

PER SERVING: 330 calories, 23g total fat, 6g saturated fat, 0g trans fat, 0mg cholesterol, 510mg sodium, 29g total carbohydrate, 3g dietary fiber, 5g protein

go local

When you purchase foods from a farmers' market, most of the money is going directly to the farmer instead of to bosses (since they are their own bosses) and marketing budgets. About 80 to 90 cents of every dollar spent by you will go to them.

starry brownies

CHOCOLATE FUDGE BROWNIES WITH STAR FRUIT

Makes 12 servings: 1 brownie each

These killer brownies are stars to my eyes. They actually have stars in them—the very edible star fruit type. By using a combination of unique cooking techniques and natural ingredients, these morsels of chocolate enchantment are eco-incredible. Brownie, you're a star—in everybody's eyes.

1½ cups turbinado or Demerara sugar

¼ cup peanut oil

3 tablespoons unsweetened applesauce

½ teaspoon sea salt

⅓ cup unsweetened cocoa powder

3 ounces high-quality unsweetened baking chocolate, chopped

2 large organic eggs

1½ teaspoons pure vanilla extract

⅔ cup stone-ground whole-wheat flour

1 star fruit, sliced crosswise into 12 thin "stars"

1. Lightly coat a 6½ × 8½-inch toaster oven pan with "homemade" cooking spray.*

2. Stir together the sugar, oil, applesauce, and salt in a large microwave-safe bowl. Cook in the microwave oven** on high power for 2½ minutes or until the mixture rapidly bubbles, stirring once midway through the cooking time. (Be careful, as this mixture will be extremely hot.)

3. Stir in the cocoa and chocolate until the chocolate is melted. Vigorously stir in the eggs one at a time and the vanilla extract. Stir in the flour until the batter is smooth.

4. Pour the batter into the pan. Arrange the star fruit on top of the batter.

5. Place the pan in the toaster oven. Turn heat to 400°F and bake until the brownies are springy to the touch, about 18 minutes. Turn off the toaster oven let bake in the off oven with the residual head until the brownies are done, about 8 minutes.

6. Cool completely in the pan. Cut into 12 pieces.

PER SERVING: 220 calories, 10g total fat, 3.5g saturated fat, 0g trans fat, 35mg cholesterol, 110mg sodium, 34g total carbohydrate, 3g dietary fiber, 4g protein

*Fill a Misto or similar spray bottle with oil of choice.
**Microwave oven cooking times will vary. See page 39.

little **green** cooking tip

One way to help prevent brownies or cakes from sticking to pans is by using cooking spray—the "homemade" type that you make by filling a spray bottle with oil, such as canola oil. Another option is to line the bottom of the pans with unbleached parchment paper.

a planet-friendly bite

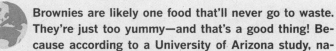

Brownies are likely one food that'll never go to waste. They're just too yummy—and that's a good thing! Because according to a University of Arizona study, nationwide household food waste is a $43 billion economic and environmental problem. Cutting food waste by half could reduce negative environmental impacts by an estimated 25 percent by reduced landfill use, soil depletion, and more.

bites & snacks

nutty blue napoleons . . . 296
pecan and blue cheese
napoleons

mini soy sombreros . . . 297
mini Mexican-style soy tacos
in crispy wonton cups

big red O's . . . 299
eco-beer-battered red onion
rounds

**crispy fish of the
gods . . . 300**
crisped Grecian sardines with
fresh herbs

crab "pancakes" . . . 302
panko-crusted crab cakes with
Asian chili-lime mayo

chicken wrap apps . . . 304
grilled chicken and feta
spiral wraps

petite turkey pâté . . . 306
mini roasted turkey
meatloaves

soiree sub . . . 308
country ham, grilled bell pepper,
and mozzarella hoagie

**not-your-fast-food
burgers . . . 309**
organic burger bites

dips, salsas, & sauces

sauce italia . . . 311
fresh tomato-basil
simmering sauce

so saucy . . . 313
tangy chili soy sauce

white velvet . . . 314
cool-n-creamy white bean "bed"

very special sauce . . . 315
tangy mayo dipping and
sandwich sauce

garlic breath dip . . . 316
garlicky veggie party dip

**tomatillo lover's layer
dip . . . 317**
layered Mexican dip with
tomatillo guacamole

soups & salads

far out far east soup . . . 319
spicy Asian soba noodle soup

brew and bean chili . . . 320
eco-brewed beer and two-bean
veggie chili

**red, white, and green
slaw . . . 322**
shredded tri-color cabbage salad

spin-stir caesar salad . . . 323
spinach salad with creamy soy
Caesar dressing

no-frills fusilli salad . . . 324
creamy fusilli macaroni salad

partyin' pasta salad . . . 325
pasta salad with seasonal
veggies and red wine vinaigrette

gone fishin' salad . . . 326
spice-rubbed tilapia-topped
cucumber salad

cool chick couscous . . . 328
poached chicken and
couscous salad with chickpeas
and herbs

vegetarian dishes

hummus club . . . 330
flaxseed hummus and veggie sandwich

groovy grain grape leaves . . . 332
lemony quinoa-stuffed grape leaves

little green pizza . . . 334
garlicky spinach flatbread pizzette

creamy crepes . . . 335
buckwheat crepes with triple crème cheese and microgreens

green gratin . . . 337
creamy baby spinach gratin

raw and wild rice . . . 339
wild rice with fresh parsley

thai a soba noodle . . . 340
cool Thai peanut soba noodles

almost dessert squash . . . 341
micro-roasted acorn squash

fish, poultry, & meat dishes

cod with kick . . . 343
Creole-style Pacific cod

curry chicken under pressure . . . 345
pressure-cooked chicken curry

chicken dunkers . . . 347
chicken skewers with fruity mustard dipping sauce

onion lover's cheese steak . . . 349
Philly-style cheese steak with extra onions

sips & sweets

fruit punch with punch . . . 351
fresh fruit rum punch

very berry cup . . . 352
fresh dairy-free strawberry smoothie

fruit-n-fudge . . . 353
hot fudgy sauce with seasonal fruit

pb&j on ice . . . 354
peanut butter and jelly ice cream

made-in-ny cheesecake . . . 356
greenmarket fruit–topped creamy cheesecake

happy planet cookies . . . 358
naturally nutritious chocolate chip cookies

nutty blue napoleons

PECAN AND BLUE CHEESE NAPOLEONS

Makes 8 servings: 3 Napoleons each

These fashionable little bites belong on the *Project Runway* of hors d'oeuvres. It'll make any green food judge "ooh" and "ahh" over their sensible eco-friendly style. They're seasonal any time of the year (though especially so in autumn). One little bite and you'll be calling these nutty napoleons "fierce!"

1½ ounces organic cream cheese, at room temperature
1 ounce organic or locally produced blue cheese, at room temperature
1 teaspoon ruby or tawny port
¼ teaspoon mild floral honey
Pinch of freshly ground black pepper
48 raw pecan halves (2½ ounces)
2 teaspoons minced fresh scallions or chives

1. Combine the cheeses, port, honey, and pepper in a small bowl with a flexible silicone spatula until smooth.

2. Using a pastry bag, pipe about ¼ teaspoon of the cheese mixture evenly onto each pecan half, flat side down. Top with a second pecan, flat-side down, and pipe about ¼ teaspoon of the cheese mixture onto each napoleon. Alternatively, create "sandwiches" by piping all the cheese mixture between two pecan halves. Sprinkle with the scallion.

PER SERVING: 90 calories, 9g total fat, 2.5g saturated fat, 0g trans fat, 10mg cholesterol, 65mg sodium, 2g total carbohydrate, 1g dietary fiber, 2g protein

little
green
cooking
tip

Merriam-Webster defines *artisan* as "one that that produces something (as cheese or wine) in limited quantities often using traditional methods." That makes the term *artisanal* worth looking for when going green. So try locally produced artisanal blue cheese in Nutty Blue Napoleons.

mini soy sombreros

MINI MEXICAN-STYLE SOY TACOS IN CRISPY WONTON CUPS

Makes 12 servings: 2 sombreros each

So you think you can dance? Then you'll want to do the Mexican hat dance around these kicked-up cups. They're like tiny, spicy chili-filled edible sombreros. Though vegetarian, they'll make the meat-eater get their groove on, too.

24 wonton wrappers, thawed, if frozen

1 (12-ounce) package soy burger crumbles

1½ cups canned diced organic tomatoes with juices

2 tablespoons finely chopped fresh cilantro

1 teaspoon chili powder

¾ teaspoon crushed red pepper flakes, or to taste

1 cup shredded soy-based Cheddar-style cheese or organic or locally produced aged Cheddar cheese

¼ cup finely diced red onion

1. Coat two mini muffin tins with homemade cooking spray* and press a wonton square into each cup. Lightly coat the squares with cooking spray. Place in the toaster oven** (do not preheat). Turn to 350°F, and bake until light brown and nearly crisp, about 7 minutes, rotating trays halfway through baking. Turn off the toaster oven and let bake in the off oven until golden brown and crisp, about 3 minutes. Let cool in the pan. (Note: Bake in batches if necessary. Store wonton cups in an airtight container at room temperature for up to 1 week.)

2. Mix the soy crumbles, tomatoes, cilantro, chili powder, and crushed red pepper in a large skillet. Place over medium heat and cook while stirring until heated through, about 5 minutes.

(continued)

little
green
cooking
tip

If you're easing into going vegetarian or doing Meatless Mondays (kicking off your week by eating vegetarian), consider cooking with veggie-based options, such as soy burger crumbles, instead of their meaty counterparts. Pair those options with highly flavored ingredients and you'll have a winning combo.

3. Divide the mixture among the wonton-cup "sombreros," about 2 tablespoons each. Top with the cheese and onion and serve.

PER SERVING: 110 calories, 1.5g total fat, 0g saturated fat, 0g trans fat, 0mg cholesterol, 420mg sodium, 14g total carbohydrate, 2g dietary fiber, 11g protein

*Fill a Misto or similar spray bottle with oil of choice.
**Toaster oven sizes and cooking times will vary. See page 39.

a planet-friendly bite

Conventionally grown produce often uses pesticides, which can affect your health as well as the health of the farm workers and environment. But cost is a factor for many people when selecting organic produce. If price is a factor, choose organic produce for fruits and vegetables that are known to carry high pesticide loads from conventional farming methods. If the produce has a low pesticide load, then it's fine to purchase the conventional, and often cheaper, produce. According to the Environmental Working Group, produce with some of the lowest loads are onions, avocados, and frozen sweet corn. So go ahead, choose conventional red onions for Mini Soy Sombreros. For more information, see Produce Picks (page 25). To download the Environmental Working Group's Shoppers Guide to Pesticides in Produce, go to www.foodnews.org.

big red o's

ECO-BEER-BATTERED RED ONION ROUNDS

Makes 4 servings: 3 rounds each

Onion lovers, rejoice! These indulgent, fried onion snacks are not rings, they're rounds. That means you're getting several rings in every bite. If separated into rings, it would mean several extra batches being fried, tacking on perhaps double the frying time— using double the energy. Eat 'em while they're hot and crispy. Make sure to dip 'em in a sauce to make them extra-tasty.

Pay attention to all of the liquids you use in cooking— even when you're not drinking them. If you usually use filtered tap water for drinking, use the same for cooking. If you use organic or locally produced wine or beer for drinking, use the same in cooking. It can make a real eco-difference.

1⅓ cups stone-ground whole-wheat flour

1 tablespoon plus 3 cups canola or peanut oil

1 large organic egg

1 teaspoon sea salt, or to taste

¼ teaspoon garlic powder, or to taste

¼ teaspoon cayenne pepper, or to taste

¼ teaspoon freshly ground black pepper, or to taste

¾ cup locally brewed beer (drink what's left in the bottle!)

2 medium red onions, peeled and trimmed, thinly sliced into
  6 rounds each (do not separate into rings)

1. Add the flour, 1 tablespoon of the oil, ⅓ cup fresh water, the egg, salt, garlic powder, cayenne, and black pepper to a bowl. With a fork, gradually stir in the beer. Continue to stir until the batter is smooth. (It should look somewhat like a thick pancake batter. Add more water, if too thick.) Let sit for about 15 minutes to allow ingredients to fully combine.

2. Heat the remaining oil in a large skillet over medium-high heat. Once the oil is hot, dip the onion rounds into the batter and gently place into the hot oil. Fry in two batches (6 battered onion rounds each) until deep golden brown and crispy on the outside, about 4 minutes per side. Let drain on a cooling rack with an unbleached paper towel underneath. Taste and adjust seasoning, if necessary.

(continued)

3. Serve with Very Special Sauce (page 315), ketchup, or a mixture of ketchup and mayonnaise.

PER SERVING: 410 calories, 20g total fat, 1.5g saturated fat, 0g trans fat, 55mg cholesterol, 600mg sodium, 46g total carbohydrate, 7g dietary fiber, 10g protein

go local

If you're ever in the New York area, check out the Brooklyn Brewery. (It's a few blocks from my apartment in the Williamsburg neighborhood.) Brooklyn Brewery runs their plant on 100 percent wind-generated electricity and transports its kegs on biodiesel-fueled trucks. I used their Brooklyn Lager—brewed with malted barley, hops, water, and yeast—when recipe testing Big Red O's and Brew and Bean Chili (page 320) for this book. Tour their Web site at www.brooklynbrewery.com. And plan to take a live tour of the brewery if you ever find yourself in Brooklyn on a Saturday afternoon.

crispy fish of the gods

CRISPED GRECIAN SARDINES WITH FRESH HERBS

Makes 4 servings: 2 sardines each

Move over canned sardines! A new sardine is in town. And it's 100 percent fresh from the Pacific Ocean. Sardines are at the top of most environmentally friendly fish lists, but they're often forgotten. In this Mediterranean-flavored preparation, they truly are like a fish of the gods. Though you don't need to kick the canned sardine habit (the cute little fishies are still heart healthful, after all), you'll probably find yourself favoring them fresh when available.

8 fresh Pacific (U.S.) sardines, cleaned and heads removed
¼ cup extra-virgin olive oil
Juice and zest of 1 lemon plus ½ lemon, cut into 8 thin wedges
2 large cloves garlic, minced
2 tablespoons finely chopped fresh mint
2 tablespoons finely chopped fresh dill
½ teaspoon onion powder
½ teaspoon sea salt, or to taste
¼ teaspoon freshly ground black pepper, or to taste
¼ teaspoon ground cinnamon, or to taste
¼ cup stone-ground whole-wheat flour
1 cup canola or peanut oil

little *green* cooking tip

Check the Environmental Defense Fund's Seafood Selector, www.edf.org, or Monterey Bay Aquarium's Seafood Watch, www. montereybayaquarium.org, before heading to the fish market for your next seafood fix. Make a list of the top eco-choices and go "fishing."

1. Place the sardines, olive oil, lemon juice and zest, garlic, mint, dill, onion powder, salt, pepper, and cinnamon in a medium bowl and toss to coat. Set aside to marinate for 30 minutes.

2. Remove the sardines from the marinade, letting excess liquid drip off. Discard the marinade. Dust the sardines with the flour.

3. Heat the oil in a large skillet over high heat and fry the sardines until crisp, golden brown, and fully cooked, about 1 minute per side.

4. Transfer to unbleached paper towels to drain. Taste and adjust seasoning. Serve with the lemon wedges.

PER SERVING: 210 calories, 15g total fat, 2.5g saturated fat, 0g trans fat, 35mg cholesterol, 680mg sodium, 9g total carbohydrate, 2g dietary fiber, 12g protein

a planet-friendly bite

Sardines currently appear to be in abundant supply. And they're quite fertile, too, spawning several times in a year.

crab "pancakes"

PANKO-CRUSTED CRAB CAKES WITH ASIAN CHILI-LIME MAYO

Makes 8 servings: 2 crab cakes each

This spectacular appetizer is made especially crispy with whole-wheat panko, also known as Japanese-style breadcrumbs. It's especially green from the addition of fresh ingredients. Plus it's quick to cook. Serve each cake with a dollop of the Asian-flavored mayo and enjoy the most brilliant bites yet.

½ cup mayonnaise
1 tablespoon Asian garlic-chili sauce
2 teaspoons fresh lime juice
7 tablespoons canola or peanut oil
¼ cup finely chopped red bell pepper
¼ cup finely chopped red onion
1 pound lump crabmeat, picked over
2 large organic eggs, lightly beaten
2 cups whole-wheat panko breadcrumbs
1 tablespoon chopped fresh cilantro (optional)

1. To make the Asian Chili-Lime Mayo, stir together the mayonnaise, garlic-chili sauce, and lime juice in a small bowl. Set aside.

2. Heat 1 tablespoon of the oil in a large stick-resistant skillet over medium-high heat. Add the bell pepper and onion and sauté until softened, about 4 minutes. Transfer to a large bowl. Mix in the crabmeat, eggs, ¼ cup of the Asian Chili-Lime Mayo, 1 cup of the panko, and the cilantro (if using). Form the crab mixture into 16 cakes, about ¾-inch thick.

3. Carefully dredge the cakes in the remaining panko, coating completely.

4. Heat 3 tablespoons of the oil in the skillet over medium-high heat. Gently transfer 8 of the cakes to the skillet with a spatula. Cook until crisp, browned, and cooked through, about 1½ minutes per side. Transfer to a platter. Repeat with the remaining 3 tablespoons oil and cakes.

little **green** cooking tip

The word *imitation* doesn't sound so green, but it can be. If you decide to use imitation crabmeat for making Crab "Pancakes," for instance, make sure it's made from Alaskan pollock—it's environmentally friendly.

5. Serve each topped with a small dollop of the Asian Chili-Lime Mayo. Garnish with additional cilantro, if desired.

PER SERVING: 340 calories, 24g total fat, 2.5g saturated fat, 0g trans fat, 100mg cholesterol, 320mg sodium, 15g total carbohydrate, 2g dietary fiber, 17g protein

use it, don't lose it

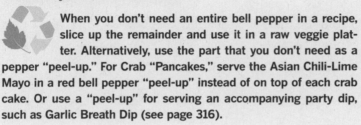 When you don't need an entire bell pepper in a recipe, slice up the remainder and use it in a raw veggie platter. Alternatively, use the part that you don't need as a pepper "peel-up." For Crab "Pancakes," serve the Asian Chili-Lime Mayo in a red bell pepper "peel-up" instead of on top of each crab cake. Or use a "peel-up" for serving an accompanying party dip, such as Garlic Breath Dip (see page 316).

chicken wrap apps

GRILLED CHICKEN AND FETA SPIRAL WRAPS

Makes 4 servings: 3 baby wraps each

Start with organic chicken breasts, pound them super-thin, and cook them in a panini grill (where both sides cook at once), and you'll have green-grilled chicken. Combine with other full-flavored ingredients, including dill and feta cheese, and you'll have everyone green with envy . . . if they don't get a bite! Make extra mini wraps if you're serving them for party appetizers.

12 ounces boneless, skinless organic chicken breasts,
    pounded to ¼-inch thickness
2 teaspoons canola or peanut oil
3 tablespoons plain soy or organic yogurt
2 tablespoons extra-virgin olive oil
Juice of ½ small lemon (about 1 tablespoon)
1 tablespoon finely chopped fresh dill
1 large clove garlic, minced
4 (8-inch) stone-ground whole-wheat tortillas*
¼ teaspoon sea salt, or to taste
¼ teaspoon freshly ground black pepper, or to taste
1 cup finely shredded romaine lettuce
½ cup finely crumbled organic or locally produced feta cheese

1. Rub the chicken breasts with the oil. Cook in a panini grill on medium-high heat until fully cooked, about 3 minutes. (Alternatively, cook in a skillet over medium-high heat for about 3 minutes per side.) Let sit for 15 minutes to slightly cool. Finely dice or thinly slice the chicken and set aside.

2. Combine the yogurt, olive oil, lemon juice, dill, and garlic in a small bowl. Spread on each of the tortillas.

3. Spread the chicken evenly on top of the yogurt sauce. Add salt and pepper and sprinkle with the lettuce and feta.

4. Roll up each tortilla tightly. Slice about ½ inch off of the ends (eat these "rejects"!) and then diagonally cut each roll into 3 pieces. Insert a bamboo or reusable pick into each piece to hold it together, if desired, and serve.

PER SERVING: 310 calories, 16g total fat, 4.5g saturated fat, 0g trans fat, 65mg cholesterol, 570mg sodium, 23g total carbohydrate, 2g dietary fiber, 23g protein

---

*For a change, try with 2 whole-wheat loaves of naan or soft lavash flatbreads instead of the tortillas. Crisp them in the toaster oven, top with all of the ingredients and serve like flatbread pizzas!

a planet-friendly bite

According to the National Chicken Council, if chickens are given outdoor access, the farmer may label their products *free range*. That outdoor access may simply be a fenced area just outside of the chicken house; chickens usually choose to not go roaming far from the chicken feed and water that's in their coop. Keep in mind that if you buy chicken that's labeled *USDA Organic*, it'll also be free-range. But if it is just labeled *free-range*, it doesn't necessarily mean the chicken was raised on organic feed.

petite turkey pâté

MINI ROASTED TURKEY MEATLOAVES

Makes 8 servings: 1 mini loaf each

Big beefy meatloaf has little to do with low-carbon cooking. On the other hand, mini turkey meatloaf is lean, green cuisine at its comforting best. It's full of whole foods to boost its green quotient. You can call it pâté to give it a persnickety appeal, but don't overthink it. The best way to enjoy this meatloaf is to just eat it!

1 pound ground organic turkey*
1 medium red onion, minced
1 large organic egg
½ cup old-fashioned oats
⅓ cup coarsely grated scrubbed unpeeled carrot
½ cup ketchup
3 tablespoons stone-ground mustard
1 large clove garlic, minced
1 teaspoon finely chopped fresh thyme (optional)
1 teaspoon sea salt, or to taste
¾ teaspoon freshly ground black pepper, or to taste
¼ teaspoon ground cinnamon

1. Add the turkey, onion, egg, oats, carrot, 3 tablespoons of the ketchup, 2 tablespoons of the mustard, the garlic, thyme (if using), salt, pepper, and cinnamon to a medium bowl. Combine well with your hands. Sculpt the mixture into 8 mini football-shaped loaves or other fun shapes, using about ⅓ cup mixture each. Place on a stick-resistant toaster oven baking pan.

2. Stir the remaining ketchup and mustard together in a small bowl. Rub the ketchup mixture over the top and sides of the loaves.

little green cooking tip

Boost your veggie intake. Go vegetarian with your entrée and turn big meaty entrées into more petite people-pleasing appetizers or sides.

3. Place the tray in the toaster oven** (do not preheat). Turn the heat to 450°F and bake until the loaves are just cooked through and a crust forms, about 18 minutes. Turn off the toaster oven. Let the loaves cook with residual heat in the off toaster oven until the juices settle, about 8 minutes.

4. Remove from the oven and serve.

PER SERVING: 130 calories, 4.5g total fat, 1.5g saturated fat, 0g trans fat, 60mg cholesterol, 580mg sodium, 10g total carbohydrate, 1g dietary fiber, 13g protein

*Choose ground turkey with at least 7 percent fat for best culinary results.
**Toaster oven sizes and cooking times will vary. See page 39.

a planet-friendly bite

In general, the fresher a food is, the greener it is. But sometimes rules are made to be broken. Certain processed foods can provide similar or greater nutritional benefit than their fresh counterparts. Ketchup is one prime example as are other tomato products, like tomato paste and tomato sauce. Due to their concentrated tomato content, these products have higher levels of the phytonutrient lycopene, which has been found to help protect against some chronic diseases.

One way to shrink your carbon footprint is to shrink-portion (or "green-size") your meat. When using meat in a recipe, go light on it, but heavy on the flavor. Big flavors mean you won't need as much meat to satisfy your appetite.

soiree sub

COUNTRY HAM, GRILLED BELL PEPPER, AND MOZZARELLA HOAGIE

Makes 8 servings: 1 piece each

Making this sub gives you a reason to celebrate—it's just too big for one or two people. So plan a soiree and show off this hero of a sandwich. It's light on the meat, but heavy on the bell peppers, peppery greens, and other inviting ingredients. It's impressive to look at, too. Shhh . . . you don't need to tell anyone how easy it is to make.

2 large red bell peppers
3 tablespoons extra-virgin olive oil
2 tablespoons aged balsamic vinegar
2 large cloves garlic, minced
⅛ teaspoon sea salt, or to taste
¼ teaspoon freshly ground black pepper
1 (14-ounce) whole-wheat Italian bread loaf, halved lengthwise
8 ounces thinly sliced fresh organic or locally produced buffalo
  mozzarella cheese
6 ounces thinly sliced organic American country ham or prosciutto
1½ cups baby arugula or leafy greens of choice

1. Cut each red bell pepper into 4 or 5 pieces. Place the peppers in a panini grill, then set the heat to medium-high (do not preheat). Grill until charred and nearly cooked through, about 4 minutes. Turn off the grill and allow peppers to "green grill" (cook in the off panini grill with residual heat) until peppers are fully cooked and softened, about 4 minutes. Set aside.

2. Meanwhile, whisk together the oil, vinegar, garlic, salt, and black pepper in a small bowl. Drizzle or spoon the vinaigrette onto the cut side of each bread half.

3. Layer the bell peppers, mozzarella, ham, and arugula on the bottom bread half. Firmly press the top of the bread over the fillings.

4. Cut the hoagie into 8 pieces and serve.

PER SERVING: 310 calories, 15g total fat, 6g saturated fat, 0g trans fat, 35mg cholesterol, 920mg sodium, 25g total carbohydrate, 4g dietary fiber, 18g protein

use it, don't lose it

Most bread, especially hard-crusted types, like whole-wheat Italian bread, should not be refrigerated. It actually stales the bread because the refrigerator draws out the bread's moisture. If you don't use a loaf of fresh bread all in one day, freeze it. Bread keeps in the freezer for up to three months, if well wrapped. Otherwise, let your fresh bread become day-old bread—which is then great for grating into breadcrumbs.

not-your-fast-food burgers

ORGANIC BURGER BITES

Makes 12 servings: 1 bite each

If you haven't had your break yet today, take one and make these "green-sized" mini bites. This recipe is my planet-friendly makeover—or "greenover"—of the fast-food favorite. Do nibble these as bites, not as whole burgers, to keep it green.

> 4 whole-grain or sesame seed hamburger buns
> ¼ cup Very Special Sauce (page 315) or Thousand Island dressing, or to taste
> 3 tablespoons finely diced white onion
> 1 cup finely chopped romaine lettuce
> 3 slices organic or locally produced Muenster or Cheddar cheese
> 1 pound ground grass-fed organic beef
> ½ teaspoon sea salt, or to taste
> 12 dill pickle chips

1. With a serrated knife, slice both halves of 1 of the buns to make 4 round bun portions, about ¾-inch-thick each. (Three of these will be used in the middle of your sandwiches. Use or freeze the remaining slice for another purpose.)

2. Onto the bottom portion of the remaining 3 buns, arrange half of each the Very Special Sauce, onion, lettuce, and cheese. Set aside.

(continued)

Burgers and subs don't need to be monster-sized. Make them mini sized or keep them big, but cut into pieces (sort of like pizza) and serve as appetizers. Alternatively, give them a vegetarian make-over. Why is this important? Research suggests a fast-food style burger may have a more detrimental impact on climate change than a gas-guzzling car.

3. Form 6 very thin, bun-size (or larger) patties with the ground beef. Add salt.

4. Heat a large stick-resistant skillet over medium-high heat. Cook 3 of the patties in the skillet until at least medium doneness, about 1½ minutes per side. Place the burgers on top of the cheese. Place the ¾-inch sliced bun portions on top.

5. Cook the remaining 3 patties in the skillet until at least medium doneness, about 1½ minutes per side.

6. Meanwhile, arrange the remaining Very Special Sauce, onion, and lettuce on top of each bun portion. Then add the pickles.

7. Place the burgers on top. Then place the top buns on the burgers.

8. Cut each burger using a serrated bread knife into 4 quarters. Skewer each quarter (mini burger) with a bamboo or reusable pick. Serve with additional Very Special Sauce on the side, if desired.

PER SERVING: 150 calories, 8g total fat, 3g saturated fat, 0g trans fat, 30mg cholesterol, 300mg sodium, 10g total carbohydrate, 1g dietary fiber, 10g protein

a planet-friendly bite

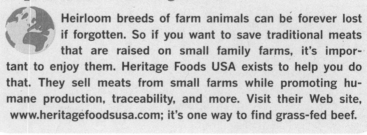

Heirloom breeds of farm animals can be forever lost if forgotten. So if you want to save traditional meats that are raised on small family farms, it's important to enjoy them. Heritage Foods USA exists to help you do that. They sell meats from small farms while promoting humane production, traceability, and more. Visit their Web site, www.heritagefoodsusa.com; it's one way to find grass-fed beef.

DIPS, SALSAS, & SAUCES

sauce italia

FRESH TOMATO-BASIL SIMMERING SAUCE

Makes 3 servings: ¾ cup each

This sauce is a happy accident. I was trying to come up with a fresh version of a jarred pasta sauce. But my first try didn't work out so well. This is it! Despite its shortcomings, it has actually turned into a most unique, versatile sauce. Use it to simmer veggies or organic poultry. Or try it in my tasty Sauce Italia Linguine (page 312). It's pretty cool how it cooks.

2 large vine-ripened tomatoes, quartered
¼ cup extra-virgin olive oil
1 teaspoon aged balsamic or red wine vinegar
4 large fresh basil leaves, finely chopped
1 large clove garlic, peeled
¾ teaspoon sea salt, or to taste

Place all the ingredients in a blender container. Cover and puree on low speed until combined, about 15 seconds. Taste and adjust seasoning, if necessary. Use as a sauce for simmering vegetables or poultry or for pasta.

PER SERVING: 190 calories, 19g total fat, 2.5g saturated fat, 0g trans fat, 0mg cholesterol, 590mg sodium, 5g total carbohydrate, 1g dietary fiber, 1g protein

little **green** cooking tip

Opal, cinnamon, and lemon are three of the many basil varieties that can grow all year on the windowsill. When recipe ready, one technique is to stack several basil leaves, roll tightly, then thinly slice. To prevent bruising, make sure your knife is sharp and leaves are dry.

sauce italia linguine

WHOLE-WHEAT LINGUINE WITH FRESH TOMATO-BASIL SIMMERING SAUCE

Makes 3 servings: 1 rounded cup each

1 recipe Sauce Italia (page 311)
8 ounces whole-wheat linguine, broken in half
1 teaspoon thinly sliced fresh basil

Pour the Sauce Italia in a small saucepan. Place over high heat and bring to a full boil. Add the linguine, making sure it's fully immersed in the sauce. (Do not add water.) Return the sauce to a boil and boil for 1 minute. Cover and turn off the heat. Let "lid cook" (cook covered while the burner is off) until the linguine is al dente and the sauce is absorbed, about 9 minutes. Top with the basil and serve.

use it, don't lose it

 Please don't refrigerate tomatoes! If you find your tomatoes are becoming overripe while sitting on the counter, it's still important not to refrigerate them. Refrigeration doesn't allow tomatoes to fully ripen and become their sweetest, juiciest best. If already ripe, it causes them to lose flavor and turn mealy. But definitely don't toss overripe tomatoes out. Rather, whip them up in a saucy recipe, such as a chili, gazpacho, or Sauce Italia.

so saucy

TANGY CHILI SOY SAUCE

Makes 8 servings: 1 tablespoon each

I enjoy this as a zippier, more complex version of soy sauce. Use it anywhere you normally use soy sauce. Think outside of traditional uses, too. Are you used to buttery veggies? Splash them with this tangy sauce instead.

⅓ cup rice wine vinegar (preferably brown rice)

2 teaspoons organic turbinado or Demerara sugar

2 tablespoons naturally brewed soy sauce

1 small red serrano pepper with some seeds, minced

1 teaspoon raw sesame seeds

Measure the vinegar in a liquid measuring cup. Stir the sugar into the vinegar until most of it dissolves, about 1 minute. Stir in the soy sauce, pepper, and sesame seeds. Store sauce in a sealed container in the refrigerator for up to 10 days.

PER SERVING: 10 calories, 0g total fat, 0g saturated fat, 0g trans fat, 0mg cholesterol, 230mg sodium, 1g total carbohydrate, 0g dietary fiber, 1g protein

little **green** cooking tip

There's no need to wash two things, when you can wash one. Mix sauce or salad dressing ingredients in the same liquid measuring cup.

use it, don't lose it

When choosing chile peppers, a general rule of thumb is the smaller, the hotter. And if you're not a fan of the heat, always remove the chile's seeds and membranes, but freeze them for later use in a recipe that can stand a little pow. Or choose a larger chile and use more or all of the seeds. The heat is caused by capsaicin—which, among many potential health benefits, may play a role in prostate cancer prevention. So, if you can handle it, eat the heat.

white velvet

COOL-N-CREAMY WHITE BEAN "BED"

Makes 5 servings: ½ cup each

Bean dips can be so much more than just dips. They can be served as "beds" on which to lay your favorite entrée. This velvety white bed is posture perfect for grilled skewers of veggies, shrimp, or organic poultry. Or use it as a spread for sandwiches if you prefer. And if you like your dip to simply be dip, enjoy it as hummus with veggies or whole-grain pita.

2 (15-ounce) cans organic low-sodium cannellini or
    butter beans, drained (do not rinse)
¼ cup extra-virgin olive oil
1 large clove garlic, minced
Juice of 1 lemon (about 3 tablespoons)
1 teaspoon sea salt, or to taste
⅛ teaspoon cayenne pepper, or to taste
1 teaspoon finely chopped fresh rosemary or herb of choice (optional)

1. Place the beans, oil, garlic, lemon juice, salt, and pepper in the bowl of a food processor and process until smooth.

2. Taste and adjust seasoning, if necessary. Stir in or sprinkle with the rosemary (if using).

PER SERVING: 240 calories, 13g total fat, 1.5g saturated fat, 0g trans fat, 0mg cholesterol, 520mg sodium, 23g total carbohydrate, 7g dietary fiber, 8g protein

little *green* cooking tip

Going green doesn't require spending lots of green. Beans are nutritious, eco-friendly, and inexpensive. Dried beans are cheaper and can be purchased in bulk, but using canned beans in a recipe is cost-conscious, too. When choosing organic canned beans, choose the less expensive store brands if available.

a planet-friendly bite

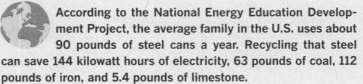

According to the National Energy Education Development Project, the average family in the U.S. uses about 90 pounds of steel cans a year. Recycling that steel can save 144 kilowatt hours of electricity, 63 pounds of coal, 112 pounds of iron, and 5.4 pounds of limestone.

very special sauce

TANGY MAYO DIPPING AND SANDWICH SAUCE

Makes 12 servings: 1 tablespoon each

I adore simple creamy mayonnaise, but when I want to punch it up, this sauce is like mayo gone mad. Use it in place of regular mayo when you want something just a little extra. It has lots of pinches of pizzazz to add fresh appeal. It's magical with Not-Your-Fast-Food Burgers (page 309) and Big Red O's (page 299).

½ cup mayonnaise

2 tablespoons French dressing

1 tablespoon minced white onion

1 tablespoon sweet pickle relish

1 teaspoon white wine or Champagne vinegar

1 teaspoon turbinado or Demerara sugar

⅛ teaspoon sea salt, or to taste

⅛ teaspoon freshly ground black pepper, or to taste (optional)

1. Stir all ingredients together in a small container. Taste and adjust seasoning if necessary.

2. Cover and chill in the refrigerator until ready to serve. Store in the refrigerator for up to 1 week.

PER SERVING: 80 calories, 9g total fat, 1g saturated fat, 0g trans fat, 5mg cholesterol, 105mg sodium, 1g total carbohydrate, 0g dietary fiber, 0g protein

a planet-friendly bite

Traditional mayonnaise is healthier than many people think. Yes, unfortunately, it does have calories. But those calories are mainly from healthful fat, usually soybean oil, but sometimes extra-virgin olive oil or canola oil. The creaminess of traditional mayo is not created though the artificial process of hydrogenation, so there are 0 grams of trans fats in mayonnaise. It's smooth due to a natural process called emulsification.

little *green* cooking tip

There's no need to head to a drive-through window. Make your own fresher, greener version of fast-food favorites. Go ahead; play a little in the kitchen in your quest for low-carbon cuisine. I did! This Very Special Sauce is my version of one that's on a famous burger at Mickey D's.

Reading some of the labels
on name-brand dips can be
kind of scary. Making your
own fresher, greener dip for
healthful veggies is a better
bet. And it doesn't take much
time. Use 1 cup organic sour
cream and ½ cup mayon-
naise as the base—then add
any fresh flavorful ingredients of your choice.

garlic breath dip

GARLICKY VEGGIE PARTY DIP

Makes 8 servings: ¼ scant cup each

Beware, garlic breath lies ahead! The name should give this dip away . . . it's garlicky all right. Serve as a brave dip for veggies or chips. Lightly brush onto green-grilled shrimp or dollop atop micro-roasted potatoes. However you prefer it, just don't eat it before a first date!

1 cup organic sour cream or soy-based sour cream alternative
½ cup mayonnaise
3 large cloves garlic, minced
3 scallions, green and white parts, minced
½ teaspoon sea salt, or to taste
¼ teaspoon hot pepper sauce, or to taste

Stir all ingredients together in a medium bowl. Taste and adjust seasoning, if necessary. Chill in the refrigerator until ready to serve. Store in the refrigerator for up to 1 week.

PER SERVING: 150 calories, 16g total fat, 4.5g saturated fat, 0g trans fat, 15mg choles-terol, 240mg sodium, 2g total carbohydrate, 0g dietary fiber, 1g protein

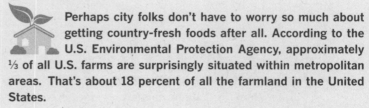

go local

Perhaps city folks don't have to worry so much about getting country-fresh foods after all. According to the U.S. Environmental Protection Agency, approximately ⅓ of all U.S. farms are surprisingly situated within metropolitan areas. That's about 18 percent of all the farmland in the United States.

tomatillo lover's layer dip

LAYERED MEXICAN DIP WITH TOMATILLO GUACAMOLE

Makes 12 servings: about 1 cup each

This dip is always requested by my friend Alyssa for every party I host. Though I have many different ways to prepare it, this tomatillo version is my new favorite. (Alyssa seems to like every version!) It's one way to take advantage of produce you pick up from the farmers' market. Experiment with whatever is in season.

1 (8-ounce) package organic cream cheese or soy-based cream cheese spread, at room temperature

1 (15- to 16-ounce) can vegetarian refried organic beans

1 large jalapeño with some seeds, minced

2 Hass avocados, pitted, peeled, and cubed

2 tomatillos, husk removed, rinsed, and minced

1 medium shallot, minced

Juice of 1 lime (about 2 tablespoons)

¼ cup chopped fresh cilantro

½ teaspoon sea salt, or to taste

1 cup organic sour cream or soy-based sour cream alternative

2 tablespoons Mexican seasoning or 1 tablespoon chili powder, 2 teaspoons ground cumin, and 1 teaspoon garlic powder

8 ounces shredded organic or locally produced Monterey jack cheese (optional)

5 scallions, green and white parts, thinly sliced

1 pint grape tomatoes, halved lengthwise, or cherry tomatoes, thinly sliced

1. Spread the cream cheese in a large 2-quart rectangular dish, 10-inch round pie plate, or other large platter.

2. Stir together the refried beans and ½ of the jalapeño; spread on top of the cream cheese layer.

3. Stir together the avocados, tomatillos, shallot, ½ of the lime juice, the remaining jalapeño, cilantro, and salt; spread on top of the bean layer.

(continued)

little **green** cooking tip

Some dip recipes suggest using not-so-natural soup mixes or seasoning packets, which come in wasteful packaging. Instead, read the ingredient label and create a greener version. For instance, my Mexican seasoning mixture uses ingredients you'll find in a taco seasoning packet.

4. Stir together the sour cream and Mexican seasoning; spread on top of the tomatillo-avocado layer.

5. Sprinkle with the cheese (if using), scallions, and tomatoes. Drizzle with the remaining lime juice. Taste and adjust seasoning, if necessary. Serve with organic tortilla chips.

PER SERVING: 180 calories, 14g total fat, 7g saturated fat, 0g trans fat, 30mg cholesterol, 410mg sodium, 11g total carbohydrate, 4g dietary fiber, 5g protein

a planet-friendly bite

 This dip is so delicious you'll be tempted to eat your serving, then another, and so on. But proper portioning is important for weight—and carbon "food" print—management. In fact, experts suggest it may take nearly ten calories of fossil fuel energy to bring one calorie of food to the American table. So by eating just-right portions (being a consumer, not an over-consumer) both you and the planet will benefit.

SOUPS & SALADS

far out far east soup

SPICY ASIAN SOBA NOODLE SOUP

Makes 4 servings: 1½ cups each

Soup's on . . . in minutes. This Asian-style soup has so many exciting flavors and textures, it's hard to imagine that it's so simple to prepare. By "lid cooking," it uses so little energy, too. Slurp it up slowly and transport yourself to Asia—at least in spirit.

5 cups low-sodium organic chicken or vegetable broth
1 cup finely chopped baby bok choy
2 tablespoons naturally brewed soy sauce
4 ounces soba noodles
2 scallions, green and white parts, minced
1 teaspoon grated scrubbed unpeeled gingerroot
2 teaspoons fresh lime juice, or to taste
1 teaspoon Asian garlic-chili sauce, or to taste
⅛ teaspoon sea salt, or to taste

1. Bring the broth, bok choy, and soy sauce to a boil in a large saucepan over high heat.

2. Add the noodles, scallions, and gingerroot and return to a boil.

3. Cover and turn off the heat. Let "lid cook" (cook covered while the burner is off) until the bok choy is tender and noodles are al dente, about 6 minutes.

(continued)

little **green** cooking tip

You don't need to buy more than one carton of broth if a recipe calls for just a tad more than a single 32-ounce carton. Water and other liquid ingredients can make up for that extra bit. For example, try 1 cup fresh water in this soup in place of 1 cup of broth. Boost flavor with lime juice or garlic-chili sauce, if needed.

4. Stir in the lime juice, garlic-chili sauce, and salt. Serve immediately.

PER SERVING: 150 calories, 2g total fat, 0.5g saturated fat, 0g trans fat, 0mg cholesterol, 850mg sodium, 26g total carbohydrate, 0g dietary fiber, 12g protein

use it, don't lose it

 Since you'll only need about half of a lime for this dish, slice up the remaining half and toss it into your accompanying beverage. Enjoy it in water, tea, beer, a cocktail, or other thirst-quencher of your choice.

brew and bean chili

ECO-BREWED BEER AND TWO-BEAN VEGGIE CHILI

Makes 4 servings: 1¼ cups each

Beer's not just for drinking anymore! It's for stewing—or "eco-brewing." As this chili is sans meat, the beer adds another layer of flavor. My favorite part of the recipe, though, is how fast it is to fix. My carbon footprint appreciates that and yours will, too.

2 tablespoons peanut oil

1 cup finely chopped red onion

1 small jalapeño with some seeds, minced

2 large cloves garlic, minced

1 cup canned crushed organic tomatoes

¾ cup low-sodium vegetable broth

½ cup locally brewed beer (drink what's left in the bottle!)

1½ tablespoons chili powder, or to taste

¼ teaspoon ground cinnamon

1 (15-ounce) can organic kidney beans, drained (do not rinse)

1 (15-ounce) can organic black or white beans, drained (do not rinse)

½ teaspoon sea salt, or to taste

¼ cup chopped fresh cilantro or flat-leaf parsley

1¼ cups shredded organic or locally produced Monterey jack or
   sharp Cheddar cheese (optional)

1. Heat the oil in a large saucepan over medium-high heat. Add the onion and jalapeño. Sauté until the onions are softened, about 6 minutes. Add the garlic and sauté until fragrant, about 30 seconds.

2. Stir in the tomatoes, broth, beer, chili powder, and cinnamon and increase the heat to high. Bring to a full boil and boil for 1 minute. Stir in the beans and salt and return to a boil. Cover and turn off the heat.

3. Let "lid cook" (cook covered while the burner is off) until flavors are combined, about 5 minutes. Taste and adjust seasoning, if necessary.

4. Stir in the cilantro. Top with the cheese (if using) and serve.

PER SERVING: 290 calories, 7g total fat, 1.5g saturated fat, 0g trans fat, 0mg cholesterol, 660mg sodium, 42g total carbohydrate, 11g dietary fiber, 13g protein

little **green** cooking **tip**

Make rich meaty soups, stews, and chilis without meat. Use hearty ingredients, like beans, and use hearty flavors, like beer.

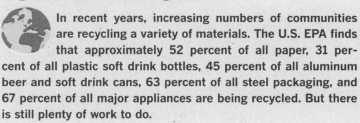

a planet-friendly bite

In recent years, increasing numbers of communities are recycling a variety of materials. The U.S. EPA finds that approximately 52 percent of all paper, 31 percent of all plastic soft drink bottles, 45 percent of all aluminum beer and soft drink cans, 63 percent of all steel packaging, and 67 percent of all major appliances are being recycled. But there is still plenty of work to do.

red, white, and green slaw

SHREDDED TRI-COLOR CABBAGE SALAD

Makes 6 servings: 1⅓ cups each

The most popular way to prepare cabbage is raw in a slaw. This quick and colorful version is tops on my charts for a refreshing side anytime that fresh red or green cabbage is available—which is most of the year. For eco-flair, serve it in bowls made from the remaining cabbage halves. Use extra cabbage in sandwiches, too.

⅓ cup apple cider vinegar
¼ cup mild floral honey
1 tablespoon stone-ground mustard
1 teaspoon sea salt, or to taste
½ teaspoon freshly ground black pepper, or to taste
¼ cup peanut oil
½ medium green cabbage, very thinly sliced
½ medium red or purple cabbage, very thinly sliced
1 large white onion, very thinly sliced

1. Whisk together the vinegar, honey, mustard, salt, and pepper in a large serving bowl. Whisk in the oil.

2. Add the cabbages and onion and toss with the apple cider vinaigrette. Taste and adjust seasoning, if necessary. Toss and serve.

PER SERVING: 150 calories, 9g total fat, 1.5g saturated fat, 0g trans fat, 0mg cholesterol, 440mg sodium, 19g total carbohydrate, 2g dietary fiber, 1g protein

use it, don't lose it

Cabbage salad (aka coleslaw) is often eaten at picnics. Unfortunately, picnics and nonbiodegradable Styrofoam plates often go together. So when shopping for ingredients for your next slaw, pass up the Styrofoam dishware section. Look for biodegradable picnic accessories, such as those made from sugarcane. Or up the fun factor—visit a secondhand store or a yard sale and create a collection of cheap, colorful china to be used for picnics for years to come.

spin-stir caesar salad

SPINACH SALAD WITH CREAMY SOY CAESAR DRESSING

Makes 5 servings: 2 cups each

This salad should be served for anyone's pleasure—*spinster* or not. Actually the name refers to how it can be made . . . whirling the spinach using a salad spinner and stirring the dressing into the spinach.

1 small jalapeño with some seeds
3 large cloves garlic, peeled
¼ cup freshly grated organic or locally produced Parmesan cheese (optional)
4 anchovy fillets (optional)
3 tablespoons extra-virgin olive oil
2 tablespoons Dijon mustard
2 tablespoons vegetarian Worcestershire sauce*
4 ounces silken tofu, drained (½ cup drained)
½ teaspoon freshly ground black pepper, or to taste
¼ teaspoon sea salt, or to taste
12 ounces fresh baby spinach

1. Add the jalapeño, garlic, cheese (if using), anchovy fillets (if using), oil, mustard, Worcestershire sauce, tofu, pepper, and salt to a blender container. Cover and blend on low until smooth, about 30 seconds. Taste and adjust seasoning, if necessary.

2. Just before serving, stir the dressing and toss with the spinach.

PER SERVING: 120 calories, 9g total fat, 1g saturated fat, 0g trans fat, 0mg cholesterol, 370mg sodium, 10g total carbohydrate, 3g dietary fiber, 3g protein

*Choose a vegetarian Worcestershire sauce, which contains no anchovies.

use it, don't lose it

Need a blender? Consider getting one with a relatively narrow container—even if costlier. I find the wider the container, the longer you need to run it to puree to ideal consistency. In the long run, a small investment up front can save you money, blending time, and use of excess energy.

little **green** cooking tip

Are you a vegetarian—or trying to be at least some of the time? When a recipe calls for a few anchovies or a touch of Parmesan cheese, other ingredients can help to make up for their taste. Since both of these ingredients provide *umami* (a sense of savory, salty taste) to this dressing, a few drops of naturally brewed soy sauce can replace their essence. Otherwise, simply add a pinch or two more sea salt in their place.

If you are often in the mood for pasta with spaghetti sauce, consider using a slow cooker to make a large batch of sauce to keep on hand in individual servings in the freezer. Slow cookers use very little energy even though you leave them on for hours.

Try this eco-sauce: Stir 1 (28-ounce) can crushed tomatoes, 1 (28-ounce) can tomato puree, 1 (6-ounce) can tomato paste, ¾ cup diced white onion, 2 large cloves garlic, minced, 3 tablespoons extra-virgin olive oil, 1 teaspoon each aged balsamic vinegar, mild floral honey, dried oregano, dried basil, and sea salt, ⅛ teaspoon crushed red pepper flakes, and 1½ cups fresh water in a 3½- or 4-quart slow-cooker crock. Cover and cook on high for 4 hours or on low for 8 hours. Taste and adjust seasoning, if necessary. Add fresh basil, if desired. Makes 16 servings: ½ cup each.

no-frills fusilli salad

CREAMY FUSILLI MACARONI SALAD

Makes 4 servings: ¾ rounded cup each

Searching for a simple, old-fashioned tasting macaroni salad recipe? Your search is over. This find is straightforward and its flavors will take you back to the good ol' days. It becomes green by the way it's cooked and cooled. And the fusilli shape gives an updated twist to the old classic—no other frills required.

1 teaspoon sea salt, or to taste
8 ounces whole-wheat fusilli or rotini pasta
⅓ cup mayonnaise
3 tablespoons sweet pickle relish
2 teaspoons apple cider vinegar
¼ teaspoon cayenne pepper, or to taste
3 scallions, green and white parts, thinly sliced

1. Bring 5 cups fresh water and ¾ teaspoon of the salt to a boil in a medium saucepan over high heat. Add the pasta and return to a boil. Cover and turn off the heat. Let "lid cook" (cook covered while the burner is off) until the pasta is al dente, about 7 minutes. Drain the pasta and place it back into the pan along with 10 large ice cubes. Toss or stir until the ice is melted and pasta is slightly cooled. Drain well.

2. Meanwhile, stir together the mayonnaise, relish, vinegar, cayenne, and the remaining ¼ teaspoon of salt in a large serving bowl until combined. Stir in the drained pasta and scallions until coated. Chill in the refrigerator until ready to serve.

3. Taste and adjust seasoning, if necessary. If desired, serve with additional sliced scallion on top.

PER SERVING: 340 calories, 15g total fat, 2g saturated fat, 0g trans fat, 5mg cholesterol, 560mg sodium, 46g total carbohydrate, 5g dietary fiber, 9g protein

partyin' pasta salad

PASTA SALAD WITH SEASONAL VEGGIES AND RED WINE VINAIGRETTE

Makes 4 servings: 1½ cups each

Pasta salad is best when fresh and using fresh veggies is key. This recipe will allow you to make it all year round. Just pick whatever veggies are in season. So hit the farmers' market, pick up a couple of veggies (try something new!), and get ready for the partyin'.

8 ounces whole-wheat rotini or penne pasta

1¼ teaspoons sea salt, or to taste

3 tablespoons aged red wine vinegar

⅓ cup extra-virgin olive oil

2 cloves garlic, finely minced

½ teaspoon freshly ground black pepper, or to taste

1½ cups bite-sized seasonal veggies, such as broccoli florets or
  halved grape tomatoes

⅓ cup very thinly sliced red onion

3 tablespoons chopped fresh basil or flat-leaf parsley (optional)

1. Bring 5 cups fresh water and ¾ teaspoon of the salt to a boil in a medium saucepan over high heat. Add the pasta and return to a boil. Cover and turn off the heat. Let "lid cook" (cook covered while the burner is off) until the pasta is al dente, about 7 minutes. Drain the pasta and place it back into the pan along with 10 large ice cubes. Toss or stir until the ice is melted and pasta is slightly cooled. Drain well.

2. Meanwhile, whisk the vinegar, oil, garlic, the remaining ½ teaspoon salt, and the pepper in a large serving bowl.

3. Add the drained pasta to the serving bowl with the vinaigrette.

little
green
cooking
tip

There's no precise science to making pasta salad. Go crazy with fresh toppings. Enjoy a little more of a veggie than you may be used to. Instead of just broccoli florets, use some of the stem. Chop up the tougher portion more finely. Or use a seasonal veggie that you've never tried before.

(continued)

All-Year-Round

4. Stir in the vegetables, onion, and basil (if using) until just combined. Taste and adjust seasoning, if necessary, and serve.

PER SERVING: 400 calories, 20g total fat, 2.5g saturated fat, 0g trans fat, 0mg cholesterol, 530mg sodium, 46g total carbohydrate, 6g dietary fiber, 8g protein

go local

What veggies are in season in your area? Your best bet is to head to your local farmers' market—or to an area market that features a variety of fresh local produce. Browse the "Seasonal Produce Guide" (page 361) for a general guide. Also check out the Seasonal Ingredient Map for a state-by-state guide to peak seasonality at www.epicurious.com/articlesguides/seasonalcooking/farmtotable/seasonalingredientmap.

gone fishin' salad

SPICE-RUBBED TILAPIA-TOPPED CUCUMBER SALAD

Makes 4 servings: 1 fillet with 1 cup cucumber salad each

The tossed cucumber salad in this dish is crunchy, flavorful, and refreshing. And the petite portion of tilapia on top makes this a light and lovely meal. So go for it—anytime you wish.

2 (7-ounce) U.S. tilapia, Pacific halibut, or Pacific cod fillets, cut in half to make 4 (3½-ounce) thin-cut fillets

¼ cup extra-virgin olive oil

1½ teaspoons ground cumin

1¼ teaspoons sea salt, or to taste

½ teaspoon freshly ground black pepper, or to taste

1 (12-inch) hothouse cucumber, halved lengthwise, very thinly sliced

1 cup cherry tomatoes, thinly sliced, or grape tomatoes, quartered lengthwise

2 tablespoons finely chopped fresh mint leaves

2 teaspoons finely chopped fresh dill (optional)

1 lemon, halved

1. Rub the fish with 1½ tablespoons of the oil. Rub with the cumin, ¾ teaspoon of the salt, and ¼ teaspoon of the pepper. Set aside.

2. Heat a large stick-resistant skillet over medium heat. Add the fish and cook until the fish is cooked through and pulls apart with a fork, about 4 minutes per side.

3. Place the cucumber, tomatoes, mint, and dill (if using) in a medium serving bowl or on a platter and toss to combine. Drizzle with the remaining oil and the juice of 1 lemon half. Add the remaining ½ teaspoon each salt and pepper.

4. Place fish fillets on top of the cucumber salad. Serve with wedges from the remaining lemon.

PER SERVING: 240 calories, 16g total fat, 2.5g saturated fat, 0g trans fat, 50mg cholesterol, 780mg sodium, 4g total carbohydrate, 2g dietary fiber, 21g protein

a planet-friendly bite

Are we going to start seeing more fish that's been frozen at sea? Rather than flying fish while fresh, freezing it when caught and then transporting it by land may help to cut down on greenhouse gas emissions—potentially as much as 10 times the emissions as transporting it by container ship, according to estimates by the Bon Appétit Management Company.

little **green** cooking tip

Don't use cooking utensils when you can use your hands for rubbing and tossing. That way, all you'll need to do is wash your hands (which you would do anyway—hopefully), not extra utensils. The food always seems to taste better when prepared in this loving way, too.

cool chick couscous

POACHED CHICKEN AND COUSCOUS SALAD WITH CHICKPEAS AND HERBS

Makes 4 servings: 1½ cups each

My colleague Lindsay was telling me about a couscous recipe she loved. Her description made me hungry, even though I had just eaten my lunch. It seemed so light yet as rich in flavor as you would find in a hip restaurant. So I had to write down all of the ingredients and create my own energy-smart version. All your trendy, cool friends will love this.

8 ounces boneless, skinless organic chicken breast or thigh,
   cut into ⅓-inch cubes
1 teaspoon sea salt, or to taste
1 cup low-sodium vegetable or organic chicken broth
¼ cup extra-virgin olive oil
1 large clove garlic, minced
¾ cup whole-wheat couscous
1 (15-ounce) can organic chickpeas, drained (do not rinse)
1 cup cherry tomatoes, quartered
3 scallions, green and white parts, thinly sliced
⅓ cup thinly sliced fresh basil
⅓ cup finely chopped fresh mint
¼ cup sherry vinegar or aged red wine vinegar
⅓ cup raw pine nuts (optional)

1. Add the chicken, ⅓ cup fresh water, and ¼ teaspoon of the salt to a small saucepan over high heat. Cook, stirring, until the chicken is fully cooked, about 3½ minutes.

2. Add the broth, 2 tablespoons of the oil, garlic, and remaining salt and bring to a boil.

3. Stir in the couscous until just combined. Stir in the chickpeas until just combined. Cover with the lid and remove from the heat. Let sit for 10 minutes, then fluff with a fork. Let sit uncovered at room temperature until slightly cool, 20 to 30 minutes. Then chill in the refrigerator.

4. Once cool, stir in the tomatoes, scallions, basil, mint, vinegar, and remaining oil. Taste and adjust seasoning, if necessary. Stir in the pine nuts (if using). Serve cool or at room temperature.

PER SERVING: 380 calories, 17g total fat, 2.5g saturated fat, 0g trans fat, 30mg cholesterol, 760mg sodium, 35g total carbohydrate, 8g dietary fiber, 20g protein

use it, don't lose it

You'll often need to buy pre-portioned produce, such as one bunch of scallions, from a store or market—which may be more than is required for a recipe. One way to prevent this is to grow your own and then pick just what you need for a recipe. No garden or no space to have one? You're still in luck. There are about 18,000 community gardens across the United States and Canada where members maintain their own plots. Learn more about these gardens and locate one near you at www.communitygarden.org.

little **green** cooking tip

Chill out! Cooling foods at room temperature before placing them in the refrigerator saves energy since your fridge won't have to work extra-hard to maintain its temperature. Just remember to chill any perishable food within 2 hours of cooking.

VEGETARIAN DISHES

hummus club

FLAXSEED HUMMUS AND VEGGIE SANDWICH

Makes 2 servings: 1 sandwich each

Hummus is one of those foods I have to have often. And I know I'm not alone. So finding this tasty way to take pleasure in it other than just as a dip, made me happy. This put a grin on my sister Rebecca's face, too! She doubled the ingredients, took it to work, and prepared it there when she was helping me test some of my recipes. She later told me that her co-workers were waiting in line for a piece of the sandwich. Who doesn't want to make a crowd-pleaser like that?

2 tablespoons extra-virgin olive oil
2 teaspoons fresh lemon juice
1 cup coarsely chopped watercress, thick stems trimmed
1 large scrubbed unpeeled carrot, coarsely grated
1 teaspoon flaxseed meal (ground flaxseeds)
½ cup (8 tablespoons) hummus*
6 slices flaxseed or whole-grain bread
2 paper-thin slices large red onion
1 medium vine-ripened tomato, cut into 4 slices
⅛ teaspoon sea salt, or to taste
⅛ teaspoon freshly ground black pepper, or to taste

1. Whisk together the oil and lemon juice in a small bowl. Add the watercress and carrot and toss to coat. Set aside.

2. Stir the flaxseed meal into the hummus until well combined. Spread 1 tablespoon of the flaxseed hummus on each bread slice. (You should have about 2 tablespoons of hummus left over for use in step 4.)

3. Arrange ½ of the watercress salad on top of the hummus on 2 of the slices (¼ of the salad each). Arrange all of the onion slices on top of the watercress salad.

4. Top with 2 of the remaining bread slices, hummus side down. Spread the remaining 2 tablespoons of the hummus on the backs of those slices (1 tablespoon per slice).

5. Arrange the remaining watercress salad and tomato on top of the hummus. Add salt and pepper.

6. Place the remaining 2 bread slices on top of the tomato, hummus side down.

7. Cut sandwiches diagonally in half. Secure each half with a bamboo or reusable pick, if necessary, and serve.

PER SERVING: 420 calories, 21g total fat, 3g saturated fat, 0g trans fat, 0mg cholesterol, 630mg sodium, 46g total carbohydrate, 10g dietary fiber, 15g protein

*Use Rock the Boat Hummus on page 190 or other naturally prepared hummus.

use it, don't lose it

Rather than placing your to-go sandwiches in plastic zipper-type bags, choose unbleached wax paper bags that are better for the environment. Better yet, use containers that can be washed and reused—over and over again.

little
green
cooking
tip

Going vegetarian doesn't have to mean eating light. Go big on veggies and other fresh sandwich toppings to create a hearty meal. Use hummus as a condiment or as the key ingredient in sandwiches, too. The fiber from the beans will provide filling satisfaction.

groovy grain grape leaves

LEMONY QUINOA-STUFFED GRAPE LEAVES

Makes 10 servings: 4 stuffed leaves each

If I had to provide a top ten list of foods that have been my favorites throughout my life, stuffed grape leaves make the cut. When I was younger, I enjoyed grape leaves that were filled with rice and beef or lamb. More recently, I loved a vegetarian version with rice and plenty of herbs. Unfortunately, both recipes required about an hour of cooking time. The stuffed leaves weren't so green after all. But here, at last, a green stuffed grape leave—with quinoa!

1½ cups quinoa, rinsed and drained
2 large shallots, minced
¼ cup finely chopped fresh mint
2 tablespoons finely chopped fresh dill
1 large clove garlic, minced
1½ teaspoons sea salt, or to taste
¾ teaspoon freshly ground black pepper, or to taste
40 fresh grape leaves, lightly blanched, or 1 (16-ounce) jar grape leaves soaked in fresh water, rinsed well, and drained
2 lemons
3 tablespoons extra-virgin olive oil
7 ounces plain organic Greek yogurt or plain soy yogurt

1. Combine the quinoa, shallots, mint, dill, garlic, salt, and pepper in a medium mixing bowl. Add ¼ cup fresh water and stir to combine.

2. Lay the grape leaves individually, dull side up, on unbleached paper towels. Remove any long stems. Place 1 tablespoon of the quinoa mixture in the center of each leaf. Roll each leaf tightly by folding the bottom end of each leaf over the filling, folding the edges over the filling, then rolling toward the leaf point, until they look like mini cigars.

3. After rolling each leaf, place seam side down, in a large skillet. (To help prevent the stuffed leaves from scorching, first lay a few large unstuffed leaves on the bottom of the skillet.) Firmly pack all of the stuffed leaves in a single layer in the skillet. Pour fresh water over the rolls until just covered (about 3 cups).

4. Cut 1 of the lemons into small wedges and set aside. Squeeze the juice from the remaining lemon (about 3 tablespoons) and drizzle over the stuffed grape leaves. Drizzle the oil over the stuffed leaves.

5. Place a heavy, heatproof plate directly onto the stuffed leaves to keep them from opening up during cooking. Place the skillet over high heat and bring to boil. Cover with a lid or recycled aluminum foil, reduce heat to low, and cook until the quinoa is nearly tender, about 15 minutes. Turn off the heat and keep covered. Let "lid cook" (cook covered while the burner is off) until the quinoa is fully cooked and the leaves are tender, about 15 minutes.

6. Remove from heat. Serve at room temperature with reserved lemon wedges and yogurt.

PER SERVING: 180 calories, 8g total fat, 2.5g saturated fat, 0g trans fat, 5mg cholesterol, 360mg sodium, 22g total carbohydrate, 4g dietary fiber, 6g protein

a planet-friendly bite

 The Environmental Protection Agency estimates that recycling and community composting programs recovered 32 percent of municipal solid waste (aka garbage!) in 2005—or 79 million tons.

Hooray, pizza is green. Well, at least it can be. Bake personal-sized pizzas so they cook quickly. Use a toaster oven instead of a conventional oven to use less energy. Enjoy crust that's made with whole grains. And top it with fresh veggies—especially those locally available and organic.

little green pizza

GARLICKY SPINACH FLATBREAD PIZZETTE

Makes 4 servings: ½ pizzette (2 pieces) each

I used to believe that the only thing worthy of being addicted to might be love. That is until I found you, my Little Green Pizza. Confession time . . . I ate a double serving after testing this. I couldn't get enough. Well, maybe it's an infatuation instead of an addiction. But it's a darn good thing any way you slice it—or don't slice it.

2 (8-inch) whole-wheat lavash flatbreads or pocketless pita breads
1 cup shredded organic or locally produced mozzarella cheese
1½ cups loosely packed fresh baby spinach
1 large clove garlic, minced
½ cup finely crumbled organic or locally produced feta cheese
⅛ teaspoon crushed red pepper flakes
2 tablespoons extra-virgin olive oil
2 teaspoons fresh lemon juice
⅓ cup thinly sliced fresh basil

1. Place one flatbread at a time on a toaster oven tray. Place in the toaster oven* (do not preheat). Broil until just lightly toasted, about 1 minute per side. Repeat with the remaining flatbread. Turn off the toaster oven.

2. Top each flatbread with the mozzarella cheese, spinach, garlic, feta cheese, and crushed red pepper.

3. Place one topped flatbread at a time back in the toaster oven. Turn the heat to 450°F and bake until the cheeses are just melted, about 3 minutes. Repeat with the remaining flatbread.

4. Immediately drizzle each flatbread with the olive oil and lemon juice.

5. Sprinkle with the basil, cut each pizzette in quarters, and serve immediately.

PER SERVING: 320 calories, 18g total fat, 8g saturated fat, 0g trans fat, 40mg cholesterol, 630mg sodium, 26g total carbohydrate, 4g dietary fiber, 13g protein

*Toaster oven sizes and cooking times will vary. See page 39.

creamy crepes

BUCKWHEAT CREPES WITH TRIPLE CRÈME CHEESE AND MICROGREENS

Makes 4 servings: 2 crepes each

These crepes may seem super-healthy, but they're sublimely rich from the melt-in-your-mouth cheese. And the sprinkling of sliced grapes provides the perfect sweet touch to balance the sharpness of the greens and the tang of the cheese.

⅔ cup plain unsweetened soymilk or reduced fat (2 percent) organic milk

1 large organic egg

¼ teaspoon sea salt

½ cup buckwheat flour

1 tablespoon unsalted organic butter, melted

4 teaspoons extra-virgin olive oil

5 ounces soft organic or locally produced triple- or double-crème or Brie cheese, thinly sliced, at room temperature

16 large red or green seedless grapes, thinly sliced

⅓ cup fresh microgreens or 1 packed cup radish or broccoli sprouts

1. Place soymilk, egg, salt, and flour in a covered container. Shake vigorously until the mixture is very smooth, about 1 minute. Chill the batter in the refrigerator, covered, for at least 1 hour. Remove from the refrigerator, add melted butter, cover and shake until combined.

(continued)

little
green
cooking
tip

Instead of cooking with all-purpose flour, try a variety of whole-grain flours—or one that's actually made from an *herb*, like buckwheat. Cup per cup, buckwheat flour works well when you'd like an earthy flavor yet a soft texture, such as in crepes, pancakes, and baked goods.

2. Add ½ teaspoon of the oil to a stick-resistant crepe pan set over medium heat. Spoon about 2 tablespoons batter into the pan, tilting the pan to make a thin circular crepe. Cook until the crepe is lightly browned, about 1 minute per side. Repeat the process with the remaining oil and batter to make 8 crepes.

3. Arrange the cheese, grapes, and microgreens on top of each crepe. Fold the edges over and arrange on a platter. Serve at room temperature.

PER SERVING: 290 calories, 20g total fat, 9g saturated fat, 0g trans fat, 95mg cholesterol, 410mg sodium, 14g total carbohydrate, 3g dietary fiber, 12g protein

use it, don't lose it

Microgreens aren't the same as sprouts; they're basically plant shoots. They're thin, delicate salad vegetables that are harvested soon after sprouting. They're so highly flavored that a tiny bit goes a long, long way. Use ⅓ cup (or less!) of microgreens in place of 1 cup sprouts or flavorful greens, like arugula.

green gratin

CREAMY BABY SPINACH GRATIN

Makes 8 servings: 1 wedge each

Beyond creamed spinach, this vibrant dish is filled with plenty of spinach and cheese to please. It's prepared in the microwave oven instead of an energy-guzzling conventional oven, so it'll please Mother Earth, too. What's more, it's downright sinful tasting. So balance this rich gratin with a lean entrée. Then savor its creamy, comforting goodness—sin-free.

2 large shallots, minced

2 large cloves garlic, minced

2 tablespoons extra-virgin olive oil

12 ounces fresh baby spinach

3 large organic eggs

½ cup organic heavy cream

½ cup organic ricotta cheese

½ cup grated organic or locally produced Swiss cheese

½ cup grated organic or locally produced Italian-style Fontina or other mild semi-hard cheese

1 teaspoon sea salt, or to taste

⅛ teaspoon freshly grated or ground nutmeg

1. Stir together the shallots, garlic, and oil in a large 2-quart microwave-safe dish. Then firmly mound the spinach in the dish. (Do not add water.) "Micro-steam" (steam in the microwave oven*) on high until the spinach is fully wilted and steaming hot, about 3 minutes. Set aside. (Do not drain.)

2. Whisk together the eggs and cream with a fork in a medium bowl until well blended. Stir in the ricotta, Swiss, and Fontina cheeses, salt, and nutmeg. Pour the egg mixture over the spinach and stir gently until combined.

3. Place the dish in the microwave. Cook on high until the gratin is puffy and no longer jiggles, about 9 minutes. Let sit for at least 5 minutes in the off microwave to allow for carryover cooking and the juices to settle.

(continued)

little **green** cooking tip

For microwave cooking, I love my round 10-inch traditional stoneware Le Creuset pie dish. Buy a piece of stoneware, if you don't already have one. It goes in the oven, microwave, refrigerator or freezer, and dishwasher. You can serve from it, too. Its versatility makes it a green piece!

All-Year-Round

4. Loosen the gratin's edges with a paring knife and cut into 8 wedges. Serve while warm.

PER SERVING: 220 calories, 17g total fat, 8g saturated fat, 0g trans fat, 125mg cholesterol, 470mg sodium, 8g total carbohydrate, 2g dietary fiber, 9g protein

---

*Microwave oven cooking times will vary. See page 39.

use it, don't lose it

In general, you can keep fresh eggs in the refrigerator in their carton (or other covered egg storage container) for at least three weeks after bringing them home from the market. If you leave eggs out on the counter at room temperature, they can age more in one day than for one entire week in the fridge.

raw and wild rice

WILD RICE WITH FRESH PARSLEY

Makes 6 servings: ¾ cup each

Raw foodies will likely appreciate this uncooked, chewy recipe more than traditionalists who like their white or brown rice steamed and mushy. It is true that wild rice is technically not rice at all; it's basically a grass. Enjoying this dish, however, is not based on a technicality; it's based on the taste and the texture. And it'll officially grow on you.

12 ounces wild rice
¾ cup finely chopped fresh flat-leaf parsley
½ cup finely diced red or white onion
⅓ cup finely diced hothouse cucumber
¼ cup extra-virgin olive oil
Juice of 1 small lemon (about 2 tablespoons)
1 to 2 tablespoons finely chopped fresh dill (optional)
2 cloves garlic, minced
1 teaspoon sea salt, or to taste

1. Pour the wild rice into a medium bowl. Add cold fresh water to cover the wild rice by about 2 inches. Place in the refrigerator for at least 24 hours (no more than 2 days), changing the water at least twice.

2. When ready to use, drain the wild rice using a mesh strainer and place in a serving bowl. Stir in the parsley, onion, cucumber, olive oil, lemon juice, dill (if using), garlic, and salt. Stir to combine. Serve.

PER SERVING: 300 calories, 10g total fat, 1.5g saturated fat, 0g trans fat, 0mg cholesterol, 400mg sodium, 45g total carbohydrate, 4g dietary fiber, 9g protein

little **green** cooking tip

When eating earth-friendly, it doesn't mean the color of your food needs to be earthy. Pick the most vibrant-colored produce (organic when possible) when it's available. So go with red instead of white onion in Raw and Wild Rice.

a planet-friendly bite

 The refrigerator uses a significant amount of energy. In fact, it's the biggest energy-consuming kitchen appliance in most households. One way to keep it running efficiently is to vacuum its coils a couple times a year.

thai a soba noodle

COOL THAI PEANUT SOBA NOODLES

Makes 10 servings: 1 cup each

Cooking large batches of foods can help you leave a smaller environmental footprint. That's because you're only cooking once, instead of two, three, or more times. You'll want this busload of noodles to come home to; they keep deliciously well for two to three days in the refrigerator. Go ahead and make the whole peanutty batch. Or throw a party—you'll have plenty of noodles for everyone.

⅓ cup rice vinegar (preferably brown rice)
¼ cup smooth unsalted natural peanut butter
Juice of 1 lime (about 2 tablespoons)
2 tablespoons sesame oil
2 tablespoons local fruit spread or homemade jam or 1 tablespoon mild
   floral honey
2 tablespoons naturally brewed soy sauce, or to taste
1 tablespoon grated scrubbed unpeeled gingerroot
1 large clove garlic, minced
¼ teaspoon hot pepper sauce
16 ounces soba noodles
2 cups mixed raw vegetables, such as thinly sliced cucumber, coarsely
   grated scrubbed unpeeled carrots, or mung bean sprouts
2 scallions, green and white parts, minced (optional)
¼ cup finely chopped fresh cilantro
¼ cup finely chopped raw peanuts

1. Whisk together the vinegar, peanut butter, lime juice, oil, fruit spread, soy sauce, gingerroot, garlic, and hot pepper sauce in a large serving bowl. Set aside.

2. Bring 6 cups fresh water to a boil in a large saucepan over high heat. Add the noodles and return to a boil. Cover with lid and turn off the heat. Let "lid cook" (cook covered while the burner is off) until the noodles are just cooked through, about 6 minutes. Drain well. (Do not rinse.)

little *green* cooking tip

Extra, extra! If a stovetop recipe stores well in the fridge for two or three days (or frozen for longer), make bigger batches so you don't have to use the stove again to make additional batches.

3. Add the noodles to the serving bowl with the peanut sauce. Toss to coat. Let sit at room temperature to cool slightly, 20 to 30 minutes. Toss occasionally to help prevent sticking. Then chill in the refrigerator until ready to serve.

4. Just before serving, splash with additional soy sauce, if desired. Toss or top the noodles with the vegetables, scallions (if using), cilantro, and peanuts. Serve cool or at room temperature.

PER SERVING: 250 calories, 8g total fat, 1g saturated fat, 0g trans fat, 0mg cholesterol, 550mg sodium, 39g total carbohydrate, 1g dietary fiber, 9g protein

use it, don't lose it

Don't forget to recycle the little paper wrappers that usually hold together bundles of the soba noodles in their packages.

almost dessert squash

MICRO-ROASTED ACORN SQUASH

Makes 2 servings: ½ acorn squash each

It could take over an hour to bake this distinctive-shaped squash in a conventional oven. So say hello to Mr. Microwave. If the only food you've ever loved from the microwave is popcorn, you'll be reawakened to a new kind of love . . . squash that tastes like freshly made caramel popcorn! This is when a vegetable can almost be dessert.

1 large acorn squash
1 tablespoon unsalted organic butter
1 tablespoon turbinado or Demerara sugar
¼ teaspoon sea salt, or as desired
1 tablespoon pure maple syrup

(continued)

little *green* cooking tip

When a recipe requires roasting, put your eco–thinking cap on and consider if it can be prepared in a greener way. Winter squash, such as acorn squash, can be roasted to a beautiful texture in a microwave oven, or "micro-roasted." And it's so much faster.

1. Using a sturdy chef's knife, cut the acorn squash in half lengthwise, from stem to end.* Scoop out the seeds and stringy pulp with a spoon. Place the halves in a large 2-quart microwave-safe dish, cut side up.

2. Coat the cut surface and the inside of each squash half with the butter. Sprinkle with the sugar and salt. Drizzle with the syrup.

3. Loosely cover the squash halves with unbleached parchment paper and "micro-roast" (cook in the microwave oven**) on high until the squash is very soft, about 10 minutes. Let sit covered in the off microwave to further steam for 5 minutes.

4. If any sauce is in the bottom of the dish, drizzle it over the squash halves. Adjust seasoning. Serve while warm.

PER SERVING: 260 calories, 6g total fat, 3.5g saturated fat, 0g trans fat, 15mg cholesterol, 300mg sodium, 55g total carbohydrate, 13g dietary fiber, 3g protein

*If having difficulty cutting the squash, soften it in the microwave on high for 2 minutes; let sit 2 minutes before cutting.
**Microwave oven cooking times will vary. See page 39.

a planet-friendly bite

Raw sugar looks and tastes like brown sugar, but it's not the same thing. Raw sugar is what's left after sugarcane has been processed to remove the molasses. Demerara is one type of raw sugar. Turbinado is raw sugar that has basically been cleaned with steam. Regular brown sugar is white sugar that's been mixed with molasses.

FISH, POULTRY, & MEAT DISHES

cod with kick

CREOLE-STYLE PACIFIC COD

Makes 4 servings: 1 cup each

Creole flavors are unmistakable. They turn this mild-tasting cod into a hot little bite. But the most surprising part of this recipe is the "micro-roasting" preparation. It turns the cod into a perfectly cooked, brothy delight.

1 tablespoon extra-virgin olive oil

1 large vine-ripened tomato, finely diced

1 medium white or yellow onion, finely chopped

1 large green bell pepper, thinly sliced

1 large clove garlic, minced

1 pound Pacific cod fillets, skin removed, cut into ½-inch cubes

Juice of ½ lime (about 1 tablespoon)

1 teaspoon finely chopped fresh thyme or oregano or
   ¼ teaspoon dried thyme or oregano

½ teaspoon paprika

¾ teaspoon sea salt, or to taste

¼ teaspoon cayenne pepper

1. Place the oil, tomato, onion, bell pepper, and garlic in a large 2-quart microwave-safe dish. Cover with unbleached parchment paper and "micro-roast" (cook in the microwave oven*) on high for 3 minutes, stirring once.

(continued)

little **green** cooking tip

When covering foods to be cooked in the microwave, 100 percent unbleached recycled parchment paper is my first choice. But unbleached natural wax paper—which is landfill safe—can be used, too.

2. Stir in the cod, lime juice, thyme, paprika, ½ teaspoon of the salt, and cayenne. Recover with parchment paper and "micro-roast" on high until the fish is just cooked through, about 7 minutes, stirring once. Let sit covered in the off microwave oven for 3 minutes to steam and tenderize the fish. Add ¼ teaspoon salt.

3. Serve over steamed quinoa or baby potatoes.

PER SERVING: 140 calories, 4.5g total fat, 0.5g saturated fat, 0g trans fat, 35mg cholesterol, 510mg sodium, 7g total carbohydrate, 2g dietary fiber, 19g protein

*Microwave oven cooking times will vary. See page 39.

a planet-friendly bite

Pacific cod caught by longline is eco-friendlier than that caught by trawling. And Pacific cod, in general, is considered a more sustainable choice than Atlantic cod, which has been overfished for decades.

curry chicken under pressure

PRESSURE-COOKED CHICKEN CURRY

Makes 6 servings: 3 chicken pieces and ⅔ cup sauce each

Under pressure? Then destress with this simple chicken curry that lets the pressure cooker do all the work. Cooking under pressure, means cooking extra-fast since all of the heat and steam is trapped inside the cooker. It will make this dish perfect for an easy family meal or casual dinner party.

3 tablespoons canola or peanut oil

2 medium white onions, finely chopped

1 tablespoon grated scrubbed unpeeled gingerroot

2 large cloves garlic, minced

6 boneless, skinless organic chicken thighs, cut lengthwise into
   3 portions each

1 cup low-sodium vegetable or organic chicken broth

1 cup plain soy or organic yogurt

1 (6-ounce) can tomato paste

1 tablespoon turbinado or Demerara sugar, or to taste

2 teaspoons curry power, or to taste

2 teaspoons sea salt, or to taste

½ teaspoon ground cumin, or to taste

1. Heat the oil in a large skillet over medium-high heat. Add the onions, gingerroot, and garlic and stir to coat with oil. Cover and cook for 5 minutes, stirring once. Remove the lid, add the chicken pieces, and cook uncovered while stirring constantly until the onions are lightly caramelized, about 2 minutes. (The chicken will not be fully cooked.)

2. Stir the chicken mixture, broth, yogurt, tomato paste, ¼ cup fresh water, sugar, curry powder, salt, and cumin into a pressure cooker.

(continued)

little *green* cooking tip

To increase veggie intake while potentially decreasing your carbon footprint, consider serving meat and poultry entrées as sides. A petite-sized dish like Curry Chicken Under Pressure can be the ideal high-flavored accent to a plate of veggies and whole-wheat couscous.

3. Close the pressure cooker lid and turn to the high pressure setting. Turn the burner on high. Once the pressure cooker hisses, adjust the heat as necessary to maintain high pressure with very gentle hissing and cook for 8 minutes, or until stew-like and chicken is fully cooked. Carefully release the pressure and remove the lid. Adjust seasoning.

4. Serve over steamed whole-wheat couscous, bulgur wheat, or quinoa. Sprinkle with chopped fresh cilantro or scallions and cashews, if desired.

PER SERVING: 250 calories, 13g total fat, 2g saturated fat, 0g trans fat, 50mg cholesterol, 870mg sodium, 17g total carbohydrate, 2g dietary fiber, 17g protein

use it, don't lose it

You don't need to let chicken bones go to waste when a recipe calls for boneless cuts. Make chicken stock with the bones and then freeze the stock for use in another recipe. But, if you prefer, just buy boneless chicken.

chicken dunkers

CHICKEN SKEWERS WITH FRUITY MUSTARD DIPPING SAUCE

Makes 6 servings: 1 skewer (5 to 6 nuggets) and 2 tablespoons sauce each

Hypermiling in a car . . . not-so-easy. Hyperfrying in a pan . . . super-easy. Instead of getting the oil piping hot and then plopping in the chicken, these nuggets are placed right in the oil before the burner goes on. This will take advantage of every bit of gas or electricity you use. That's what hyperfrying is all about. And the results here . . . a sophisticated take on chicken nuggets. You'll love them with the zippy dipping sauce. But if you need something quicker or kid-friendlier, serve with organic French tomato or other favorite salad dressing instead.

½ cup fresh or thawed frozen raspberries

⅓ cup stone-ground mustard

2 tablespoons local fruit spread or homemade jam or 1 tablespoon mild floral honey

1½ cups plain unsweetened soymilk or whole organic milk

1 large organic egg

1 tablespoon white wine vinegar

1 tablespoon plus ¼ teaspoon sea salt

1 pound boneless, skinless organic chicken breasts, cut into 1-inch cubes

1½ cups stone-ground whole-wheat flour

1 teaspoon freshly ground black pepper

½ teaspoon cayenne pepper

½ teaspoon garlic powder

4 cups canola or peanut oil, or to taste

1. Mash the raspberries with a fork in a small bowl. Stir in the mustard and fruit spread until well combined. Set aside or chill in the refrigerator.

2. Whisk together the soymilk, egg, vinegar, and 1½ teaspoons of the salt in a medium bowl. Add the chicken cubes. Set aside.

3. Combine the flour, peppers, garlic powder, and 1½ teaspoons of the salt in a separate medium bowl.

(continued)

little **green** cooking tip

Be a kid again by turning adult-sized food (chicken breasts) into child-sized food (chicken nuggets); it'll require less cooking energy.

4. Dip each chicken cube into the flour mixture until well coated. Lay on a large baking pan or bamboo or Paperstone cutting board.

5. Add the oil to a large skillet. Add the chicken nuggets, then turn the heat to medium-high. Fry the chicken until brown on one side, about 8 minutes. Using tongs, flip each piece over and fry until brown and the chicken is fully cooked, about 2 minutes. (The chicken will have a textured coating, but it won't be extra-crispy.) Turn off the heat. Remove the chicken (smallest pieces first) to unbleached paper towels or a metal rack to drain. Add remaining ¼ teaspoon of salt.

6. Once cool enough to handle, insert chicken nuggets onto 6 (6- to 8-inch) bamboo or reusable skewers. Serve warm or at room temperature with the fruity mustard dipping sauce.

PER SERVING: 320 calories, 11g total fat, 1g saturated fat, 0g trans fat, 60mg cholesterol, 910mg sodium, 33g total carbohydrate, 5g dietary fiber, 22g protein

go local

To find sources of organic or locally raised chicken, start by asking the butcher at your neighborhood market. Also, check out www.localharvest.org, where you can search by the product term *chicken* and your zip code or city and state.

onion lover's cheese steak

PHILLY-STYLE CHEESE STEAK WITH EXTRA ONIONS

Makes 4 servings: 1 sandwich each

If you're from Philly, you'll need to pardon my recipe. I know it's not traditional. But I wanted to give your city some sisterly love because your town's favorite recipe was my inspiration. And the bright flavors and utter ooziness of this eco-friendly version is inspiring . . . a bit too inspiring. I have a hard time stopping at just one. See if you can stop!

⅓ cup mayonnaise

½ teaspoon hot pepper sauce, or to taste

3 tablespoons canola or peanut oil

1 extra-large white onion, thinly sliced

12 ounces grass-fed organic New York strip steak (shell steak),
    cut into very thin long strips or chopped into tiny bite-sized pieces

½ teaspoon sea salt, or to taste

½ teaspoon freshly ground black pepper, or to taste

4 (1-ounce) slices organic or locally produced provolone or
    soy-based American-style cheese

4 whole-wheat hamburger or sandwich buns or
    4 (4-inch) portions of a 16-inch Italian bread loaf

1. Stir together the mayonnaise and hot pepper sauce in a small bowl until well combined. Set aside.

2. Stir together the onions and oil in a large stick-resistant skillet. Place over medium-high heat and sauté until the onions are slightly softened, about 5 minutes. Cover (no need to lift off the lid to stir) and cook until the onions are fully softened and caramelized, about 4 minutes. Stir well to evenly distribute the caramelized onion and then stir in the meat. Sauté until the meat is just cooked through, about 2 minutes. Add salt and pepper.

(continued)

little **green** cooking tip

When meat is cut into tiny bite-sized pieces, it'll only use a couple minutes of cooking energy . . . maybe less! Plus, when beef is organic and grass-fed, it'll be free of antibiotics and better for the environment than it's conventionally produced counterpart.

3. Spread each bun with the mayonnaise mixture. Place ¼ of the meat mixture into each bun. Top with the cheese. Enjoy immediately.

PER SERVING: 590 calories, 39g total fat, 10g saturated fat, 0g trans fat, 65mg cholesterol, 890mg sodium, 32g total carbohydrate, 5g dietary fiber, 29g protein

a planet-friendly bite

 Sometimes the fun of cooking is to *not* follow a recipe. So if you want a bite without beef, turn into a "top chef" and create your own beef-free version. Try this recipe using organic chicken instead—just cook the chicken until it's well done, which may take an extra minute. Or skip the meat and poultry altogether and add green bell pepper in addition to the onion to create a full-flavored veggie Philly-style sandwich.

SIPS & SWEETS

fruit punch with punch

FRESH FRUIT RUM PUNCH

Makes 1 serving: 1¼ cups each

You know you need to get some fruits into your diet, so what better way than mixed into a spirited cocktail? With this potent punch you'll be able to check off getting your fruit servings for the day.

Juice of 1 small lemon or 1 lime (about 2 tablespoons)
½ cup seasonal fruit juice of choice, such as freshly squeezed orange juice
¼ cup light- or medium-bodied rum
1 tablespoon mild floral honey
1 slice of lemon or orange, for garnish

1. Add the lemon juice, fruit juice, rum, honey, and 3 large ice cubes to a cocktail shaker; shake vigorously for 1 minute.

2. Strain into a tall glass over additional ice. If desired, garnish the rim with a lemon slice.

PER SERVING: 260 calories, 0g total fat, 0g saturated fat, 0g trans fat, 0mg cholesterol, 0mg sodium, 33g total carbohydrate, 0g dietary fiber, 1g protein

little **green** cooking tip

Move over mixed drink mixes and glow-in-the dark potions. If you're going to have a drink, make it count. Take advantage of local seasonal fruit by incorporating freshly squeezed juices into spirited cocktails.

go local

Rum, which is made from sugarcane, is often from the Caribbean. But some rum is made in the U.S. In Houston, Texas, there's an artisanal distillery, Au Natural Spirits. In Keslo, Tennessee, Prichards' Distillery makes rum in small batches. Visit the Ministry of Rum to find out more: www. ministryofrum.com.

All-Year-Round

When fresh fruit is at its seasonal, and cheapest, peak, buy a bunch and freeze whatever you don't use. That frozen fruit is ideal for making smoothies. Then no ice will be required to blend to a cool, creamy consistency. The fruit will be the "ice"— nutritious, delicious ice.

very berry cup

FRESH DAIRY-FREE STRAWBERRY SMOOTHIE

Makes 2 servings: 1 cup each

Yum! This'll taste like a velvety thick and rich strawberry milkshake. But there's no dairy in this drink—just 100 percent vegan-friendly indulgence.

1 cup vanilla soy or rice frozen dessert
1½ cups sliced fresh strawberries or slightly
   thawed frozen strawberries
¼ cup plain unsweetened soymilk, cold
1 tablespoon local strawberry or other fruit spread or
   homemade jam or 2 teaspoons mild floral honey
2 fresh whole strawberries, for garnish

1. In a blender container, add the frozen dessert, strawberries, soymilk, and fruit spread. Cover and blend on low speed until smooth, about 1 minute.

2. Pour into two glasses. Garnish the rim of each with a strawberry, if desired. Serve immediately.

PER SERVING: 210 calories, 4g total fat, 0g saturated fat, 0g trans fat, 0mg cholesterol, 70mg sodium, 40g total carbohydrate, 6g dietary fiber, 3g protein

go local

Frankly, smoothie recipes aren't really necessary. Just toss whatever fruit and liquid you want into a blender and puree—adjusting ingredients to taste for desired consistency and flavor. That said, toss your smoothie ingredients of choice into whatever kind of blender you desire, even a bike blender! Check it out at www.bikeblender.com.

fruit-n-fudge

HOT FUDGY SAUCE WITH SEASONAL FRUIT

Makes 3 servings: ¼ cup each

Thank goodness there's a way to make luscious, low-carbon choco-late decadence! This warm, fresh, and fudgy sauce is so good that you might just want to eat it straight by the spoonful. But it's also divine with nearly any fruit. My favorite pairings are with fresh ripe strawberries or cherries. Drizzle this rich, memorable sauce over angel food cake, too. It's an experience worth experiencing often.

¾ **cup turbinado or Demerara sugar**
½ **cup plain unsweetened soymilk or whole organic milk**
½ **teaspoon pure vanilla extract**
1 **ounce high-quality unsweetened dark chocolate, finely chopped**
4 **cups bite-sized fresh seasonal fruit of choice**

1. Combine the sugar, soymilk, and vanilla extract in a small sauce-pan. Stir in the chocolate and place over medium heat. Cook while stirring occasionally until the sauce is bubbling, about 6 minutes. Then continue to cook while stirring constantly until the sauce is a rich brown color, nearly smooth, and just begin-ning to thicken, about 6 minutes.

2. Turn off the heat and cover. Let "lid cook" (cook covered while the burner is off) for 5 minutes. Remove from the heat and stir continuously until silky smooth and desired thickness, about 5 minutes.

(continued)

little ***green*** cooking tip

In addition to being or-ganically produced, look for chocolate that's Fair Trade Certified. It means the choc-olate was produced using environmentally sustainable practices and the farmers were paid fairly.

3. To serve, drizzle it over the fruit or enjoy it as a dipping sauce, like fondue, with the fruit on bamboo or resuable skewers. Or, if you just can't wait, fingers will do—as long as you don't mind finger licking!

PER SERVING: 320 calories, 6g total fat, 3g saturated fat, 0g trans fat, 0mg cholesterol, 25mg sodium, 70g total carbohydrate, 6g dietary fiber, 4g protein

use it, don't lose it

What should you do if your fudgy sauce becomes more like thick chocolate paste? It's not a loss. Reheat it in a microwave-safe bowl in the microwave oven on high for a few seconds. Or, even better, just pour a mound of it onto unbleached parchment paper, let it rest for at least 10 minutes to fully set, then slice and enjoy your homemade fudge!

pb&j on ice

PEANUT BUTTER AND JELLY ICE CREAM

Makes 4 servings: ½ cup each

What's the most famous pairing of them all? Peanut butter and jelly, of course. It's difficult to top the perennial favorite pb&j. But if you blend those popular flavors with ice cream—the yummiest food of them all—it's tops in my book!

1⅓ cups whole organic milk
¼ cup turbinado or Demerara sugar
¼ cup smooth unsalted natural peanut butter
¼ cup finely diced fresh seasonal fruit, such as strawberries or raspberries
1 tablespoon local fruit spread, such as cherry or strawberry or homemade jam
1½ teaspoons pure vanilla extract

1. Add all ingredients to the container end of an ice cream ball.* Add ice and rock or kosher salt to the other end, per ball instructions. Toss the ball around for 20 minutes, scraping down sides of the ice cream in the container after 10 minutes.

2. Scoop into cones (organic ice cream cones are available now!) or bowls and enjoy.

PER SERVING: 210 calories, 11g total fat, 2.5g saturated fat, 0g trans fat, 10mg cholesterol, 35mg sodium, 23g total carbohydrate, 1g dietary fiber, 6g protein

*See http://icecreamrevolution.com for information about the ice cream ball.

go local

If you find yourself in the New York City area, make sure to find your way to Peanut Butter & Co. to try their natural peanut butter. Check out their Web site: www.ilovepeanutbutter.com. And if you'd like to go the organic route, head to an area market where you might find Brad's Organic Peanut Butter. Visit www.bradsorganic.com for more. If there are no Big Apple plans in your future, both peanut butters can be ordered online.

little **green** cooking tip

Going green can save you money. Making your own ice cream can be cheaper than buying it from the ice cream shop. And a manual maker—ice cream ball or hand-churned model—is cheaper than the electric version. Yippee for luscious, low-carbon, cost-conscious ice cream.

made-in-ny cheesecake

GREENMARKET FRUIT-TOPPED CREAMY CHEESECAKE

Makes 8 servings: 1 wedge each

I live in New York. That means rich, creamy, decadent New York-style cheesecake is (too) easily within reach. Whether you're a New Yorker or not, this light and fluffy version of it takes the cake for its greenness. It's baked in less than 20 minutes . . . in a toaster oven. Then the delicious cake is topped with fresh fruits of the season. That's the way to take a bite out of the Big Apple, for sure.

1 large organic egg
2 large organic egg whites
¼ cup turbinado or Demerara sugar
¾ teaspoon pure vanilla extract
¼ teaspoon pure almond extract
¼ teaspoon lemon zest (optional)
⅛ teaspoon sea salt
10 ounces organic cream cheese, at room temperature
1 (9-inch) ready-to-use graham cracker piecrust (with no trans fat)
3 cups bite-sized fresh seasonal fruit of choice, such as raspberries, blueberries, sliced strawberries, or pitted cherries
1 tablespoon mild floral honey
1½ teaspoons fresh lemon juice

1. Whisk together the egg and egg whites in a medium bowl until well blended. Stir in the sugar, both extracts, lemon zest (if using), and salt until well combined. Stir in the cream cheese until combined and just tiny lumps remain. (This may take a couple of minutes.) Then beat with an electric mixer on low speed until velvety smooth and fluffy, about 1 minute. Pour into the piecrust.

little *green* cooking tip

Want to take a physically green challenge? When a recipe says to mix a batter with an electric mixer until smooth and fluffy, try to use your own muscle energy and a regular whisk—whisk vigorously by hand. I actually tried it for step 1 of this recipe, but failed. Let's see how you do!

2. Place the filled crust on a toaster oven tray, then place in the toaster oven* (do not preheat). Turn the heat to 400°F and bake until the crust rim is brown, about 7 minutes. Turn the heat down to 325°F and continue to bake until the cheesecake is nearly set and very slightly cracked, about 10 minutes. Turn off the toaster oven. Let the cheesecake cook with residual heat in the off toaster oven until fully set, about 8 minutes.

3. Cool on a rack for 30 minutes. Then chill in the refrigerator until well chilled, at least 1½ hours.

4. Add the fruit to a medium bowl. Drizzle with the honey and lemon juice. Very gently stir to combine.

5. Slice the cheesecake into 8 wedges. Top with the fruit.

PER SERVING: 300 calories, 19g total fat, 9g saturated fat, 0g trans fat, 65mg cholesterol, 280mg sodium, 29g total carbohydrate, 3g dietary fiber, 6g protein

*Toaster oven sizes and cooking times will vary. See page 39.

use it, don't lose it

When a recipe calls for egg whites, don't toss out the yolks. Make a classic hollandaise sauce, zabaglione, or crème brûlée with them. Or mix them into lean organic ground chicken or turkey along with an equal portion of oats to create extra-moist, extra-nutritious poultry burgers. But what if you have too many yolks to use right away? For a sweet recipe, add ½ tablespoon mild honey per 1 cup of yolks; for a savory recipe, add ½ teaspoon sea salt per 1 cup of yolks. Pour into an ice cube tray and freeze. (The honey and salt will help preserve the eggs.) Remove frozen yolk cubes and store in an airtight container. Thaw in the fridge when ready to use.

happy planet cookies

NATURALLY NUTRITIOUS CHOCOLATE CHIP COOKIES

Makes 12 servings: 2 cookies each

What would life be without the chocolate chip cookie? Well, luckily you don't have to worry about that. And if you're going green, you still don't need to worry. These New Age hyperbaked goodies will definitely make you—and the planet—happy. They're green chocolate chip cookies with an extra dose of healthfulness that actually taste good!

1 cup stone-ground whole-wheat flour
1 teaspoon baking soda
½ teaspoon sea salt
½ teaspoon ground cinnamon
⅛ teaspoon cayenne pepper (optional)
½ cup canola or peanut oil
1 cup turbinado or Demerara sugar
1 large organic egg
1 tablespoon apple butter
1½ teaspoon pure vanilla extract
½ cup old-fashioned oats
4½ ounces high-quality semisweet chocolate chips or chunks

1. Combine the flour, baking soda, salt, cinnamon, and cayenne (if using) in a medium bowl. Set aside.

2. Whisk together until combined the oil and sugar in a large bowl. Whisk in the egg, apple butter, and vanilla extract until smooth.

3. Stir the flour mixture into the oil-sugar mixture until blended. Stir in the oats, then the chocolate chips until combined. (Don't worry if the mixture seems a bit stiff; it's because of all of the hearty ingredients and is supposed to be that way.)

4. Line two baking sheets with unbleached parchment paper. Drop the dough by rounded tablespoon onto the sheets, 12 cookies each.

5. Place in the oven, then turn the heat to 375°F (do no preheat oven). Bake until they just spread out to cookie shape, yet are still undercooked to the touch, 10 to 12 minutes. As quickly as possible (so you don't let out too much heat), open the oven and swap the trays—move the tray on the top rack to the bottom and bottom rack to the top. Close the oven, then turn the oven off and let the cookies continue baking in the off oven until desired brownness and crispness, about 5 to 8 minutes. Remove from the oven and let cool completely on the baking sheets on racks. (Note: The cookies will continue to cook slightly once out of the oven, too.)

PER SERVING: 260 calories, 14g total fat, 3g saturated fat, 0g trans fat, 20mg cholesterol, 210mg sodium, 35g total carbohydrate, 2g dietary fiber, 3g protein

a planet-friendly bite

 It has been estimated that just 6 percent of the energy output of a conventional oven is actually used for cooking the food! That means a typical oven is 94 percent hot air—and a major waster of energy.

little **green** cooking tip

You can bake eco-friendlier and healthier cookies all at the same time! Choose whole-wheat flour over all-purpose. Choose oil rich in monounsaturated fat over butter—and perhaps use a little less than called for in the recipe. Then make them as natural as you can otherwise.

seasonal produce guide

Below is a chart that provides a general guideline for knowing when select produce is grown and typically available in the United States. Regional variations will occur. If you find produce at times of the year other than what's indicated below, it may be because it is shipped in from another country—which can tack on many food miles. Aim to use produce that's in season in your local area.

PRODUCE	IN SEASON IN THE CONTINENTAL UNITED STATES
Apple	All year (most varieties peak in autumn and winter)
Apricot	Spring, summer
Artichoke	All year (peaks in spring and autumn)
Asian pear (most varieties)	Summer, autumn, early winter
Asparagus	Spring, early summer
Avocado	All year
Bean	
French, haricot vert, green	All year
Fava	Spring, summer, early autumn
Beet	All year
Berries	
Blackberry, blueberry	Spring, summer, autumn
Cranberry	Autumn
Raspberry, strawberry	All year
Wild Strawberry (fraise des bois)	Spring, early summer
Bok choy (most varieties)	All year
Broccoli	All year (peaks in autumn, winter, early spring)

PRODUCE	IN SEASON IN THE CONTINENTAL UNITED STATES
Cabbage	
Red, green, white	All year
Savoy	Autumn
Brussels sprouts	Autumn, winter
Carrot	All year (peaks in autumn, winter)
Cauliflower	All year
Celery	All year
Celery root (celeriac)	Autumn, winter, spring
Chard	Spring, summer, autumn
Cherry	Summer
Corn (most varieties)	Spring, summer, early autumn
Cucumber (most varieties)	All year (hothouse variety peaks in spring, summer, autumn)
Date	All year (peaks in late autumn)
Eggplant	
Baby purple/Indian, baby white	Spring, summer, early autumn
Common (purple), Chinese, Japanese, Thai	Spring, summer, autumn
Endive	
Belgian	All year (peaks in winter, early spring)
Curly	All year (peaks in summer, autumn)
Fennel	All year
Fig (most varieties)	Summer, early autumn
Garlic	All year
Ginger	Late autumn, winter, spring, early summer
Grape	
Common green or red	Spring, summer, autumn, early winter
Globe, common black	Summer, autumn, winter
Grapefruit (pink, red, ruby, white)	All year
Greens	All year

PRODUCE	IN SEASON IN THE CONTINENTAL UNITED STATES
Guava	Autumn, winter, early spring
Kiwi	
Baby kiwi	Autumn
Green kiwi	Autumn, winter, early spring
Kumquat	Late autumn, winter, spring, summer
Leek	
Chinese	Late autumn, winter, spring, summer
Baby leek, leek	All year
Lemon	
Eureka (most common in U.S.)	All year
Meyer	Autumn, winter, spring
Lime	
Key lime	Summer
Persian (most common in U.S.)	All year
Lychee	Spring, summer
Mango	
Altaulfo, Haden, Kent, Tommy Atkins	n/a (available all year from outside U.S.)
Keitt	Summer, autumn
Melon	
Watermelon	Spring, summer, early autumn
Cantaloupe, common green honeydew	All year
Microgreens	All year
Mushroom	
Common white/button, cremini, enoki, oyster, portobello, shiitake, wood ear	All year
Chanterelle	Summer, autumn, winter
Morel	Spring, early summer
Porcini	Summer, autumn
Nectarine (white- and yellow-fleshed)	Spring, summer, autumn

PRODUCE	IN SEASON IN THE CONTINENTAL UNITED STATES
Okra	Spring, summer, early autumn
Onion	
Scallion/green onion/ spring onion	All year
Storage onion—boiler, cipolline, pearl, red, white, and yellow	All year
Sweet onion—Maui	All year
Sweet onion—Texas Sweets/ Oso Sweets	Winter, spring, summer, early autumn
Sweet onion—Vidalia/Georgia	Spring, early summer
Sweet onion—Walla Walla	Summer
Orange	
Blood/Moro	Winter, spring
Navel	Autumn, winter, spring
Valencia	Summer, early autumn
Papaya	
Green	n/a (available all year from outside U.S.)
Strawberry, yellow-fleshed	All year
Parsnip	Autumn, winter
Passion fruit	Summer, autumn, winter
Pea	
English	Spring, summer
Snow, sugar snap	Spring, summer, autumn
Peach (white- and yellow-fleshed)	Spring, summer, autumn
Pear	
Bartlett, Bosc	Summer, autumn, winter
Comice, Seckel	Autumn, winter
Anjou	All year
Pepper	
Bell pepper	All year (peaks in spring, summer)
Chile	All year (many varieties peak in summer, early autumn)

PRODUCE	IN SEASON IN THE CONTINENTAL UNITED STATES
Pineapple	All year
Plum	Summer, autumn
Pomegranate	Summer, autumn, early winter
Potato	
Creamer, regular	All year
Fingerling	Autumn, winter, early spring
Pumpkin (most varieties)	Autumn
Radicchio	Spring, summer, autumn, early winter
Radish	All year
Rapini (broccoli rabe)	All year (peaks in autumn, winter, early spring)
Rhubarb	
Hothouse	Winter, early spring
Field-grown	Spring, summer, autumn
Shallot	All year
Sprouts	All year
Star fruit (carambola)	All year (peaks in summer, autumn, winter)
Summer squash	
Summer green, summer yellow, zucchini	Spring, summer, autumn, early winter
Baby crookneck, baby zucchini, pattypan	Spring, summer
Sweet potato (most varieties)	All year (most varieties peak in autumn)
Tangerines (Mandarin Oranges)	
Most varieties	Winter
Clementine	Winter, early spring
Tomatillo	All year
Tomato (most varieties)	All year (peaks in summer, autumn)
Winter Squash	
Green acorn, banana, butternut, spaghetti, kabocha	All year
Other varieties	Summer, autumn, early winter

find a farmers' market

Farmers' markets are central locations where a variety of farmers sell their agricultural products directly to you. In 2008, there were more than 4,600 farmers' markets in the United States—and that number is still growing. It's easier than ever to find a farmers' market in your area. That means locally produced fruits, veggies, herbs, honeys, and more are readily available now, too.

In addition to a farmers' market, joining a community supported agriculture (CSA) program is another way to access locally grown foods. A CSA is a regional community of growers and consumers who share the benefits (and risks) of food production. The CSA season often runs from late spring or early summer through the fall. As a member (or "shareholder") you'll receive a weekly allotment of produce—or whatever else your CSA membership provides, which can include eggs, flowers, and more.

To find a farmers' market or a CSA near you, visit these links:

Biodynamic Farming and Gardening Association
A comprehensive national listing of CSA sites
www.biodynamics.com/csa

Farm Locator
Find a farm that can sell directly to you
www.newfarm.org/farmlocator/index.php

Local Harvest
Search by location or search by product to find farmers' markets, CSA listings, and more
www.localharvest.org

National Sustainable Agriculture Information Service
Search by state to find a local food directory
http://attra.ncat.org/attra-pub/localfood_dir.php

USDA Farmers' Market Search
Search by farmers' market name, state, city, county, zip code, and/or form of payment for a full listing of farmers' markets in the U.S.
http://apps.ams.usda.gov/FarmersMarkets

the big green glossary

Below is a list of low-carbon culinary techniques and terms that are used throughout *Big Green Cookbook*.

Earth-style
Use of every edible produce part, such as skins and seeds

Eco-brew
Cook with a locally brewed or organic beer, such as in chilis or stews

Ecotarian
A person who eats foods based on environmental sustainability

Eco-wrap
Edible, no-cook wrap, such as lettuce leaves

Green grill
Grill in the off position with residual heat

Greenover
Eco-friendly recipe makeover

Green sauté
Sauté in a hot skillet with the residual heat while the burner is off

Green-sized
Just right–size portions, such as small portions of meat

Hyperbake
Bake in an oven without preheating it, and use residual heat after turning it off

Hyperfry
Fry in oil without preheating it

Residual heat
The remaining heat that can be used for cooking after turning off the heat source

Lid cook
Cook covered while the burner is off

Micro-bake
Cook or "bake" a sweet food in the microwave oven

Micro-roast
Cook or "roast" a savory food in the microwave oven

Micro-steam
Steam in the microwave oven

Micro-stew
Stew in the microwave oven

Peel-ups
Produce peels used as serving cups or bowls

for more information

For additional tips on following a lower-carbon lifestyle, for details about climate change, or to find out more about organizations that support improving the environment, browse this selected list of Web sites.

American Humane Association
www.americanhumane.org

Carbonfund.org
www.carbonfund.org

ClimateCrisis.net
www.climatecrisis.net

The Climate Project
www.theclimateproject.org

The Daily Green
www.thedailygreen.com

Discovery Channel's Planet Green
http://planetgreen.discovery.com

Earth Day Network
www.earthday.net

EarthLab
www.earthlab.com

Environmental Defense Fund
www.edf.org

Environmental Working Group
www.ewg.org

Fair Trade Certified
www.transfairusa.org

Food Alliance
www.foodalliance.org

Global Green USA
www.globalgreen.org

Green for All
www.greenforall.org

Green Living Ideas
www.greenlivingideas.com

Greenopia
www.greenopia.com

The Hunger and Environmental Nutrition Dietetic Practice Group
www.hendpg.com

The Huffington Post's "Green"
www.huffingtonpost.com/green

Ideal Bite
www.idealbite.com

Intergovenmental Panel on Climate Change
www.ipcc.ch

Live Earth
http://liveearth.org

Marine Stewardship Council
www.msc.org

Monterey Bay Aquarium's Seafood Watch
www.mbayaq.org/cr/seafoodwatch.aspx

National Geographic's Green Guide
www.thegreenguide.com

Natural Resources Defense Council
www.nrdc.org

Organic Consumers Association
www.organicconsumers.org

Rainforest Alliance
www.rainforest-alliance.org

Sierra Club
www.sierraclub.org

Slow Food USA
www.slowfoodusa.org

StopGlobalWarming.org
www.stopglobalwarming.org

TreeHugger
www.treehugger.com

United Nations Environment Programme
www.unep.org

U.S. Climate Action Network
www.usclimatenetwork.org

USDA Agricultural Marketing Service— National Organic Program
http://ams.usda.gov/nop

U.S. Energy Star Program
www.energystar.gov

U.S. Environmental Protection Agency—Climate Change
www.epa.gov/climatechange

Water Keeper Alliance
www.waterkeeper.org

The We Campaign
www.wecansolveit.org

World Resources Institute
www.wri.org

World Wildlife Fund
www.worldwildlife.org

For more *Big Green Cookbook* information, go to
www.biggreencookbook.com.
And for more information about Jackie Newgent, RD,
author of *Big Green Cookbook*, go to
www.jackienewgent.com.

---

index

A

Acorn Squash, Micro-Roasted, 341–342
Alcohol, organic, 24, 27, 240
Almond(s)
  Artichoke Heart Dip with, Baked, 57
  Dates, Raw Almond–Stuffed, Wrapped in Organic Bacon, 185
  measuring, 185
  Orange-Bulgur Stack with Tomatoes, Herbs and, 209–210
Almond Butter
  in Mushroom Pâté, Wild, Cumin-Accented, 246–247
  and Peach Toastie, 132–133
American Humane Certified, 28
Antibiotics, in meat production, 28
Appetizers. See Dips; Hors d'Oeuvres; Salsa
Apple(s)
  Champagne Arugula Salad with Walnuts and Red Delicious Apples, 204
  Gravy, Golden Delicious, Rosemary-Roasted Organic Turkey Breast with, 284
  Pancakes, Granny Smith, with Cinnamon Butter, 273–274
  -Papaya Sauce, No-Cook, 187
  peels, 274
  in season, 361
  Smoothie, Triple Fruit, 238
  Sundae, Hot Fuji Apple, 243
  Sweet-n-Sour Savoy Cabbage, Golden Delicious, 222
Appliances. See also Microwave oven; Ovens; Refrigerator
  blender, 163, 323
  dishwasher, 9, 35
  Energy Star-qualified, 8, 9
  panini grill, 42, 111
  renewable energy source for, 9–10

slow cooker, 14, 324
small must-haves, 11, 13, 14
unplugging, 10, 98, 163
Apricot(s)
  Beet, Thinly Sliced, and Goat Cheese Salad with Fresh Apricot, 68
  Goat Cheese Salad, Nut-Crusted with Apricot Vinaigrette and, 124
  -Jalapeño Chicken Thighs, Grilled Organic, 93–94
  in season, 361
Artichoke(s)
  Heart Dip, Baked, with Almonds, 57
  micro-steamed fresh, 58
  Scallion, and Spinach Dip, Creamy, 194–195
  in season, 361
Artisanal cheeses, 178, 296
Arugula
  Baby, Orzo Salad, 69–70
  Blood Orange and Maytag Blue Cheese Salad with Blood Orange Vinaigrette, 266
  Champagne Salad with Red Delicious Apples and Walnuts, 204
  Fig, and Country Ham Salad with Fig-Balsamic Vinaigrette, 130–131
  Quinoa with Eggplant, Pine Nuts and, Cool, 144–145
  Submarine Wrap with Vine-Ripened Tomato Salsa and, 234–235
  -Watermelon Salad with Feta Cheese and Pine Nuts, 125–126
Asian(-Inspired)
  Cabbage Slaw, 64
  Chili-Lime Mayo, Panko-Crusted Crab Cakes with, 302–303
  Mandarin Orange Salad, Leafy, 261
  Peanut Vinaigrette, 107

Soba Noodle Soup, Spicy, 319–320
Asparagus
  in season, 361
  Tip and Mushroom Omelet, with Shaved Parmesan, 79–80
Autumn menus, 36
Avocado(es)
  in Bacon, Organic, Lettuce, and Tomato Sandwich, 160–161
  Black Bean and Hass Avocado Salad, 63
  in Grapefruit, Red, Shrimp Salad, Gingery, 71–72
  growing, benefits of, 118, 154, 189, 318
  Guacamole
    with Fall Fruits, 188
    Studded with Fresh Strawberries, 118
    Speedy, 253
    Tomatillo, Layered Mexican Dip with, 317–318
  -Honeydew Puree, Grilled Mahi Mahi on, 153–154
  peel-ups, 63, 91, 92, 161, 188, 197
  in Tomato Soup, "Cream" of, Raw, 196
  Tuna Tartare, Seared Ahi, and Florida Avocado with Fresh Lime, 91–92

B

Baba Ghanoush (Eggplant Dip, Middle Eastern Skillet-Smoked), 192–193
Bacon, Organic
  Canadian, Kumquat, 287
  Dates, Raw Almond–Stuffed, Wrapped in, 185
  Lettuce, and Tomato Sandwich, 160–161
  micro-roasting, 160
  portion size, 160